RESULTS

Reach beyond the barriers.

Evolve into your best self.

Select the right three projects.

Utilize your time effectively.

Lead yourself, others, and your schedule.

Thrive in your physical, psychological, and people environments.

Succeed by flourishing in all areas of your life.

RESULTS

"Saiyyidah is focused, thorough, and everything she does is amazing. In RESULTS Saiyyidah shares her unique perspective on getting things done. She shares her unique method and system and provides you with a clear picture on what it takes to accomplish your goals. This is a great guide to making things happen and getting the right things done."

— **Ajit Nawalkha, co-founder Evercoach by Mindvalley**

"I've known Saiyyidah for many years, and she is the one who does the work and gets it done. So, it's no wonder she's written a book on the subject! She totally walks her talk... so if you want to get more done, buying this book would be a brilliant start!"

— **Shaa Wasmund MBE, International Bestselling Author**

"Saiyyidah Zaidi is incredibly dedicated to making a difference in this world. She practices what she preaches. You want to learn from someone who does the hard work of growth learning themselves, and Saiyyidah is a master learner. She has distinctions and advice that can truly help you grow."

— **Brendon Burchard, #1 New York Times Bestselling Author**

"Saiyyidah has a remarkable talent for combining deep learning across an impressive range of subjects with an ability to generate practical, action-focused ideas and solutions. A highly original thinker, in RESULTS, she brings together her expertise in project management, coaching and positive psychology to help you achieve your goals. Readers of this book will benefit hugely from the author's insights and the techniques, models and tips gathered from her years of experience as a coach and as a senior leader in the public sector. Written with clarity, compassion, and an eye to a successful outcome, anyone looking to achieve meaningful personal growth will get something valuable from RESULTS."

— **Liz Gooster, Business Coach, Partner, The Alliance**

"Saiyyidah is a constant student of life and business. Her greatest gift is making the complex simple! The wide range of deep learning she has in positive psychology, project management, personal growth, and business results is the basis for a great experience. I know Saiyyidah will help you move forward. Saiyyidah doesn't just suggest the possibility of taking your ideas and making them a reality, she shows you how."

— **Ethan Willis, #1 New York Times best-selling author and CEO of Roundsquare Ventures**

"Results is a book full of science-based principles broken down so it is easy to understand. The reminders on how to check emails and use the different time blocks was a great refresher, even for me. Looking at planning your results for 10 years' time might be a lot for someone starting out with their life, but for an experienced business owner it works as perfectly as Saiyyidah suggests. The book is so comprehensive and complete. People who read this will leave with so much value—this is not fluff!"

— **Dr Neeta Bhushan, co-founder Global Grit Institute**

"Saiyyidah gets things done and makes things happen. I've known her for over a decade, and she is one of the best people I have ever worked with. Saiyyidah is deeply reflective, has great values and is one of the top action takers I know. Spend time with her and that great approach will rub off on you too."

— **Muhammad Alshareef, Founder, DiscoverU**.

"Saiyyidah Zaidi is a remarkable individual with an amazing back story and a tremendous depth of experience, all of which she brings to bear in this excellent book. Saiyyidah is a thought leader whose wisdom and insights deserve a wider hearing."

— **Professor Anthony Reddie, University of South Africa, and Centre for Religion & Culture, University of Oxford**

RESULTS

"Saiyyidah Zaidi looks at the world through not just one, but a number of lenses. She has the rare ability of understanding what those lenses are. This self-awareness means she is tuned to inter-sectionality in her own life, but crucially others' lives too. Saiyyidah knows what it is like to hold a number of identities that sometimes overlap, often clash, and occasionally run in parallel. She is always focused on making inter-sectionality a fruitful learning opportunity for herself. Equally important to Saiyyidah is her being the sort of person who, when others encounter her, they go on their way enriched and empowered to embrace their own challenges of identity."

— **Dr Eric Stoddart, Lecturer in Practical Theology & Distance Learning; Associate Director, Centre for the Study of Religion & Politics**

"I suspect there are actually several Saiyyidah's—how can one person achieve all she has already?! I admire her thirst for learning, and her generosity in sharing it, without ego or attachment. I still remember the impact of her guidelines years ago, on how to support a colleague in the workplace as they fast during Ramadan: they were clear, warm, very practical and supportive, and I'm sure must have made a difference to many hundreds, perhaps thousands, of people. Just like Saiyyidah herself."

— **Anne Scoular, Founder, Meyler Campbell and Author of The Financial Times Guide to Business Coaching**

"Saiyyidah is a brilliant coach who looks at problems with a unique lens. She amazes me with her insights and solutions every time. I have known her for five years, and I have learned the most valuable lessons of my life with her. Here she moves people from charcoal to the transformation of a dazzling diamond."

— **Fouzia Usman, Founder of Ummah Stars/Senior Oracle Applications Engineer**

"Saiyyidah Zaidi is a master of high performance and results. She has a deep understanding of how to ignite motivation and unlock the potential to perform inside all of us. Through her easy, pragmatic yet powerful approach, she has been able to help me navigate my bustling lifestyle. RESULTS is a fresh perspective to completely revolutionizing your life through her contemporary perspective. I trust her for her insight and confidentiality as I have come to know her over the years, and I will be forever grateful for her presence in my life. If you work with Saiyyidah, it can only mean you are ready to take your life to the next level."

— **Jasir Soomro, Student and Community Organizer**

"Saiyyidah gets straight to the point with her coaching and teaching. She'll tell you exactly what it is and show you how to do it. That is why she is such a refreshing voice in personal development."

— **Helene Walker-James, Executive Coach**

"I have known and worked with Saiyyidah over many years. I always trust her professional integrity and passion for helping people achieve their goals and become their best version. She has spent years defining and mastering her coaching skills to serve her clients and students better, and I trust her to provide me with solid, unbiased advice while maintaining trust. Over the years Saiyyidah has helped me define goals, look at the bigger picture on a strategic level in business and life and provided me with advice that I might not like at the time but I know is valid and comes from a place of pushing my personal boundaries to achieve higher."

— **Elena Nikolova, Founder Muslim Travel Girl**

"Saiyyidah brings a unique combination of intellectual exploration, depth and rigour along with a grounded practicality and straightforwardness. She has the ability to identify key insights and to provide guidance on how to put them into practice."

— **Ann Orton, Meyler Campbell faculty member and Partner / Coach with The Alliance**

RESULTS

RESULTS

The Art and Science of Getting It Done

SAIYYIDAH ZAIDI

Results.Partners Library titles may be purchased in bulk for educational, business, fundraising or sales promotional use. For permissions requests, speaking inquiries, and bulk order purchase options, email s@results.partners

ISBN-13 979-8550000335

Cover design, illustrations, and interior design: Saiyyidah Zaidi

Names: Zaidi, Saiyyidah, author.

Title: RESULTS: The Art and Science of Getting It Done

Subjects: Personal Growth, Positive Psychology, Project Management, Success

More resources at RESULTS.Partners

DEDICATION

To you and your future results…

CONTENTS

RESULTS

INTRODUCTION

"For the past 33 years, I have looked in the mirror every morning and asked myself: 'If today were the last day of my life, would I want to do what I am about to do today?' And whenever the answer has been 'No' for too many days in a row, I know I need to change something."

Steve Jobs — (1955-2011)

RESULTS

"Are you settling?"

My fourteen-year-old son Musa has always been a huge Nike fan. If it isn't Nike, he doesn't want it. Kids and their labels! In August 2019, we were driving from Los Angeles to Sundance in Utah where I was attending a conference. It was in our plan to stop at The Outlet Malls in Barstow, California. "We have three hours. That is it. We can split into teams and go into different stores, but we can't be more than three hours," I said. The kids rolled their eyes, but it was what we had all agreed the day before—after all, they had a project manager mum!

Musa and I trawled through all the shoe stores. He found some trainers that fit, but I could tell he was less than satisfied with the shoes. The ones in the Nike store were over $150, and I was not prepared to pay that much for a pair of shoes that my growing son may only wear for six months. Towards the end of our three hours we were all starting to get a little irritable. Three hours in the glorious Californian sun going from store to store is not the same as sight-seeing or enjoying the beach!

RESULTS

At the end, Musa came running to me and said, "I'll have these. I want these." His dad was ready to go to the checkout and pay for the trainers so we could leave. I knew how he felt. Musa looked at me for approval.

"Musa, honey, are you settling for these shoes?" I asked.

"No," he said firmly.

"Do you understand what I mean? Do you know what settling is?" I asked him.

"No," said Musa.

"Settling is when you accept something that you don't really want because you can't have what you do want. There are times in life when you may want to settle, but if something is really important to you then please, honey do not settle."

Musa was silent. He did not say a word. He picked up the trainers and put them back. I could see that Musa was disappointed in not having the thrill of buying some new shoes that day, but I also knew that he had just learned a lesson that would serve him for life.

#

As human beings, we spend a lot of time accepting second best. That is not good enough. Sometimes it is our need to do something—anything—that motivates us. Other times it's our desire to feel as if we are making progress and take some form of action that creates the double-edged sword: we want to move forward, but we don't know how to make that happen. A common response is "do something, anything just to fill the time."

Action for the sake of action has no real meaning; it will not get you where you want to go. It is focused, deliberate action guided by informed decision making that enables you to move closer to your end goal. Focused deliberate action creates momentum towards your vision and helps you to close the gap between where you are now and where you want to be. It enables you to avoid settling.

Human beings are naturally goal oriented. Our behavior, thoughts, feelings, and actions are all determined by what we want to do. Yet sometimes we are just not getting it done, or we are getting the wrong thing done. Sometimes we are just settling.

The late Professor Anthony Grant articulated the problem perfectly in his diagram the Goal Hierarchy Framework illustrating the outcomes of goal neglect.[1]

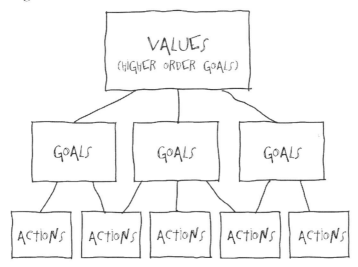

Goal Hierarchy Framework (Grant, 2012)

It is your values that give direction to your goals and actions. When there is no connection between the values, goals, and actions, when you fail to pay attention to the value (higher-ordered goals) everything else results in goal dissatisfaction and disengagement.

RESULTS

When you consider the relationships between values, goals, and actions in the previous image, and the example below what do you see?

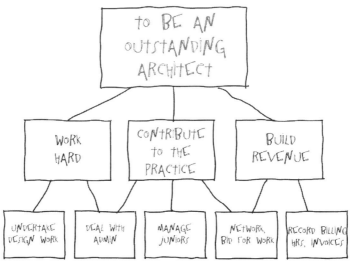

How to be an Outstanding Architect, image based on Grant's The Goal hierarchy framework illustrating the outcomes of goal neglect (Grant, 2012

I see ambition, hope, and a dream. What I also see is no clear definition of the vision, what does "to be an outstanding architect" actually mean? Does that goal connect with the person's values, strengths, and broader desires for life?

Whilst working hard, contributing to the firm, and building revenue are all good project goals, how does one know that they have been achieved? What timeline is attached to these goals? How much revenue to build? Is "working hard" something that excites this person, day in, day out?

To me, "deal with admin" is a necessary function but not something exciting enough to provide sufficient motivation and will, especially when paired with "read prior cases" and "document billing hours."

Therein lies the problem: insufficient excitement to motivate and summon one's will.

There is a missing link between the person, the values (as illustrated in the previous diagram), the goals, and the action undertaken. When there is a disconnect between these elements, individuals struggle to take the right action.

And when that happens, people settle.

The Problem of Settling

People know what they want to do, but they are not getting it done.

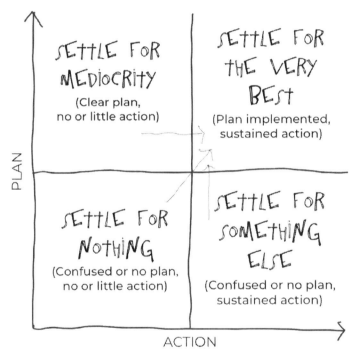

The Problem of Settling™

It is not for want of trying, but rather because they don't have a process in place that shows them how to align what they take action on with their values and overarching aim for life, or they don't have the project management skills to move them forward. So, many people are just settling. In my experience I have seen people and projects fall into one of the following four quadrants:

1. No plan and inaction (settling for nothing)
2. Clear plan, and inaction (settling for mediocrity)
3. Action and no plan (settling for something else)
4. Action and clear plan (settling for the very best)

Settling for Nothing

At some point in your life you will have wondered, "What do I do?" You may have even asked, "Where am I?" When this happens, you want to take stock of where you are and create a *next steps* plan. Settling for nothing can cause anxiety and unease, but with the right support, steps, and desire, you can avoid the stress of settling for nothing and instead, find your way so you have something meaningful to settle for.

Settling for Mediocrity

This is where you know exactly where you want to go and what you want to achieve, but you are doing little (or nothing) to move you towards your goal. You are settling for mediocrity. It is important to identify the reasons why there is no progress being made so you can remedy the situation, otherwise your dreams will stay on the shelf, clearly outlined in a nice, neatly printed plan and gather dust. (I have had this happen to me many times!)

Settling for Something Else

Being sidetracked is one of the most common impediments I have seen people face, and this is when they settle for something else. A lot of time is spent being busy, but the work itself has no strategy, therefore it can appear that you are doing the right thing, but in actuality, you are working on items that are less significant or on someone else's agenda.

Settling for the Very Best

This is where we want to be—making progress with *our* plans and moving forward. You schedule time daily to work on your project or goal in addition to your business-as-usual tasks, and you are able to get it done. You are aiming for the very best version of you and striving to realize the vision you have created for your life and your associated projects. And this is exactly where you will be when you use the RESULTS Method™ to map out your direction, destination, and the actions it will take to get there.

The only thing I want you to settle for is the very best!

The RESULTS Method™

BEFORE		AFTER
RESISTING	**R**EACH	ACCEPTING
UNFULFILLED	**E**VOLVE	FULFILLED
CONFUSED	**S**ELECT	CLEAR
UNORGANIZED	**U**TILIZE	FOCUSED
AVOIDING	**L**EAD	IMPACTING
SPORADIC	**T**HRIVE	CONSISTENT
REDUCING	**S**UCCEED	INCREASING

The RESULTS Method Before and After

RESULTS

Each phase of the RESULTS Method has a recognizably significant effect not only on the general progress in any project you are pursuing, but also on your psychological and physical states. The previous illustration compares how you feel at each phase before and after applying the RESULTS Method and its processes to your life.

We start with where you are right now. I'm sure you know that there is more to achieving your desired results and succeeding than simply having a goal, creating your plan, and implementing it. If it were that easy, everyone would be doing it!

Reach Beyond: What's next?

Asking yourself "What's next?" is the perfect place to start! Let's **reach** beyond who you are now so you can deal with personal showstoppers such as doubt, struggle, imposter syndrome, self-sabotage, and any other self-defeating mindsets or beliefs right at the get-go. By understanding how to accept these, you put yourself in a strong place to deal with any personal resistance in your life so you can move forward. As you deal with the cause of what is holding you back, you will open to evolving into the true, authentic you at a much deeper level, enabling you to get more done.

Evolve: Who am I?

Understanding who you are is essential for you to employ the potential that you have within you in an authentic way—you allow yourself to **evolve** from unfulfilled to fulfilled. I know that you are more than capable of making your life a success, but when that success is not in alignment with who you are, it is bittersweet. I have seen many people make significant progress in their life, but their internal conflict haunts them for years to come. This is partly because they have not done the work to understand who they are and how that impacts every aspect of their life; and partly because they are working on projects and goals that are not in line with their true vision for life. By knowing your values, strengths, and communication style, and by acknowledging what you do not know about yourself, you put yourself in a strong position to answer the next question, "What do I work on?"

Select: What do I work on?

Your time, money, resources, effort, and energy can be allocated to *any* project, but it is important to **select** the *right* project from the beginning. When your project is in line with your current needs and long-term vision, you avoid being misdirected and mismanaging whatever you have invested. This is what creates the shift from being confused to being clear and gaining clarity on what you work on. This way your ultimate results are intrinsically tied to your actual choice of project. Selecting the right projects, aligned with your vision, is essential to the successful use of any of the RESULTS Process tools I share with you.

Utilize: How do I get it done?

By learning to **utilize** your time and resources effectively, you set yourself on a dynamic course to make the kind of progress you have always sought. Sure, you may still encounter hiccups along the way, but by knowing how to utilize the 10 different time blocks and the BART (boundaries, authority, responsibility, task) system, you move from being unorganized to being focused on what truly matters to you.

Lead: How do I follow through?

It is difficult to acknowledge but many of us are avoiding leadership. When you follow the RESULTS Method, you learn to **lead** in a way that is authentic and will enable you to take control of the logistical responsibilities you have to yourself (self-care, health, etc.), to your relationships (family, friends, community, etc.), and to your projects (tasks, plans, delegation, etc.). In this phase, you will discover how to

RESULTS

lead on your terms so you can increase your impact. This phase will give you an incredible amount of peace as you move forward in your projects because you will have everything handled and will lead in a way that enables you to flourish. You will also create your weekly rhythm taking account of your personal preference for time management. This is really powerful.

Thrive: How do I deal with obstacles?

We all know that challenges and obstacles will come your way. Finding a way to **thrive** means that you will move from being sporadic in your results to consistent, and this has a strategic impact on your outcomes. Taking control of your three environments (psychological, physical, and people) enables you to navigate past any challenge or obstacle that comes your way. Many of the events of 2020 were completely unexpected and threw the majority of us off course— people lost jobs; companies closed; and simple, yet basic, necessities like food shopping became really difficult. Many have called it the Great Reset. There was a big difference in how people, communities, and countries responded. Watching what others are doing and then following or ignoring them is not always helpful. With the strategies you will learn in the **Thrive** phase of the RESULTS Method, you will know what to do when you feel like you are being thrown off course and will be in a stronger position to overcome any obstacles and keep following your plan or adjust it as necessary.

Succeed: How do I have continuous success?

Well, that is the million-dollar question! Yet, despite popular opinion, succeeding is not about results alone. With RESULTS, you will **succeed** by moving from a state of thriving to one of flourishing, and you will do so in a way that enables you to continuously build on your progress. You will discover a simple strategy so you can review, rest, and revitalize your plans and your approach when necessary so you can continue on your quest for progress at home and at work. You will discover how to master your morning and evening in order to have daily buy-in into your dreams.

If in the past you have ever had success and then fallen back into your old ways or known that you have settled for less than you want, you will finally learn how not to do that again and avoid "reduced circumstances "[2] (having less than you once had). With the RESULTS Method, you will establish how you can be consistent and increase your alignment with who you are and how you want to show up in the world. By absorbing and implementing the RESULTS Method, you will make progress, move forward, get it done, and do it on your terms!

I will also show you how to repeat the RESULTS Method time and time again—you will be provided with a menu of options in the Succeed phase so that whatever you decide to do after you have read and implemented the book once, you will know what to do next.

As a lifelong planner, the essentials are clear so you can:
- know what can cause you to go off plan,
- know who you are and what you stand for,
- be ready and committed to work on your project,
- have the confidence to make the decision to pivot if necessary,
- work out your logistics,
- develop and maintain a clear plan of how you will make it happen,
- recognize the difference between internal and external navigation,
- and know what your immediate priorities are in line with your vision and values.

After that, it really is a rinse and repeat cycle, and you do it again and again and watch how you get more done and scale.

At the end of going through the RESULTS Method, the minimum you will take away is a Quarterly Action Plan, Weekly Rhythm, Monthly

RESULTS

Moves, Annual Power Plan, and Daily Schedule. You will also know how to establish personal accountability to get it done. You'll also know where to find support and assistance so you can maintain that momentum.

This is your time for results, and I am so excited for you.

The RESULTS Process™

You need to have the *right* process in place, alongside the right method to make your vision reality. To be fruitful, that process must take account of who you are, what is going on in your life, be able to create space for curiosity about what you would like to focus on, as well as offer the practicality of how to get it done.

I am sharing the diagram of the overall structure of the RESULTS process with you before we begin so that you can see how it all links together.

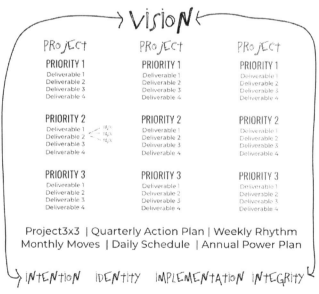

The RESULTS Process™

At each phase you link back to your vision using the RESULTS GPS (more about that in a minute) and underpin your practice with the use of permission slips, Post-it notes, and pitstops. Having strategic plans that support you in the short and long term and linking to your overarching vision and foundational intention, identity, implementation strategy, and integrity results in your being more connected to your aims in the moment.

Right now, you might look at this and wonder how you can do it. Remember, I am here to guide you through this process, and I have done this before, hundreds of thousands of times, so you are in safe hands. I am giving you the operational tactics and tools, the method, and the process for implementation—take what serves you and let the rest go.

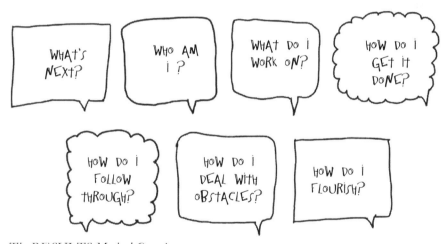

The RESULTS Method Questions

By asking yourself the right questions, you notice your future in ways you never imagined. Asking the wrong questions, or not asking any questions at all, can create psychological paralysis, and you remain stagnant. When it comes to creating change, it can be easy to focus on what is wrong, and that is why I love the perspective that positive psychology and a flourishing approach brings. Adopting a lens of curiosity and reframing the questions you ask yourself allows you to focus on what you truly want. Throughout this book, I will ask you questions that are devised to enable you to search deep within or to make a clear decision about where you want to go next in your life. I will share with you the Self-Interview™ process I have created.

ABOUT THIS BOOK

I know many of you have big dreams, clear goals, and solid plans, but something has got in the way of achieving them. The power of the RESULTS Method is that it covers the three core components to success: you, your projects, and your process.

One of my superpowers is to take science and translate it into actionable steps that you can apply in your own life. I do this in my own life and with my coaching and leadership development clients, so that is exactly what I do in this book. I am committed to taking research-based principles and showing you how you can use them in your day-to-day life, or business, so that you can get the tangible results you seek. I will show you how to stop being complacent, remove the internal competition, and help you create (and implement) a solid, values-based plan that focuses on you and the results you want and gives you the quality of life that you want to experience on a daily basis.

In your hands, you hold a uniquely-charged combination of personal growth, positive psychology, behavioral science, project management, and high performance that will enable you to manage the projects, ideas, and other activities that you've been working on for many years and to make significant progress in them. This book requires you to rethink your goals, aspirations, and desires and then to identify and navigate the obstacles that are keeping you from attaining them.

Within days of your reading and implementing the practical insights you'll find within these pages, you will experience change in certain aspects of your reality. Your effectiveness, your levels of energy, and the effort it takes you to complete your tasks may all change as a result.

Bold statements, right?

Absolutely.

Yet, I have endeavored to give you a book that will give you the tools and strategies to think again about how you plan everything from your weekly chores, your career, your health and personal growth, even your relationships with those dearest to you. The processes outlined in the RESULTS Method help you organize your personal life and your work life. They will enable you to take the ideas or projects that are important to you and create a clear plan of action—a plan that you will *actually use*. Once you know how to create your personalized plan, your view on personal and professional growth may change forever.

This book is written for everyone. Regardless of whether you're seasoned in personal growth, you're just starting on your journey of self-development, or even if you're a cynic. In fact, in the research phase, I deliberately included a broad range of opinions to ensure that a variety of feedback was taken into consideration. I did not want to write another book that would sit on your bookshelf or stay in the depths of your Kindle vault! I am offering you a book that you can use as a manual and return to every time you start a new project. The plan that you have for your life may be outcome focused. Sure, outcomes can be measured and adjusted incrementally, but a really innovative approach is to start with your intention. I will show you why initiating your goals and projects with your intention and values will accelerate your results, and in turn, allow you to experience a life where you are flourishing and thriving because you are living in accordance with your identity and integrity.

This book is the gateway to your true RESULTS.

RESULTS

It is designed to disrupt the personal development field because the focus is no longer just about goals and dreams; it is now also about implementation and action. You will be given practical tools to change how you plan your year, quarter, month, and week and also, how you live and experience the day. No doubt there will be some discomfort and uneasiness, for that is normal when you are going through change. Lean into that resistance because it is by stretching and being uncomfortable that you will grow.

This is an invitation for you to change your lived experience by finally getting it done!

If you already have some knowledge of project management, you will acquire a new perspective of some of the principles that you are familiar with and will learn to apply them to your personal and professional growth in a way that makes you more effective. If you know nothing about project management, do not worry because I will break it down and show you how you are already the project manager of certain aspects of your life. If you are a coach or regularly participate in personal development, this book will help you to create a streamlined process for implementing your ideas and desires.

You might be here because you know me, or because a friend recommended this book, or you found it in a library. Regardless of how you got here, please take this as the invitation for you to change your life and get the results you seek.

I came up with the idea for this book because I had spent too many years and a ridiculous amount of money and effort getting training, taking courses, being coached, yet something was preventing me from making the progress that I sought in my life and business. Then one day I stepped back and looked at my skill set as a whole.

There was a missing link.

That missing link is the process I have laid out for you in this book: the connection between positive psychology, personal growth, and project management. Once you use this process in your life, you will achieve the RESULTS you desire through:

Reaching beyond where you are now,
Evolving by understanding yourself more,
Selecting the right, specific projects to work on,
Utilizing your time and resources more effectively,
Leading yourself, others, and your projects,
Thriving in an authentic way, and
Succeeding in true alignment with who you are.

If you are starting to feel a little overwhelmed or your inner cynic is starting to ask questions, take a look later in this chapter for the outline for your first 100 days. While I was writing this very book, I happened to join a new learning community, and although the knowledge blew my mind, I had no idea where to start, it was overwhelming. I suggested that they create an onboarding plan for the first 100 days (see later) I intuitively realized what a great idea it was, so I have created such a plan for you, to guide you through your reading and how you use and implement the RESULTS Method. I have taken other measures to enhance your journey using the RESULTS Method to help you truly take advantage of its benefits.

The Online Experience

The RESULTS Method comes with its own custom designed course with additional content, templates, training, and more. As you want to explore a particular concept further you can use the online resources to deepen your understanding.

When we read books, especially books that call us to action, we often want to discuss ideas, share our own thoughts, call out when we have an Aha! Moment, or simply ask others about their experiences implementing the steps presented. Right? I want to facilitate a place for you where you can collaborate with other readers. With that in mind, I have created the RESULTS Community where you and other readers can share your insights, what you've learned, how you are using the RESULTS Method, and maybe even hear from me every now and then. The community turns this book into an interactive experience and gives you the added value of belonging to a group rooting for you and offering support. At *www.results.partners/bookresources* you will also find the complimentary RESULTS Circuit Breaker online training along with videos and additional templates (which you can use at your own pace).

Teaching and Learning Methodology

I have written this book so that it can be used by anyone. Maybe, you are a professional mapping out your personal career plan, a parent at home who wants to make their ambitions a reality, a student who wants to explore options other than going to university, or someone who is feeling a little stuck and frustrated and is looking for more than motivation.

You have big hopes and dreams, and I want you to realize them. Once you understand the concepts in this book and connect those together, you will see how each element is interrelated. After reading it and using the processes, you will never look at a personal development book in the same way.

I know coaching is not accessible to everyone. My first experience of coaching was in 2009 when I saw a job opening that I wanted to apply for: the problem was that it was two grades higher than the role I was in and had a 50 percent increase in salary attached to it. It was unheard of for someone like me to get a promotion like that, but I was determined to give it a go—at best I would get the job; worst case, I'd gain some insights about myself. I asked a few people for their thoughts, and a friend who worked in human resources suggested that I hire a coach. I worked with my coach on this for six months. We had some sessions in a park, some in a coffee shop, and others over the phone. We worked hard, and…. drum roll please… I got the job!

I am not meant to be writing this book. Statistically, I should be in a repetitive office job somewhere pushing a pen, living in social housing, and predicted to get a divorce. When I was young, I decided that statistics would not define my life. I became a coach so that I could help others attain their dreams, even if they seem unrealistic to them, just like my dreams seemed impossible to me.

When I work with someone as their coach, my aim is for them to also realize their aspirations no matter how small or audacious. The definition of a coach is "someone whose job is to teach people to improve at a sport or skill,"[3] they are "unlocking a person's potential to maximize their performance."[4] With this book, I am here, not just as the author of the book, but also as your coach. Throughout my life, one of my values has been to help and support others, I have written this book to share the RESULTS Method and process with you, to enable you to enhance your life by using the potential that is already within you to create and implement plans.

As your coach in this book, my aim is to:

- Help and guide you as you seek change in the way that you want, supporting you in the direction you want to go.
- Help you become who you want to be at every stage of your life taking account of your current and future potential, capacity, and capabilities.
- Create a psychologically safe space to build awareness and empower choice, leading to authentic change.

However, this book will not:

- Replace therapy—if a deeper intervention is needed, then like all reputable coaches I make referrals to the appropriate therapists and counselors. There is no shame in therapy, I have had it myself several times, and I urge you to find the right support in your locality.
- Tell you how to live your life or make decisions for you. In this book I provide you with the method and process, you integrate it into your life because you are the expert there.
- Be a "one-size-fits-all" answer. I am an advocate for enabling different experiences and ways of implementation. You need to create the lifestyle that you want, and you do it in a way that fits where you are right now and where you want to go (as hard as it is for me to admit, I no longer have the capacity that my 27-year-old self did!).

One of my missions in life is to bring coaching within the reach of everyone who is interested. An alternative to working with a coach in a group or privately, is to benefit from me as your coach through this book. Or you can read the book with a friend, in a book club, or another community group. And of course, you can discuss RESULTS The Art and Science of Getting It Done with your personal coach.

Writing Style

As this book is in your hands, I consider you to be one of my clients, and my writing style is conversational in tone to reflect the connection that I share with people I work with. I am also writing to you as though we were in a classroom–where yes, I am teaching you– but, you have the freedom to be relaxed as you learn at your own pace. This is a process of discussion, rather than me simply transferring information for you to digest alone. This relationship creates the perfect environment not only for learning, but also for me to be vulnerable, to share stories, to tell you where I went wrong and what lessons I learned, as well as tell you the things that worked well for me and my clients[1] and how you can learn from the people who have previously used the RESULTS Method before you.

Drawings

Throughout my life I have scribbled on napkins for problem solving or for explaining processes to others. I believe if I can't draw it on a napkin, it still needs work to move it from science to simplicity. I've even drawn out solutions on napkins for strangers in coffee shops and airports! All the illustrations in this book are my own, drawn on my virtual napkin (the iPad) as I sat at my writing desk and reminisced about life before 2020.

Respect

Lastly, I value and respect your time. I have poured my heart, soul, and the best of my knowledge into this book for you so that you are able to take advantage of my decades of experience in the fields of positive psychology, project management, and personal growth.

And since I know your time is precious, as is mine (I really dislike it when something wastes my time), I have filled this book with tools, concepts, and ideas that you may not have seen before, as well as new perspectives on others you may be familiar with. I do not want to insult you by writing a book with waffle when trying to explain a simple concept or to confuse you by not explaining something sufficiently. That said, I am human and prone to error, if something doesn't make sense or you want to know a little more you can contact me on social media with the hashtag #resultsbook or by email at s@results.partners.

---

[1] *The names, personal characteristics of individuals, and details of events have been changed in order to disguise identities or protect the privacy of the author's clients and students. Any resulting resemblance to persons living or dead is entirely coincidental and unintentional.*

RESULTS

This book contains applicable knowledge, ideas, and processes. It is divided into seven phases. Each phase can be used independently, but when used collectively, you will find an impactful philosophy for getting it done!

The aim is to give you maximum information, in a clear way, so that rather than spending your time with your head in this book, you understand the guidance within its pages, apply it, and come back every now and then, to refer to it as you would an instruction manual.

My ambition is that you get the results you seek to change your life, your business, or your projects and make your vision a reality. And now that you have this book in your hands, you now have *me* on your team.

While gaining results and moving forward in life can feel like magic, the truth is that it isn't. Attaining the results you seek is all about leaning into yourself and your resources, having a clear plan that you visit every day, and consistently working according to your plan.

#

By discovering and implementing the RESULTS Method you will make progress, move forward, and get it done!

As a lifelong planner, the essentials are clear: you must know what can cause you to go off plan, know who you are and what you stand for, be ready and committed to work on your project, have the confidence to make the decision to pivot if necessary, work out your logistics, develop and maintain a clear plan of how you will make it happen, recognize the difference between internal and external navigation, and know which needs handling. After that, it really is a rinse and repeat cycle, and you do it again and again and watch how you get more done while you are flourishing and thriving.

Remember, at the end of going through the RESULTS Method, the minimum you will take away is a Quarterly Action Plan, Weekly Rhythm, Monthly Moves, Daily Schedule, and Annual Power Plan for what you should do next. You will also know how to establish personal accountability to get it done.

This is your time for results.

100 Day Plan

Are you still with me? Awesome!

Having a plan for learning (or reading) is important. Let me help you to create your 100-day plan to guide you in reading and implementing RESULTS.

Traditionally a 100-day plan is created with you to support a promotion in the corporate world (we have seen politicians talk about their first 100-day plans— they use it as a way to communicate the change they are implementing). The aim of the 100-day plan is to support successful integration into a new role or situation. When I learn something new that I want to implement immediately, I create a 100-day plan. This provides me with two things: a learning plan, and an implementation strategy. As you embark on a change in life having a 100-day plan helps you to imbed that change in a way that supports the shift from where you are now to where you want to go.

For the success of any project you need four things: process, plan, deliberate practice, and progress. Here, the RESULTS Method is the process. You create the plan based on the guidance and tools given in the book. Commit to personal practice and see the progress in your projects.

It is that simple.

The RESULTS Cycle

However, I know that just because it is simple that doesn't mean you will do it. With that in mind I invite you to be kind and compassionate to yourself, as you would a friend. Your intuition will tell you if your practice is sufficient at the end of the day. You will know if you have lived a day in integrity with who you are, so please do the work and ensure that you are clear on what deliberate practice and integration of the RESULTS Method looks like for you and then act on it.

The first time you start a job (and here you are becoming the CEO of your life!) having a 100-day plan is really useful. A few weeks ago, I joined a new mastermind, and one of the facilitating team members asked for open feedback. It was a really powerful experience for me because in all my times of having attended masterminds and high level training, I had never been asked to offer feedback on the course structure and materials in such an open and transparent way—in a way that would result in marked improvement for them and their clients. So, this was different. In our discussion, I shared honestly, "I love what I'm learning, and I have lightbulbs going off every day. But I don't really know where to start in terms of implementing this learning, and I would benefit from a 100-day plan." As soon as I said these words, I watched the questioner as she, seemingly inspired, wrote my suggestion down. They are now working on creating a 100-day plan for new attendees.

I have been in other environments where additional teaching or coaching is provided during the first 100 days. Sometimes coaching is just not enough—take a minute to realize the significance of these words that I, a coach myself, am saying to you! The individual needs to buy into the plan, to be wedded to it, believe in it, and be determined to make it happen—to put in practice what has been taught. This goes beyond instruction or coaching; it permeates the fields of being supported, motivated, and actually doing the work.

Creating a 100-day plan the first time you use the RESULTS Method gives you the ability to create a replicable structure for your life, introduces you to practicing the different facets and phases of the method, and enables you to incorporate it in your daily life.

	M	T	W	Th	F	S	S
1							
2							
3							
4							
5							
6							
7							
8							
9							
10							
11							
12							
13							

100 Day Plan template

Mark the "weekend" days you will take—this can be a traditional Saturday/Sunday or Thursday/Friday depending on where you live in the world. It can also be any two days of the week. The minimum number of days off per week to have is one—this rest enables you to process thoughts, problem solve, come up with new ideas, and also to refresh and revitalize.

Once a month, the last Friday or last day of the month, take at least half a day to review your progress and reset your plans. There is more about this in the **Succeed** phase, for now know that this time is essential in your RESULTS plan as it will help you to assess your progress and make any necessary adjustments.

At the end of the 100-days or Quarterly Action Plan take two days to review and reset in some detail. A sample agenda that you can use is provided in the **Succeed** phase.

Planning to finish in a week?

I am inspired by your aspiration to read the book in a few days. There is a lot to do in this book. I know some people advocate reading books quickly, skimming through them, or listening to the audiobook at 1.25 or 2.0 speed. Sure, you can follow any of these techniques. However, if you choose to read *this* book in a week, then it is important for you to approach this task as your singular priority for those days. Take the time necessary to read *and* implement. Whilst I love that you are reading this book to gain the wealth of knowledge and insights, I would hate for you to simply read it and then put it up on the shelf without ever taking that knowledge and moving forward. Reading RESULTS is an active process: you must read, reflect, and do. And if you get to the end of the first week and feel overwhelmed, it is ok to change gears and rewrite your plan. There are some alternatives to the plan of finishing the book in a week (which are perhaps more likely to integrate into your life given how much you have on your plate).

If you happen to be reading this book for the second time, then refreshing your knowledge of the concepts alongside creating your new Project3x3 is perfect. As you will see later in the Project3x3 and in the Succeed phase, I ask you to set aside two days to dedicate yourself to creating your next Project3x3, and after that you'll be taking a week off so dive in and review the phases and in any of the specific areas where you may need a refresh, and go get it!

Planning to finish in two weeks?

The first time you read RESULTS, I urge you take about two weeks, or a month. It gives you time to familiarize yourself with the concepts, to create your Project3x3 and then add in the details. You will end up with four clear RESULTS plans: Project3x3, Monthly Moves, Weekly Rhythm, and Daily Schedule. These four pages will be your map for the next few months, and as you learn more about yourself and the process, you'll see how to navigate your way to success and flourishing.

Planning to take a month or two to read?

I am really glad that you know yourself and your situation enough to say it will take more than a month for you to read this book. I myself have rushed through books that I know I should have given more time and attention. I would end up disappointed because I was still as stuck as I was when I started! You will avoid that frustration by giving yourself the amount of time you need to benefit fully from this book.

You can find a template to help you with all versions of the 100-Day Plan at *www.results.partners/bookresources*

Can't choose?

That's ok. Just keep reading and discover what to do next.

Use the template shared on page 27 to create a 100-Day plan for how you will read and implement the RESULTS Method.

What to do next?

I know you are busy. I know you have a lot to do, so, I am glad that you are here. I know you are committed to changing your life and making progress. At the same time, I know that there is a chance that you might not come back to this book, and it may end up in your home library or on the office shelf.

Instead, why not take a step or two towards the change you are looking for? There are two action steps that you can scratch off the list right now:

1. Join the RESULTS Circuit Breaker at *www.results.partners/circuitbreaker*

It is a free training and only requires about 10 minutes a day. You will get a video training, templates, or tool to use in each of the seven categories of the RESULTS Method. With this additional online support, you'll:

- Learn how to move beyond your personal showstoppers.
- Deal with doubt, self-sabotage, and imposter syndrome.
- Understand more about who you are, and why you are that way.
- Discover the three parts to The Architecture of Action™.
- Identify the three most important projects for you to work on.
- Discover smart tactics to plan your RESULTS and take care of your responsibilities while leading and thriving.
- Implement the fundamental skill that will keep you on track, avoid boreout and burnout, and help you to finally take action and make progress in your life.

You are welcome to share the link or your results with your family, friends, peers, or colleagues. Whilst the RESULTS Method is a process, we each have our own way of implementing it, and it is essential to know that no two people will do it the same. Always feel free to come back and learn how you can be a better planner and implement more effectively.

I've even added an option to allow you to do the RESULTS Circuit Breaker in two weeks, or a month so that you are in charge of how you integrate the RESULTS Method into your life.

In the electrical world a circuit breaker is a switch designed to protect an electrical circuit from damage caused by excess electricity from an overload or short circuit. Its basic function is to interrupt the current flow after a fault is detected. I have created the RESULTS Circuit Breaker to do just that for you—to protect you from burnout and overload, to interrupt your current processes and redirect your energies in a more efficient and effective manner. When you access the RESULTS Circuit Breaker online, you will be given the opportunity to receive video, audio, and email training from me, but it is not compulsory. You do you.

2. Read the next two chapters.

I ask you to start today if you can or certainly over the next couple of days. In the next chapter you will learn how you have reached this place where so many people have a huge amount of knowledge, but there is still little or no ineffective implementation. You will leave with a real understanding of how you can reach beyond where you are now, and you will no longer wonder why you are not moving forward or making the progress in life or your projects that you desire.

You can get it done. Just turn to the next page...

ORIENTATION

"You have brains in your head.
You have feet in your shoes.
You can steer yourself in any direction you choose.
You're on your own, and you know what you know.
And you are the guy (or gal) who'll decide where to go."

Dr. Seuss (Theodor Seuss "Ted" Geisel) (1904-1991)

RESULTS

When it comes to getting results, we, all know that implementation is absolutely necessary. Yet, there are times when you struggle to get it done or make progress despite having a clear plan of action set out. Before we get into the RESULTS Method and its processes, I would like to share with you what I refer to as the RESULTS GPS (Goal Priority System).

Where are you going?

The Goal Priority System starts with you understanding your intention and identity. You put yourself in a place where you select the right things to work on right now, so you are able to implement with integrity. This focus on understanding one's self first is a significant difference between the RESULTS Methodology and a standard goal-setting approach where you envision a future, create a plan, and then work hard to stay on track. In the latter approach, because something is missing you may experience a disconnect and not be able to acknowledge or celebrate your progress. Traditional goal-setting has some flaws: it doesn't always require you to understand your values, needs, and deeper intentions; it might be carried out with no regard for the bigger picture of your life and circumstances; and it does not eliminate setting goals that are inconsistent with who you want to become. These flaws can all be reconciled by setting your goals based on your intention, identity, integrity by focusing on who you are, so that you are able to consistently show up ready to get the work done while implementing!

The more clarity you have over these four elements the more likely you are to self-regulate your results. These are the elements that I will ask you to assess in each step of the RESULTS Method by performing the Self-Interview (more about that later).

The RESULTS GPS is your Goal Positioning System, and it is core to your success.

The RESULTS GPS™

But a word of warning, your intention, identity, implementation and integrity can work against you—they can hold you back just as easily as they can propel you forward. It could be that someone hurt your feelings, an incident happened in the past, or you interpreted things in a way that left you feeling vulnerable or wounded; as a result, your intentions (even subconsciously) become self-protective. It is possible to create a mechanism to keep you safe that works so well that it also keeps you stuck in life. Remember there is a difference in operating from a place of fear and wanting to be safe. Having an intention that will serve you properly is critical. Other instances when intentions can go against you are when you intend to show that you are the leader at the cost of your team, when you intend to be right at the cost of your relationships, or when you intend to be a good employee at the cost of your homelife.And when you get your intention misaligned with who you are, the rest of it also goes in the wrong direction.

In much the same way, your identity, integrity, and implementation might be swayed by untrue beliefs about yourself dictated or learned from others, unconscious self-deception, and previously acquired, faulty practices. You can thwart your own progress to the extent that these misguided beliefs or practices determine your course.

Intention

"Actions are according to intentions, and everyone will get what is intended." — Al-Bukhari[1]

Understanding the intention *for* everything you do is critical to the success *in* everything you do. Have you ever reflected on your intention for sleep, going to work, waking up? It could be that you are doing these things because it is the norm, but when you increase the clarity regarding your *intention* for doing something, you activate another layer of your being to support the choices you make and the actions you take. As we will see even the research shows that actions are determined by their intentions—whether you will do something or not depends on your intention for the action.

When you have a clear intention for wanting to make progress in a certain area of your life, or for working on a particular project, you make choices in a different way. You are guided by clarity when choosing what to say yes and no to. Allowing the day to take you where it wants or working on other people's agendas are no longer options.

RESULTS

With a clear intention, you can spend time working on what is important for you, rather than what happens by accident. Intention setting is an important part of any project or plan. Imagine studying for a degree, traveling, building a house, or going to work without a clear intention. I know you have it within you to do all of these and anything else you put your mind to incredibly well. However, just because you are good at something does not mean you have to do it.

By having clarity on what you intend to do and how you intend to do it, you can wisely and consciously allocate your most valuable resource—time, and when you can do that, you will enhance your life experience as a whole. You will sense an increased satisfaction with life, feel joy, reap positive financial results, build more memories, and face less "fear of missing out." Setting intentions will make you more effective by positioning you to reflect on what you desire from a broader, holistic perspective rather than the restricted reflections of the heart or head, and you will be better able to articulate what you desire. Setting intentions will enable you to see things that you might not have otherwise seen and do things that you might not have otherwise done.

Intentions can change over time. The longer you leave off reflecting on your intention, the more likely it is that you will forget or lose sight of why you are attending to a particular task or item. Being mindful of your intentions is a pivotal element in attaining the results you want. Professor Peter Gollwitzer's research into human behavior in relation to goals and plans confirms that intentions matter and that without clear intentions, we can become distracted and go off course. We miss the target because the intention relates only to the goal and not to the implementation. In other words, we can have action without ever achieving our stated goal simply because our intention is unclear or unknown.[2]

As a personal growth and project management specialist, I can tell you that if your intention is not clear, then you will struggle with implementation or will feel like you are wading through wet concrete every step of the way. I want you to set your intentions clearly. Do not worry if this is the first time you are doing such an exercise. It is my job to guide you through this and all of the RESULTS Processes. Always remember, as you are here, I am by your side. At any point you can contact me on social media with the hashtag #resultsbook, and I will endeavor to reply.

Setting intentions can make you more effective. Knowing what your intentions are for undertaking any project will result in your carrying out the behaviors necessary for you to make progress on the task that you are working on. By acknowledging your intention, you gain clarity on why you are doing what you are doing. How does it work? Simply, by acknowledge your intentions. For example: intentions for sleeping— to be rested and ready for the next day; for eating—to have the energy you need to perform the day's tasks; for reading this book—to finally get the results you are seeking in life, and so on. Clarity in articulating and writing down your intention is essential.

In project management terms, intention is directly linked to your ability to implement (see later in this chapter). Implementation is the hardest part of any project. Executing a plan in a way that will deliver the anticipated results requires a solid understanding of how the plan fits in within the overall intention, taking into account "business as usual" as well as anticipating the new and being ready to deal with obstacles. Yet we wonder, shouldn't everyone have values, vision, a mission, or purpose for their life or organization? Of course, it is important to spend time working on each of these elements, but at the end of the day they all lead to your strategic intention, which is based on your values and who you are. When you have clarity on your intention, you will feel more inspired to work on what is important for you and for those who are impacted by you at work and at home. Once you know your values, strengths, and a bit more about who you are, I will ask you to prepare a compelling future vision. This will be something that you come back to at all phases, ensuring what you are doing is in line with your aspirations.

RESULTS

In each chapter I will give you opportunities and questions for reflection; your honest input will enable you to know your intention for that phase.

Identity

> 'What we *know* matters, but who we *are* matters more.'
> — Brené Brown

Knowing your identity helps you to know who you are as a person, the qualities that make you different, your reputation, and the characteristics that make others think of you. Your identity is constantly changing. When you were younger perhaps you wanted to be a lawyer, doctor, engineer, firefighter, entrepreneur, writer, or architect. If you are doing something different now than what you were doing a few years ago, your identity has changed. Even if you are doing the same thing, your identity has changed in other aspects of life in that now you might also be a parent, manager, caregiver, etc.

Identity is the set of qualities, beliefs, looks and how you show up in the world. Your psychological identity is what you think about yourself, your self-esteem and the mental model you have of who you are. By understanding yourself and who you want to be you have clarity on your current and future identity.

Affirmations can help with that.

Affirmations are a well-known tool in personal growth and positive psychology. Both anecdotal evidence and research[3] verify that affirmations work. Claude Steele gives us three concepts for how affirmations are effective in his self-affirmation theory:

- Self-affirmation increases our awareness of our self-talk and the identity we create for ourselves.

- Affirmations are not associated with being perfect or exceptional, they are articulating the descriptions that we personally value.
- Affirmations help us to maintain our integrity with who we authentically are by motivating us to live the attribute.[4]

There was a time that—despite the evidence—I was still cynical about the power of affirmations. This all changed when I attended a conference in 2017 that changed my perspective on the "I am…" exercise considerably. Professor Anthony Reddie of Oxford University invited attendees to participate in an exercise he called "I am…." I remember that I viewed this exercise slightly differently to affirmations because for the first time I saw it in relation to the core of what I wanted to be. It was a powerful moment as I had not articulated my true essence of until that moment. (You yourself may find that you come across familiar ideas in this book, and my hope is that you will see them in a more powerful light just like I did with the "I am…" exercise.)

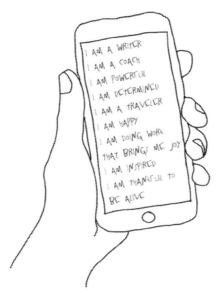

How you can use 'I am…' affirmations

RESULTS

This simple activity enables you to articulate who you are with clarity. I have used this with individuals, organizations, and families, and it is a powerful and speedy way of expressing who you think you are. Find a piece of paper and pen and write the words "I am…" 20 times on the page. Then complete each sentence with a statement of who you are. My answer is never completely the same, but the top five to seven statements are usually consistent.

I reiterate, research on affirmations and positive self-talk confirms the power of this practice as a technique that will enable you to develop a more optimistic identity, as well as being more likely to achieve your goals and aspirations.[5] The regular use of affirmations and positive self-talk generates confidence as you work on your goals. You create the belief that what you desire is achievable and when obstacles arise you find a way to navigate around them. Spending time listening to how you talk to yourself can help you identify what could be holding you back.

For example, shift from saying, "This is an impossible deadline. I'll never be able to meet that," to "There is a lot to do, but I will do what I can," "I'll keep everyone up to date as I make progress," or "I am sure we can get this done." Seek the positive in a situation and use your self-talk to confirm your potential and worthiness. Instead of "I'm so stupid. I messed that one up again," recognize the opportunity and tell yourself, "I didn't do as well as I had wanted, but I've learned much and will do better next time. This has really helped me."

Commit now to trying the "I am…" exercise for yourself. You can download the tool for "I am…" in the online resources section available at *www.results.partners/bookresources*. Understanding more about who you are is important to everything you do—it affects how you show up at work, in relationships, and even in the coffee shop! Knowing yourself is so important that the second phase of the RESULTS Method is dedicated to you gaining a better understanding of who you are. In that phase, I introduce you to some fantastic tools that will help you get to know more about yourself. I also share a framework which will enable you to increase your self-awareness and personal insights throughout your life. Now is a wonderful time for you to start thinking about the elements you would like to include in defining your identity. This strategic move will enable you to be more impactful in your life, implement with more joy and ease, and enable you to look at who you want to be in the future (as well as who you are now).

As you become more intentional, you might discover that you have assumed certain identities that you will choose to release as you go through the RESULTS Method. Such a decision, when well-made, can empower you as you continue pursuing results.

One more thing on identity: if you look inside and see something that you do not like or do not want to be, then know that it is not set in stone. If that is the case, part of your plan could be to work on that aspect, articulate who you want to be, and then step into that being. Your identity is malleable and can be molded to include new aspects or exchange undesirable ones. When I was pregnant with my first child, I had no real idea of how I would be as a mother, but I read and sought advice, and I learned how to be one. When we were teenagers, many of us had a specific career aspiration, yet in reality we had no understanding of how to perform in that role—we learned how to carry out specific functions and then assumed that identity. Whatever you are currently doing, whether you are a lawyer, engineer, writer, coach, parent, student, or entrepreneur, remember that you had to learn how to step into that role and embrace it as part of your identity.

Implementation

> "All our dreams can come true, if we have the courage to pursue them." — Walt Disney

In 1990 Napster came out as a music streaming service and signaled a change in the music industry as we knew it. Music engineer and

RESULTS

record label owner Jimmy Iovine was in partnership with rap artist Dr Dre at Interscope Records, and they both recognized that Napster could be the end of their entire business: people would no longer buy records or CD's, instead they would download the music. Given that their business was in a difficult state, they explored various options including trainers (which had been successful for Nike and Michael Jordan), but Iovine said to his business partner, "No man, your thing is audio," and Dr Dre replied, "Yeah, I can see that."[6] Within moments Dr Dre came up with the name Beats. I just want you to pause to reflect on the power of this. Beats was streaming music before Apple iTunes and any other music streaming service. That is huge. It was an idea before its time.

The initial concept for Beats was to stream music online, but when they realized the true area of their genius—the quality of audio (Dr Dre) and implementation (Iovine)—the concept moved from music streaming to raising the bar in home audio. It was Iovine's attitude towards life that took a thought, turned it into an idea, and made it a success. In Netflix's *The Defiant Ones* Iovine says, "I just said I have got to do whatever it takes." Later in the documentary, he says, "You have got to be of service. Do whatever you can to be in the room with the best people you can…. If that means sweeping, sweep. If that means setting up a microphone, set it up. Learn from the best and get in that room somehow."[7] Yet without their partnership and the ingenuity of sounds held by Dr Dre, Iovine's idea might have never become reality.

It was not just the ingenious idea and the personalities involved that made it work. Initially it was the right idea, but as the technology was not available to support it and the market itself was not interested in expensive headphones in 1990, the time was wrong. Ultimately, this idea took twenty-four years to come to fruition, when, on August 1, 2014, Beats Headphones was sold as the largest acquisition in Apple's history when Apple bought it for $3 billion in cash and stock. Now that is the power of the right time, right people, right skills, right idea!

When it comes to implementation, I want you to be ready. And being ready requires saying no to some things so you can say yes to others. If you have an idea do not ignore it; instead write it down, play with it, and wait until you sense the time is right. At the right time, the right people and all the resources you need will show up. There is no rush to implement, but there is a need to show up for your life.

You already know that implementation is the hardest element of any project and plan. Despite having a great plan, it is possible to be stuck in paralysis, not because you don't have the know-how but because of any of the following factors:

- inadequate or zero commitment
- lack of clarity
- not *your* goal
- lack of alignment
- too many other commitments
- insufficient confidence or certitude
- the wrong time
- unprepared society
- unavailable technology or infrastructure

And I am sure a myriad of other inhibitors are coming to your mind right now.

The RESULTS Method addresses the key issues that cause a lack of implementation. It must start with you and dealing with some of the obvious challenges that are already present.

Integrity

"The supreme quality for leadership is unquestionably integrity. Without it, no real success is possible, no matter whether it is on a section gang, a football field, in an army, or in an office."
— Dwight D. Eisenhower

RESULTS

Integrity is how you show up and what you do. The word integrity conveys moral strength, personal confidence, and a praiseworthy steadfastness to one's inherent truths. The Cambridge Dictionary gives the meanings of being complete and whole and of not compromising one's beliefs or high standards.[8] One thing is for sure, integrity takes a whole lot of determination, and it is certainly never easy.[9] It requires following your convictions and doing the right thing in all situations, as if no one is watching you. *The Economist* has identified integrity as one of the top attributes of leadership.[10] When you are focusing on leading your life and getting the results you desire, I believe a discussion on integrity is mandatory.

Often, we work on a project or have an idea because we are seeking some form of external reward. I have no problem with that per se; in fact, under the right circumstances, I advocate external rewards. However, in my experience, there needs to be a solid connection between who you are and your intended result; otherwise, you will not operate from a place of integrity, and that means when you are tired, distracted, or simply cannot be bothered, you will forget your true intention, identity, and no longer implement. There is no need here for a philosophical debate regarding who regulates integrity nor the details of what it means academically, that discourse would fill several other books! In relation to the RESULTS Method, integrity is you having the conviction to follow through, knowing your own honor—and keeping it, being genuine to yourself, and checking in regularly to ensure that you are living your life from a place of truth and authenticity.

Integrity is a bit like confidence. You know you want more of it, but it's hard to describe what it really is and to define exactly when you do have more of it. I propose that living a life of integrity requires you to be clear on your values and to live by them (don't worry, you will be exploring and identifying your personal values in the **Evolve** phase).

Integrity is valuing honesty *and* being honest with yourself so that you do not fall into self-deception or naively accept others' stories about you or what you should be doing. Operating from the perspective of integrity is prioritizing excellence—not someone else's excellence but your own. Integrity also entails undertaking a journey of continuous improvement, so that you are constantly evolving into the best of who you can be (we will discuss this further in the **Reach** and **Evolve** phases).

You can work on developing your personal integrity by:
- Communicating honestly and transparently—even with yourself!
- Being reliable and following through on your commitments.
- Ensuring your actions are consistent with the language you use—both written and verbal.
- Knowing your values and showing up in a manner that reflects those values.
- Acknowledging when you might not have got it right and being willing to be an active participant in a cycle of continuous improvement.
- Caring for yourself, your plan, and your projects (or revising or deleting them if they are no longer of value to you and your aspirations).

Living with integrity is a lifestyle choice. It is possible you may not have considered it from that perspective before, but that is partly because in today's social media fueled lives, we have been seduced by pretty pictures of what life should be like, rather than what it really is. Influencers influencing and social media algorithms mean that we often question what truth is, and questioning the truth has become so pervasive in society. It is easy to understand why a discussion on integrity could be overlooked as you work on understanding yourself more or spend time reflecting on where best to allocate your resources and effort. The truth is that in order to be true to yourself you need to maintain integrity between who you are today and who you want to become to realize your vision.

RESULTS Self-Interview™

At the end of every phase, I request that you conduct a process I created called the Self-Interview. I'll provide the questions; you do the work. Warren Berger is a journalist who interviewed employees of companies like Google, Netflix, and Airbnb for his book *A More Beautiful Question*. In it, Berger says that questions are the key to innovation and breakthroughs, and that those who ask the best questions have the most innovative and successful ideas.[11] As a professional coach and researcher, I know that responding to a simple, well-worded question with deep and honest reflection provides an opportunity for life-changing awareness, understanding other perspectives, and the ability to make deep change.

By asking appreciative and inquisitive, open-ended questions such as the ones you will find at the end of each phase, you will discover more about your strengths and how to create a flourishing change.* The questions have been designed using an Appreciative Inquiry[12] approach, meaning that there are no right or wrong answers and your well-being is at the heart of everything. The more curious you are, the more you will discover. These questions will act as prompts for you to reflect, gain clarity on your personal perspectives, and give you insights on where you are in your RESULTS journey.

Now, I know that some of you will have a resistance to writing, and that is okay; I have been there too. Let me be clear, the Self-Interview is not a "brain-dump" of words for the sake of feeling good about completing the exercise—a brain-dump may make you feel you've completed the task, but there is no substantial evidence that it improves

---

* While conducting a Self-Interview is effective, working with an experienced coach to guide you through the introspective process and help you notice the nuances of your responses has its advantages. It can enhance your experience and quicken the journey of self-discovery, but it is not necessary. You can do the work alone and remember done is better than perfect.

your well-being or desire to take action. In my experience as a lifelong learner, and reflective practitioner in both my personal and professional life, I have found that writing out your thoughts, reflections, and feelings is therapeutic and leads to important insights about yourself that you might not otherwise garner. Research shows that students who write about emotional topics have improved grades in the months following the study,[13] and senior professionals who have been made redundant are likely to find a new job more quickly after writing.[14] Therein lies the power of self-reflection and writing. However, writing can also unlock difficult reflections.

In his book *Principles,* Ray Dalio shares his framework for progress:

$$PAIN + REFLECTION = PROGRESS$$

We have all been through difficulties and some form of pain. Dalio's premise is that progress comes through the reflection of that pain[15]. I like what Dalio says. To me this premise really comes to life when you are aiming for audacious goals or when you have little capacity and what seem like small goals are actually really bold for you. There is no avoiding the obstacles and challenges that come up in a journey of progress. The pain and struggle you feel as a consequence are signs that you are looking for alternative solutions to continue progress (you will find out more about this in the **Thrive** phase). By navigating your obstacles, your learning and personal evolution will be rapid. I know from personal experience that the challenges we face test and strengthen us. It is through the reflection that the appreciation comes.

If you neglect to reflect, all that you have is the pain. This is why in every program I teach, I advocate reflection.

RESULTS

The Centre of Journal Therapy offers a nice little acronym for guidance on how to approach such reflective exercises so that you can WRITE effectively:

What are you going to write about?
Review or reflect on the topic and start writing.
Investigate your thoughts and feelings.
Time yourself.
Exit smart.[16]

I encourage you to have a dedicated journal for your RESULTS self-interviews (or you can download the template waiting for you in the online book resources).

Let's take a moment now to consider these questions briefly.

Self-Interview

Insight: What is your biggest insight from the orientation?

What can you notice about yourself?

Intention: When you explore your boldest hopes and highest aspirations, what is it that you ultimately want?

Identity: Why does your work on this really matter to you?

Implementation: What is the smallest or most immediate action you are willing to take?

Integrity: What can you do to deepen (*strengthen, expand, intensify, grow*) your commitment to follow through?

Before
RESISTING

After
ACCEPTING

REACH

"If you always put limits on everything you do, physical or anything else, it will spread into your work and into your life. There are no limits. There are only plateaus, and you must not stay there, you must go beyond them."

Bruce Lee - (1940-1974)

RESULTS

This inconsistent performance will affect him…

Daniel's office gives him views over the Thames. He is a 34-year-old lawyer and is on partner track. Gloria, his manager, contacted me asking for help. She said, "Daniel's potential is there, he does really incredible things. But he has blips—there are times when he does really well, and then there are times when he is average. This inconsistent performance will affect his partner track."

Daniel is typical of many people who are capable but might not use their full potential due to inconsistency. In working with Daniel, it was clear that there were times in his life that he truly believed in his skills and capability, and other times when he felt insecure. He thought that he could cover up for his uncertainties, but his colleagues noticed. Daniel identified with the traits of imposter syndrome. By working with him and helping him to understand the intricacies of the impact of his imposter syndrome and identifying the cause of his doubt, Daniel was able to stop resisting his latent talent and start accepting himself for who he was. Subsequently he was able to get the results he sought more consistently. One year after our last session, he contacted me to say he'd been made a partner.

Daniel's story shows the power of applying your potential and accepting who you are, and the undesirable consequences you can face when you have resistance in your life rather than surrendering to the possibility of the unknown.

You have a great deal of potential, but there are a number of factors (I call them Showstoppers) which could be holding you back. We give ourselves excuses, but we should be truthful about our potential. Jose Mourinho, one of the greatest professional football managers of our time, made it clear: "You should demand more from yourself. It should not be me demanding more from you. Nobody else. You. You should demand more from yourself."[1]

Daniel's story shows you that by addressing the factors that are restricting your progress, you will be able to realize your capabilities and use your potential to make progress rather than give in to resistance.

It is normal to have days when you find it hard. You do not need anyone's permission to have short "pity parties" or tantrums (more about that in the **Succeed** phase) or even have the odd off day. It is when the odd days turn into weeks or months that there is a problem and you may start to settle for a life that you did not, and do not, want.

So, what do you do?

What's next?

This is probably the most important question you will ask yourself as you seek to persevere in the challenge of achieving your long-term goals. Your answer will determine how you allocate your energy, effort, and effectiveness. I believe that by reaching beyond where you are now, you will always find the right answer. You may experience some discomfort at first because many of us are strangers to introspection, but don't stop.

I have coached and trained a wide variety of people from C-suite executives to stay-at-home parents, and even mature teenagers. One thing is common with most of them and the majority of the population for that matter: at some point, insecurities settle in and throw people off course.

In this phase, you are going to learn how you can identify the areas of your life where you may be feeling resistance, and then you will discover how to develop acceptance of the cause of the resistance so you can progress. You will learn how to deal with doubt, make imposter syndrome your friend, cultivate the essence of real resilience, avoid self-sabotage, and develop a growth-focused mindset. I suggest that you read this chapter at least once a year to truly experience the insights and opportunity available to you when you pause and think about where you are in your journey. I know that doubt, derailment, and self-sabotage will try and come back every now and then. Your job is to recognize when they do and then to address them. It is crucial that you do not ignore these stumbling blocks or else one day you could be thrown off course.

At the end of this phase, you will create a plan for dealing with the causes of resistance in your life, and you will then be ready to ask the pivotal question, "Who am I?" which is covered in the phase that follows.

Showstoppers

As you read the various points shared in this phase, remember that not all of them will apply to you, but they are showstoppers that can hold you back. It is good to know what is preventing you from making progress and discovering how to respond to it in a different way. It is also helpful to know what might be holding others back, so that you are able to support those close to you. In some cases, you will find insight instantaneously and will intuitively know what you need to do or how you need to respond in a different way. In other cases, you may need more of an intervention to respond i.e. counselling, therapy, or coaching.

I have identified six Showstoppers which can hold you back and prevent you from reaching beyond your current circumstances. You may resonate with some, and you may start to understand the behaviours of colleagues and friends. This is a real education in what holds us back, and you have the opportunity to move from resistance to acceptance.

Self-doubt and Self-sabotage

Self-doubt is not a new or modern obstacle. In fact, in 1604, William Shakespeare wrote about the dangers of self-doubt in his play *Measure for Measure* "Our doubts are traitors and make us lose the good we oft might win, by fearing to attempt."[2] (In other words: "Our doubts work against us and make us lose the good things we often could win by making us scared to try."[3])

Self-doubt is very persuasive and can hold you back from so many things—it prevents you from starting or finishing projects. Self-doubt is that feeling you have when you question yourself or your abilities and then allow those thoughts to get out of control. Occasionally self-doubt can be helpful: it helps you to recognize that you may not always be right and that humbleness and openness to learning is empowering. But most of the time self-doubt results in you standing in your own way. I believe that us getting in our own way is one of the most common forms of unidentified self-oppression, and it is not discussed enough. The desire to "keep up with the Joneses" can be crippling, and as soon as your eyes are open, and you start comparing yourself to others you may feel unworthy which can reinforce the feeling that you are right to doubt yourself.

Self-sabotage comes from a fear of failure, that fuels procrastination (more about that later). By allowing yourself to fall down the hole of self-sabotage, you stop doing the things that you are capable of, and eventually, you begin to believe that you're incapable of moving forward because you have forgotten how well you do when you do the work. Self-sabotage is a subversive way to shift the blame away from ourselves and onto something outside ourselves. You convince yourself that it wasn't you or your capabilities that failed, it was the situation. But the reality is that had you done the work, you would have made progress. But you didn't, and that's why you feel stuck.

With self-sabotage, you create a self-fulfilling prophecy where what you say and do becomes the truth to you. Rather than focusing on developing a great plan and working on the results you want to create, you speak to yourself negatively over and over again, and eventually that talk forms indents in your neural pathways. If you tell yourself some form of "I'm not worthy," "I'm incapable of doing this," "I'm no good," eventually these thoughts become ingrained in your psyche and become your truth. Two simple words lay at the core of this way of thinking: "I can't." When you are convinced you can't, you make less effort. With less effort, you decrease your chances of succeeding, ultimately reinforcing your own negative beliefs and creating a vicious cycle of further self-sabotage.

By denying your own sense of achievement you're contributing to a larger issue related to a lack of self-compassion. While you are kind and encouraging towards friends in need, you are probably much harsher with yourself. Self-compassion researcher Kirstin Neff says self-compassion is when you are compassionate with yourself despite the situation being challenging.[4] This research demonstrates that lack of self-compassion relates to self-doubt. Individuals who are kinder to themselves tend to accept, rather than deny, their deficiencies and are better able to encourage themselves to do better. Those with high self-doubt have a greater need for approval from others; they worry more about failures and negative evaluations and are harsher in their self-judgments. This leads to a tendency toward isolation.

I propose the solutions to self-doubt and self-sabotage involve you developing self-compassion. It requires you to challenge yourself to go beyond your current capabilities to discover the other talents you have. Vincent Van Gogh put it rather nicely when he said, "If you hear a voice within you say you cannot paint, then by all means paint and that voice will be silenced."[5] A significant reason why the **Reach** and **Evolve** phases compel you to look inside to understand yourself (and articulate your best self) is because the internal strategies you discover will assist you to connect with who you are. By understanding yourself more, you can be more open to accepting help from others and seeking support. Connections can be built both in the online and virtual world, so do not think that if you are unable to meet people physically that you are unable to shake off self-doubt. You can do it!

Imposter syndrome

If you feel any insecurity, self-doubt, uncertainty, fear of failure, perfectionism, or self-criticism, you could be experiencing imposter syndrome. These feelings are normal and are experienced by between 9 and 82 percent of the population depending on the assessment used.[6] Imposter syndrome is common amongst men and women and across all age ranges from teenagers through to late-stage professionals. Whilst it is normal that these feelings may prevent you from making progress in your life, work, or of having the impact that you seek, it is *not* normal to allow this to happen when you have the tools for responding to imposter syndrome.

Imposter syndrome (or imposter phenomenon) is a mindset pattern where someone, who despite having many accomplishments and achieved successes, has a persistent fear of being exposed as a fraud.

They feel like a fraud despite there being no evidence to confirm it. In their article, Clance and Imes say that imposter syndrome has five main elements of which any two need to be present in order for you to fall into this trap. These elements are: the imposter cycle, the need to be special or the best, characteristics of being superman/superwoman, fear of failure, and denial of ability or discounting praise.[7]

To determine if you have imposter syndrome (or to discover where it shows up in your life, as most people have this in some way shape or form) you can look at the imposter cycle below.

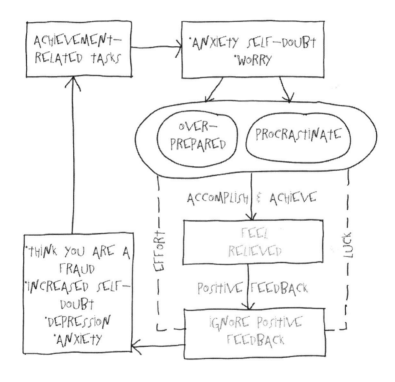

Clance's (1985) model of the Imposter Cycle, as depicted in Sakulku & Alexander (2011).

As you look at the diagram above, you are probably starting to think of times when you have had something to do but you got stuck procrastinating. Several years ago, I attended a two-month visioning course and created a beautifully illustrated and structured 10-year-plan. Yet despite its perfect preparation and binding, it still sits on my shelf untouched; perhaps I have left it unactioned because it was over-prepared or because of the insecurities I had due to imposter syndrome—I did not believe in myself.

Valerie Young is a researcher in Imposter Syndrome, and her TEDTalk[9] on the subject is very insightful. Young says that people with imposter syndrome fall into one of five groups: the perfectionist, the superwoman/man, the natural genius, the soloist, and the expert.[10] The cycle first starts with an achievement-related task, maybe a project that was assigned to you. If you think back to school and reflect on the things that made you anxious, worried, or gave you feelings of self-doubt, those things are probably still making you feel as if you are a fraud even today.

What did you do in response to that task? Did you procrastinate and then panic to complete the assignment? Once you finished, did you have a positive sense of completion and relief. When you were given positive feedback did you shrug it off thinking that you did not deserve the praise? Rather than acknowledging your skills and capabilities, did you feel that your achievement was met only because of luck or the extra hard work you put in?

In the imposter cycle, because results are attributed to hard work or luck—rather than your ability and action—no matter what you do, when the results come in, you will *not* believe that your ability and action played an important part in those results. Consequently, you always ignore or discount positive feedback, even when it is accurate. Whenever you have a project to work on, this cycle repeats and heightens, and so with every new project or task your feelings and perceptions of fraud, self-doubt, depressive symptoms, and anxiety increase. And as this perpetuates, your self-identification as a fraud intensifies which in turn increases the feeling that you lack ability and you fear that at any point you might be exposed as a fraud. Removing or addressing self-doubt before something happens can help to reduce or eliminate feeling like an imposter. If you do feel like an imposter, then it is highly recommended that you seek the support of friends, family, a coach, or a therapist. Imposter syndrome is not a psychologically defined illness or a mental health issue, but its impact on your life can cause anxiety or mild depression and thus become a mental health issue.

Imposter syndrome can take place in any new environment (new city, new home), academic environment (school or university), at work (new job, office, or promotion), social interactions (meeting new people), or in relationships (family, friends, spouse).

Research (and my own personal experience) relating to responding to imposter syndrome suggests the following:

- **Talk about it**—others may also be struggling with similar feelings. When I first did this so many other felt they were able to share their own experience which was both reassuring and empowering for me.
- **Seek understanding**— the syndrome is well researched. Knowledge can help disrupt a negative script.
- **Know what triggers negative feelings**. — Big groups do it for me. Now that I know this, I can have a different conversation with myself when I am revising my well-researched lecture at 3 a.m. on the day it's due to be presented!
- **Record achievements** — disrupt the script of "I know nothing."
- **Think "good enough"**— perfection is impossible, particularly when an issue is complex.
- **Be curious** — especially about feeling particularly stupid or incompetent—while this is an internal feeling, it may also be a clue about an external trigger such as something difficult emerging in a conversation; something no one feels confident about managing. Bracketing this off as just another example of

incompetency is to miss the opportunity to talk about what may really be going on.

- **Recognize self-doubt**— this is a core skill, and to learn it, one must be prepared to radically question what one assumes to be true. Dismissing this doubt as "just imposter syndrome" can mean missing moments of productive reflection.
- **Pay attention to hours worked**— while it may be routine in some work cultures to work long hours, this shouldn't be a reason not to have conversations about why we work so hard and why we collectively agree to this.

Queena Hoang investigated the impact of imposter syndrome in the workplace and classroom. Her research suggests that having a mentor who has walked the path before you can minimize feelings of self-doubt and allow for a smoother transition and less overwhelm when moving towards a new situation.[11] Having the support of someone to cheer you on and say, "You got this!" can have a profound impact on how one accepts rather than resists imposter syndrome. Find someone who can give you that encouragement or join the RESULTS community and get the support there.

If you feel as if you have imposter syndrome know that you are not alone. Individuals such as Michelle Obama, Maya Angelou, Tom Hanks, Nicola Sturgeon, Emma Watson, Robbie Williams, and I have all openly spoken about it. The sense of being an imposter is real and can be personally debilitating, but it is more than a personal experience. If 50 percent of the people in a group are privately struggling with imposter syndrome, it will have a profound impact on the way the group functions. Speaking up, despite feeling like an imposter, is an important skill for all of us if we are to remain thoughtful, curious, and help others to continue learning.

In order to write this book, I had to overcome my own imposter syndrome. This was hard work! However, once I realized the extent to which it was impacting my life, I resolved to master it, and I did that by deciding that imposter syndrome would be my friend, not my foe. As contradictory as it sounds, that worked for me and I am sure it can for you too. Sure, there are still days when it feels impossibly hard to do anything, but because I have done the work outlined in this chapter and the next, it is easy to remind myself of the values I have and contribute to others and why I do what I do. I share this with you so that you know the same opportunity awaits you.

Struggle

Struggle is part of our lives, and rather than ignore it, I invite you embrace it. Let me explain why.

When you are clear on the progress you seek from life and things don't go to plan then you may become frustrated. That frustration can show up as a major obstacle and derail you, or it can give you an opportunity to pause, reflect, and keep going.

As I am writing this book, I am plagued with internal struggle, haunted by imposter syndrome, taunted by the question of whether that I am the right person to do this work despite knowing it is much needed.

The struggle is real. It will show up in different ways—you know that. Rather than fight it, why not acknowledge it? When people are in a hurry to get things done and it doesn't work out in the way that they want it to, they psychologically beat themselves up and this is one of the biggest oppressions known to humanity—the oppression that you inflict upon yourself!

We are all in a rush to get things done, and that is fine, but remember most of the time your expectation of what you can do is far greater than the reality of what you will deliver. It comes back to the idea that we will overestimate what we can do in a year and underestimate what we can do in ten (more on that when we discuss Planning Fallacy later).

Rather than ignore the self-oppression and struggle that you have created for yourself, why not accept it as part of the process. I ask you to be patient and do the work, your progress (even if slower than you would like) will speak for itself.

I can tell you, if I allowed the struggle to engulf me, I would not have finished this book. There are plenty of things I have done in the past where the struggle has engulfed me, and I just stopped. Getting intimidated or frustrated to the point of throwing in the towel is not of service to you or me. When you are patient and focused then your results will come. They will show themselves time after time. Remember when you were a toddler and you were struggling to walk? You were patient, but you continued despite the stumbles and falls, you eventually learned to walk on your own two feet. So, I know you have the tools to persevere inside you. All you have to do is reach inside, find your potential and possibility, and put them both to work!

As you work through this book, be patient with yourself; you will stumble, but you just need to get up and keep going. That is how you make your plan work; that is how you navigate your internal dialogue. Your persistence will result in actions, and those actions will take you forward in small steps.

Persistence, patience, and planning are the key ingredients of making progress in life and dealing with struggle.

Derailment

A stable sense of who you are is important for psychological well-being and psychological safety. Derailment happens when someone goes off course, just like a train goes off its tracks. People who are "derailed" have trouble coming to terms with how their life course has unfolded over time and consequently they do not easily identify with their older self. It has been suggested that derailment is a feature of depression, but that it is not unique to depression.[12] However, by engaging with unlikely goals or future visions you may de-couple the link of derailment and depression.[13]

Psychological safety is one of the most important elements in life. It goes beyond Professor Amy Edmundon's definition of "giving candid feedback, openly admitting mistakes and learning from each other."[14] Psychological safety is about the culture you create internally and externally. At the time of writing, in 2020, many people are living in fear or panic due to an increased global feeling of stress related to the pandemic and its impact. Working from home, not being able to read the cues of colleagues which creates a sense of belonging in the workplace, leads to increased anxiety, and derailment.

You can also develop psychological safety by creating a virtual community. Whilst the 11 a.m. huddle meeting may feel like a chore, today it is a vital tool for building well-being and community. In terms of psychological well-being, knowing who you are is critical to this, and we will work on building this awareness in the **Evolve** phase. Know that self-change has many potential benefits for responding to derailment,[15] so the work you are doing here will keep you on the right track.

One of the most important elements to avoid derailment is having a good relationship with yourself and others. The feeling of psychological safety provided because of the natural support system fostered by friends and family is powerful. Having people who will cheer you on in life will build joy and provide the opportunity for you to ask for help when you need it and enable you to increase belief in yourself. A trusted support system is a major factor in avoiding derailment; when you have people who are looking out for you, they will also assist you in seeing the signs of derailment.

RESULTS

Disengaging with your goals is a process, and recovering from this disconnect is sped up within a learning environment thereby moderating any detrimental effects of derailment. Interestingly, it has also been suggested that rumination (over thinking) and excessive pondering is a "casual influence" on depressive symptoms.[16] Maybe individuals who develop depression as a result of feeling derailed are actually doing so as a result of increased rumination about a lost cause.[17] By being here and following the steps I set out for you in RESULTS and using the processes I share, you are doing the work to avoid derailment.

Procrastination

When you put something off, it is not because you are being lazy; chances are it could be to do with delaying tactics. The origin of the word procrastinate is from the Latin word *prōcrāstinātus* meaning to put off until tomorrow. When you put something off until tomorrow, you tend to feel guilty.

Sometimes you might even go into a cycle of procrastination on a particular task because you have a negative association with it. When you look at all the reasons for procrastination, it is the emotional element that links them—the association of anxiety, insecurity, frustration, self-doubt, etc. Procrastination is not a time management problem; it is a self-regulation problem and awareness can help.

Your dislike of a task correlates to how you feel about it. The cost of procrastination can be significant to both the project and you. At the minimum, it can result in a job poorly done, but it can also stop projects before they even start. On a physical and psychological level, procrastination can cause chronic stress, symptoms of depression or anxiety, or high blood pressure.

Reason	RESULTS Method Solution
Deadline (too far away or too close)	· If a deadline is too close and the stress means you will not meet it, move the deadline or ask for a change. · If it is too far away, then create a self-imposed earlier deadline and start taking small steps towards it. This is not always easy, so take a look at the 10 different time blocks (see **utilize** phase) and pick one of those for the project where your deadline is far away.
Perfectionism	· Realize that nothing on earth is perfect! If you insist on seeking perfection (like I used to) then redefine what perfection is (for me 80 percent was perfect). · Start doing the work. Even a messy napkin sketch is better than keeping the thoughts in your head. In fact, many parts of this book were sketched out on a napkin, back of a receipt, or in a note on my phone. · You are seeking progress, not perfection.
Boredom	· Do your tasks in the best time for you. You know your personal rhythm. Some people are morning people, others prefer evenings. There is no right or wrong. Break the boring task up into smaller tasks, set an alarm for the amount of time you will work on it, and start.
Resentment	· You don't like the fact that the task is now yours! Occasionally we all need to do something we don't want to. Decide to either grit your teeth and do the task, or use the Eisenhower Model and delegate or delete it (we will come to this in the **Lead** phase).

Ideas for how to respond to procrastination.

RESULTS

When given a task that makes you feel anxious or insecure, the amygdala (the "threat detector" part of the brain) perceives the task as a genuine threat to your self-esteem or well-being. Even if you intellectually recognize that putting off the task will create more stress for yourself in the future, your brain is still concerned with removing the threat in the present. Daniel Goleman named this the "amygdala hijack."[18]

Telling yourself to stop procrastinating will not do much, as you probably already know! In essence, procrastination is about emotions, not productivity. The question then is, how do you get the work done? Since the reason is rooted in emotion, the solution must address the emotion. You need to find a better reward than avoidance, and the solution must be dependent on yourself and not anything external.

It would be wrong to suggest that procrastination is something that goes away; it is something that you face every day—even if related to small or strategic parts of your day. When you start to encounter procrastination during your RESULTS journey, respond by cultivating curiosity, taking the next small action, and making your temptations inconvenient.

Cultivate Curiosity

If you're feeling tempted to procrastinate, bring your attention to the sensations arising in your mind and body. What feelings are pulling you to procrastinate? Where do you feel them? What do they remind you of? What happens to the idea of procrastinating when you are more attentive to these feelings? Does it become more or less intense? Do other emotions arise? How do the sensations in your body shift as you continue to focus your awareness on them? Use the discoveries within your answers to navigate through the desire to put off what needs to be done.

Take the Next Small Action

By focusing only on the "next action," you do something to move you forward. At the start of a task, you can consider the next action as a possibility, as if you were acting: "What's the next action I'd take on this if I were going to do it, even though I'm not?" Maybe you would open your email. Or perhaps you would put the date at the top of your document. Don't wait to be in the mood to do a certain task. Just start with a small action.

Make Your Temptations Inconvenient

It's still easier to change your circumstances than change yourself. Put obstacles between the thing that you want to do while procrastinating—hide apps or use an app that sets time blocks on certain apps on your phone, turn off notifications and remove chat apps from your computer, and always keep drinking water with you. Shut the door to the room you are working in and tell others you are in a meeting with your project. By putting obstacles between yourself and your temptations, you create a degree of the right kind of resistance. You are adding friction to the procrastination cycle and making the reward value of your temptation less immediate.

Fixed Mindset

As a young researcher, Professor Carol Dweck, author of *Mindset: The New Psychology of Success,* was fascinated by how some children faced challenges and failures with self-confidence while others shrunk back. In her book, Dweck identified two core mindsets, or beliefs, about human traits that shape how people approach challenges: fixed mindset and growth mindset.[19] A fixed mindset is when you believe that your abilities are set in stone and are not flexible; that they were predetermined at birth. Someone with a growth mindset believes that their skills and qualities can be changed and molded through effort and perseverance.

RESULTS

More recently, Dweck noticed a new trend: a widespread embrace of what she refers to as "false growth mindset"[20]— which she says is a misunderstanding of the idea's core message. The growth mindset's popularity had led some to believe that one could simply encourage effort or encourage a growth mindset by saying "try hard." For example, you might congratulate someone for trying on a test even though they failed it, believing that this would promote a growth mindset. But this empty praise can actually lead to a false growth mindset.

The false growth mindset is when you think you have a growth mindset, but you either don't really have a growth mindset or you don't really understand what it is. It is false to think that you can have a growth mindset all the time; reassuringly, Dweck says, "Everyone is actually a mix of fixed and growth mindsets."[21] You can have a growth mindset in a certain area, but there can still be something that triggers a fixed mindset in you—this is normal. For example, if you are really challenged or outside your comfort zone, a fixed mindset can be prompted where you think "of course that other person can do it, but not me!"

The whole idea of growth-mindset praise is to focus on the learning process. When you focus on effort, you learn how effort leads to progress. By commending the effort that led to the outcome, you link the praise to outcome. But it is not just effort, it is also strategy, so you are effectively acknowledging the effort and encouraging the creation of a plan to get the results you seek. Know that if you are stuck, effort alone is not enough—you also need energy and effectiveness for results, more on that later. Continuing with an ineffective approach will not get you the results you seek. All of this is part and parcel of the process of learning and implementing.

I believe that at some point in your life, you make a strategic decision to lean towards a fixed mindset or a growth one. As you can imagine, the benefits of a growth approach are significant—they can enhance your skill base, growth, and overall health and happiness.

Dweck tells us that there is a significant link between what you believe and what you do.

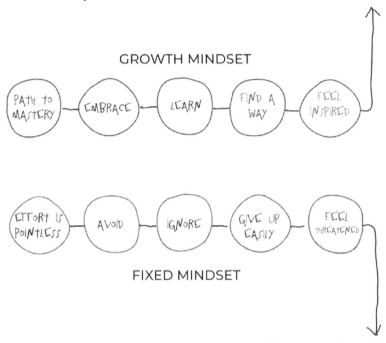

Illustration by Saiyyidah Zaidi based on Dweck's Mindset.[22]

"I'm not good at it" is what you might say when you are given a complex problem to solve. Rather than retreating behind such words, why not view the situation as a challenge and look at how you could solve it. Ignoring your own (and others') negative talk and criticism will help you to find your own inspiration and success. When you believe things about yourself like "It's hard for me to lose weight," "I'm not good at mathematics," "I'm not a natural athlete," "I'm not creative," "I'm a procrastinator" then it is very likely that these beliefs will cause you to avoid experiences where you might feel like a failure because you don't attempt anything that will prove you wrong. As a result, you don't learn as much, and it's difficult to progress. In *Mindset*, Dweck briefly mentions imposter syndrome as a symptom of a fixed mindset (you can revisit that section a few pages ago if needed).

If you believe you have a growth mindset it is important to ensure that it is not a false growth mindset and to work out how you can move from a fixed mindset to a growth one. With a growth mindset you know that change is possible. Note, if you do not make the progress you seek, it could be because you have a false growth mindset or a fixed one. It is necessary to step back and reflect so that you can understand what is making you feel stuck or fixed. There are ways of thinking, identities that you can adopt, and habits or rituals that will move you forward or hold you back. I outline the ones I would like you to assume throughout the book.

Think growth.

Daniel Kahneman, author of *Thinking Fast and Slow*, offers two theories on how we think. He says that we have one thought system that is automatic and intuitive; it is the one that enables us to make day-to-day decisions with ease. The other system is more conscious and deliberate and helps us to problem solve.[23] Both serve us well when it comes to adopting a growth mindset.

Become curious as to *how* you think—it is the foundation of how you show up every single day. By effectively using both the intuitive and more conscious thinking methods driving your thought processes, you are able to see both problems and possibilities and then use these as the basis for your personal and professional growth. It is important to take responsibility for how you think.

When you think that getting *that* job or completing *that* project will transform you into the person you want to be, then you are operating from a fixed mindset— you are defining who you are by the results.

This is a major problem in our society when the focus in on achievements not on alignment, more about that later. Yet, deep change is rooted in your clear intention and identity, not by focusing on the results you want. And it is your daily actions and your convictions that enable you to become the person you want to be and deliver on the projects that are important to you.

	Fixed	Mixed	Growth
Challenges	Avoid challenges	Only take on a challenge if you have previous results in that area	Challenges excite you. What's the next one?
Mistakes	Mistakes are failures, you hide them or lie about them.	Mistakes are just a setback	You reflect, learn and apply your learning. Nothing to worry about here.
Feedback and criticism	Feedback is a threat. Criticism is the same.	It depends on who is saying it and if it is mean or not.	Feedback and criticism are motivators and enable learning.
Implementation	You avoid implementing, or you apply ineffective strategies.	You implement but if something goes wrong you quit.	The process has ups and downs. It's all part of the fun.
Perseverance	If you struggle you quit.	If you have encouragement and support, you might keep going.	You get it done with grit and grace.
Asking questions	You don't ask questions, or don't know what to ask.	You might ask, but if its outside your comfort zone you won't.	You ask questions about everything.
Risks	You do not take risks at all.	If the task is familiar, you'll take a risk, otherwise you'll do exactly what is needed.	You plan, start with confidence, errors are ok, and you share your learnings with others.

RESULTS Effort (based on Effective Effort Rubric, Carol Dweck, Mindset Works.) [24]

RESULTS

As you know by now, your beliefs can sabotage your behavior. There is a powerful relationship between mindset and achievement. So how do you develop a growth mindset?

The three key strategies for nurturing a growth mindset are: focusing on the process not the product of it, encouraging reflective learning on the go, and setting clear goals and monitoring progress.

Using the right language for ourselves and how we communicate is also a contributing factor. Reflect on the RESULTS Effort Rubric to see where you are on the mindset spectrum. Depending on where you are, decide to progress toward a mixed or growth mindset.

It is as simple as making a decision and then doing the work. The Stages of Change will help you with this.

Stages of Change

Do you view anything you want to achieve as a problem or as a possibility?

It doesn't matter how you answer this question because both are right. What is critical here is that this is your decision to grow. The moment you realize that you have a problem or a possibility and you decide to do something about it, *that* is the time in which you enter the contemplation phase of the Stages of Change. Contemplating and decision making can make people feel uncomfortable. You might not know the options available or how to make a decision and stick to it, or you might not have all the information you need to make a clear selection. Throughout your life, you are required to make decisions— simple ones such as what to have for breakfast and larger ones such as what should you put in your Project3x3 (more on that in the **Select** phase).

Change comes in many shapes, sizes and forms. Sometimes we pick it, and sometimes change chooses us. When I was first introduced to Prochaska and Norcross's Stages of Change Model (see illustration),[25] I felt I finally understood the times I did well with change and the instances I did not. This five to six step concept will give you a valuable awareness of change, and for this reason, I'd like to introduce it right at the start so you can use it as a point of reflection for all the times things have gone, or not gone, to plan.

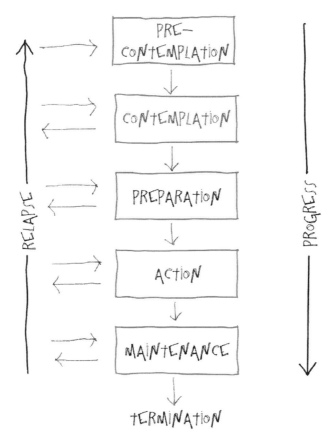

Prochaska and Norcross's Stages of Change

Pre-contemplation is the time when change may be on your radar, but you are not certain. You might ask yourself things like "How can things be better?" or "What will happen if things stay the same?"

RESULTS

Contemplation happens once you have seen that there is a need for change, but there is also the option for present conditions to stay the same. This is the time when talking to good friends, colleagues, or a coach is a great idea. Seeking feedback will help you to brainstorm what is really happening with you and to consider the available options.

Preparation is when you have made the decision to change, but you are still not sure if it is something you want. You are moving towards action and are seeking confidence and clarity.

Action is the stage when things are actually changing because you are doing things to move you forward.

Maintenance refers to something that you have decided to continue for life, and at this point there are two options: exit the Stages of Change Model or relapse. In the **Thrive** and **Success** phases, I propose that "maintenance" and "sustainability" are not useful words to use in this context as they imply that you are able to continue something for life, which I think is impossible without an element of struggle.

Relapse is when you realize that the new habit, consistent action, or objective you wanted has not quite worked out, and you are required to go back to the pre-contemplation stage. It is quite normal to spend a lot of time in the relapse stage. Yet when you are in relapse, it is beneficial to look at the reasons why you are there because the insights you gain will give you valuable information about yourself that will guide you to make progress where you are flourishing.

Adoption (also known as Termination) is when the change has become part of your life and the behavior change is completely embedded.

By sharing the Stages of Change with you, I want to reassure you that change is not easy, at times we lose our way. Yet we know that we need to change, and the RESULTS Method offers you a solid, structured process for how you can bring about change and progress in your life and on your terms.

When we look at why people end up in the relapse stage (or do not begin a course of change), it is often due to at least one of the six previous Showstoppers.

In order to have effective change and account for relapse it is the Architecture of Action model that needs to come to play.

The Architecture of Action™

Any plan and RESULTS Process has three key elements contributing to the implementation and outcome of that plan. The diagram below illustrates how these elements impact each other and create a synergy that will either boost or hinder the entirety of the plan and its delivery. You can see that there is a choice to stay where you are or to make progress. Either way, there will be results. But whether those results are the ones you seek (or not) depends upon how you handle these three elements.

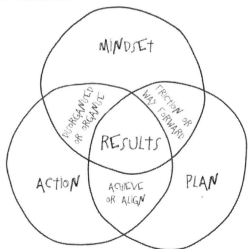

The Architecture of Action™

RESULTS

In this book I share with you the MAP that will help you to maximize your approach to get the results you want: Mindset, Action, Plan.

The basis for the RESULTS Method can be depicted in the same three arenas as the three elements shown above, and each influences the element of the corresponding field. So that Positive Psychology has a boosting impact on our Mindset; effective Project Management propels our Action forward; and Personal Growth directs the proficiency of our Plans.

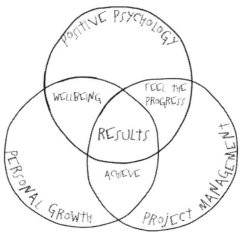

The Architecture of Achievement™ (*Relationship between project management, positive psychology and personal growth.*)

These clear links will help you to create and implement a solid plan. As a business coach, I have found that this framework has helped many companies and individuals really lean into their potential and create exponential results that enabled them to thrive and flourish. Let's look at each element more closely, so you have an understanding of the strategies that I will share with you.

Positive Psychology

Professor Martin Seligman and Mihaly Csikszentmihalyi, founding fathers of positive psychology said it is "the scientific study of positive human functioning and flourishing on multiple levels that include the biological, personal, relational, institutional, cultural, and global dimensions of life."[26] Their colleague Christopher Peterson said positive psychology is "the scientific study of what makes life most worth living."[27] However, positive psychology "is not to be confused with untested self-help, unverified tools, or secular religion—no matter how good these may make us feel." Peterson also said that positive psychology is "neither a recycled version of the power of positive thinking nor a sequel to the secret."[28]

There are three focuses in positive psychology:

1. Positive experiences (like happiness, joy, inspiration, and love).
2. Positive states and traits (like gratitude, resilience, and compassion).
3. Positive institutions (applying positive principles within entire organizations and institutions).[29]

A key element of positive psychology is the desire to flourish; Dr. Lynn Soots describes positive psychology as "the product of the pursuit and engagement of an authentic life that brings inner joy and happiness through meeting goals, being connected with life passions, and relishing in accomplishments through the peaks and valleys of life."[30] Flourishing underpins much of the work we will do in this book, and we will come back to it at the end when we look at long-term success.

Personal Growth

The aim of personal and professional development is to help you manage your own learning and growth throughout your life. It is important that you continue to develop your skills and knowledge and keep up-to-date and ensure that you continue to live life striving to move forward. Personal growth is about you developing an awareness of who you are, your identity, and developing your talents and potential to the full.

Project Management

"At its most fundamental, project management is about people getting things done" (Dr. Martin Barnes, APM President 2003-2012).[31]

APM Body of Knowledge, the project managers handbook, says "Project management is the application of processes, methods, skills, knowledge and experience to achieve specific project objectives according to the project criteria within agreed parameters."[32] What makes project management different to management alone is that it is time specific.

Project management is seen by many as restrictive or technical, but that is partly because of how it is used in industry. In my view if you have ever planned a holiday, move, or party, you are already a project manager!

As you can see at the intersection of these three arenas—the mindset (positive psychology), action (personal growth), and plan (project management)— is the place where you are able to get it done. You are able to gain clarity on your intention and identity, select the right ideas for you to implement, and create a plan in integrity with you and your circumstances. Throughout the book we will work on how you can hit your targets more consistently, and overcome obstacles to reach your goals. You will consistently move forward and have more confidence, clarity, and conviction in your abilities and will, therefore, be able to meet your achievements with more success.

Now that your awareness of the RESULTS Method has increased there may still be something holding you back. This is the time for you to start looking at how you give yourself permission.

Permission

My husband was sitting next to me, and yet, in the room with 2000 others, I felt alone and uncertain. It was always like this when I filled in the mastermind application at personal development events where I wanted to work further with the teacher. Being a lifelong learner, I knew that it was the right time to do it, but I lacked the confidence to make the decision.

It was September 2019, and we were in the ballroom of the Grand Marriot in Phoenix, Arizona. Usually I attend these events by myself, but this time it was different—I had finally managed to persuade Idris, my husband, to come with me. He kept telling me that "it was good," but I knew he was a little bored.

Then, the time came when the event staff handed out the forms inviting us to join the mastermind. This is something I'd wanted to do for a while so I could learn some of the subtle nuances to help my business grow. While sitting next to Idris, I completed the form as I always did. I had the resources and flexibility to join the mastermind, but something was still holding me back—like it always did. I began to slide the form inside my folder with the other papers. From the corner of my eyes I could see Idris looking at my paper. "You should do this," he said. I was uncertain. "Are you sure?" I asked. Idris knew I was ready; he'd known for years! I said a quick prayer and thought "Gosh, what am I about to do?" I stood up and walked to the registration desk and handed in my form.

A few months later I was at another event speaking to 2000 people telling them this story. I asked them, "Do you think my husband was giving me permission in that moment?" I could see that they all looked a little uncomfortable: I suppose a woman talking about her husband giving her permission sounds a bit outdated or oppressive. I allowed them to sit with that thought for a moment more. I then said, "He was not giving me permission. He was giving me support." His encouragement that I "should do this" was actually a subtle reminder that I needed to give myself permission.

#

Support comes in many ways. I know I've said it before, but I can't say it enough: if you need support, then know that I have your back. Also, look out for people who are already in your network. Support is someone telling you, "You can do this." It is someone who is in your corner, cheering you on and offering valuable direction and insight: a coach, a friend, a mentor. The most important attribute of your supporters is that they have your back and will stand by you and encourage you, but you need to be doing that for yourself as well. You know that there will be times when it gets hard, but the right support will get you through the day-to-day, and permission will enable you to get over the mindset games you are playing with yourself.

I know if you search, you can find the external support that you need, but can you muster the internal support you require? Perhaps *you* still need to give yourself permission.

Permission Slips

In her book *Dare to Lead* Brené Brown tells us to create "permission slips."[33] Remember when you were at school and the teacher would give you a permission slip to allow you to go to the library or restroom during lesson time? It is just like that, except now you are giving yourself permission to act or feel in a certain way. With a permission slip, you set an intention for how you want to behave in a particular situation. In Brown's *Daring Classroom*, she asks her students to consider creating permission slips at the start of every lesson so they consciously select the mindset and presence they will have during that class.[34] Writing permission slips is something I want you to do.

I know some of you will be reading this and thinking that you are *above* this concept. Friend let me tell you, I have three master's degrees with distinction, various coaching certificates, plenty of project management and leadership qualifications… and guess what, I still write myself permission slips! It does not matter who you are, what you know, or what your experience is, the permission slip is an effective tool for self-awareness and for summoning your courage. A permission slip is not a note promising anything; it is setting an intention with no repercussions. Permission slips are personal, for you to keep in your pocket or somewhere safe.

These are the recent permission slips I have given to myself recently:

"I give myself permission to write this book."
"I give myself permission to tell others about my imposter syndrome."
"I give myself permission to share my knowledge and experience."
"I give myself permission to belong amongst my peers."
"I give myself permission to ask for help and advice."

I have created some templates for you to create your own permission slips. You can go to *www.results.partners/bookresources* to get yours.

I..

GIVE MYSELF PERMISSION to

....
....
....

Please do make sure you physically write out your permission slip and not just make a mental note. The difference appears subtle, but in actuality, the very act of writing and the physical evidence that ensues (i.e. the note on the paper) is far more impactful than any intangible thought. You don't need permission, understanding, acknowledgement, approval from anyone else.

You need it from you.

Self-Interview

Insight: What is your biggest insight from the **Reach** phase?

Intention: When you explore your boldest hopes and highest aspirations, what is it that you ultimately want?

Identity: Why does reaching beyond really matter to you?

Implementation: What is the smallest or most immediate action you are willing to take?

Integrity: What can you do to deepen your commitment to follow through?

EVOLVE

"The whole point of being alive is to evolve into the complete person you were intended to be."

Oprah Winfrey

RESULTS

You are the most important project you work on.

Mary's manager wanted to put her on the promotion track so she would fill his role when he retired. Mary loved the idea and got in touch with me to benefit from the support of a coach guiding her in her transition up. Following a 360 review where Mary's managers, peers, and other colleagues provided feedback about her, she realized she was spending so much time focusing on her weaknesses that she had forgotten what her strengths were!

The education system and society seem to encourage us to work on our deficits rather than play to our strengths. As we saw earlier when exploring Carol Dweck's mindset work, simply focusing on your strengths is not a solution, as it is missing the element of continual improvement.

Mary and I went back to basics and started to create a holistic vision for what Mary wanted to be and how she wanted to show up in all aspects of her life— including being ready for the promotion. She wanted to jump right in and immediately describe her vision, and I explained that we could do that but without Mary spending some time to know who she was, the vision itself might be disconnected with her own unique, personal truths. In that moment, she said she realized that perhaps she had been so preoccupied with doing an outstanding job at work and at home that she lost the essence of who she was. This was a hard moment for Mary in our coaching, yet she knew she had it within her to **evolve**, and that she did!

#

You are the most important project you will ever undertake. If you make haphazard attempts or altogether skip the work of understanding yourself, then you may find it difficult to succeed in the projects you tackle. Real satisfaction and success come when you achieve alignment with who you are and what stage of life you are in. By starting with your values, who you are, what you represent, and how you want to show up in the world, you increase the likelihood of actually delivering on your project and making it a reality. When you fail to engage with the truth of who you are you could be working and living your life for a cause that you either do not know or are not engaged with. If that happens, you may one day look back on your life and wonder, "Why?"

Who am I?

To evolve knowing your values is a good place to start. It is no surprise that the most successful companies have a mission statement and their values clearly articulated. There is no reason why you as an individual cannot adopt this approach to life. When you practice these techniques not just for yourself, but also for your family, you will find that your communication and care improve, and you will get to know yourself and those you connect with at a deeper level. You will become more in tune with who you are. Knowing and living by the values that are important to you makes you feel more in alignment with who you truly are. With this your lived experience brings a deep sense of joy and you move from unfulfilled to fulfilled.

Everyone has both strengths and areas for improvement. One of my key messages is that if an area needing improvement is one that you are sincerely not interested in developing then, please, delegate any associated tasks either by outsourcing or by asking someone else who shares responsibility for that task to take control of it. (In exchange, you could take charge of something that they might not prefer doing.) The approach of focusing on your areas of improvement is not as effective as focusing on your strengths. There is much talk about the power of utilizing your strengths in positive psychology, which is why I call it to attention here. In addition, tapping into your strengths is also important in project management and self-development.

Effective communication is a key factor to achievement in any area. Communication is two-sided: internal communication and external communication. Internal communication is a combination of *how* you speak to yourself and *what* you tell yourself; and external communication is your manner of speaking and relating with others. Being aware of how you use language on both sides of the communication track can help you gain a greater understanding of yourself and others. For this, I like to use the *love languages* developed by Gary Chapman. It is a brilliant tool to increase communication style awareness. The entire purpose of RESULTS is for you to amplify the self-awareness you have about who you are and how you communicate your plan and projects with the world. Self-awareness is important because the more you know who you are, your strengths, values, and communication style, the more you can use these aspects to create and work on your personalized plan to move forward. And—huge bonus— you can also use this knowledge to work on improving the things that you do not like about yourself (let's face it, we all have some of those!).

Increasing your self-awareness in these three areas (values, strengths, communication styles) enables you to be vigilant for potential hazards that you may face and take them into account when creating your plan. A big gain that you get out of knowing yourself better is that you will become more authentic and be truer to who you really are. When I am coaching a group of executive or individual clients simply aspiring to make more progress in life, one of their common core outcomes is that they learn to be more of themselves in their day-to-day activities. This will be your experience as you follow through with what you learn in the **Evolve** phase of the RESULTS Method.

Let's get to it by looking at assessments in general.

Assessments

If you have ever taken a personality assessment on social media, you have taken a psychometric assessment you know the value of the information you receive. Tools such as Myers Briggs Type Indicator,[TM1] Big 5,[2] DISC,[TM3] Kolbe Index,[4] and Hogan Personal Inventory[TM5] provide an insight into your personality. There is a lot of debate about the accuracy and effectiveness of non-validated assessments and their uses. My advice is to only use assessment tools that have been researched, can show their validity, and *only* use them if they are useful to you. When used in the right way these assessments can be helpful in providing insight into individuals' thought processes, behavior, and how they operate. However, obsessing about the results and changing your behavior to conform with the results is not useful. The primary aim of these assessments is not to fit you into a stereotype. If you feel that is happening, then please use any information gained here warily. In my experience as a coach and leadership trainer, I have found that leaning into any resistance you feel about these results can also help you to understand yourself more.

The values, strengths, and communication style I share with you in this phase provide you with results that you may or may not agree with, with assertions that you can take or leave. The intelligence gained is there for you to reflect upon, and you should only use these tools if you find truth or value in them. The key with these assessments is how you use the information you have gained—if there is no behavior change and no impact then taking the assessments is pointless.

In the RESULTS Method, we use three assessments to gain insight in three areas: values, strengths, and love languages (communication styles). Find the reports from any other assessments you have completed and also use that information in the "Who am I?" reflections.

Values

Roy Disney, nephew of Walt, captured the significance of knowing your values when he said, "When your values are clear to you, making decisions becomes easier."[6]

Do you recall the four factors that make up your GPS? They are intention, identity, implementation, and integrity. One of the core elements of all of these is knowing your values, mission, and vision.

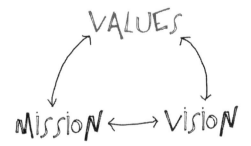

Your values are crucial in defining and aligning you with your goals. Your mission is how your values show up in your day-to-day life. Your vision is what you ultimately want.

RESULTS

In order to know what you really want in life, you need to know what your values are. This applies to individuals and businesses. We all know of companies that have stated values but do not live by them, and we also know of organizations that have a very clear purpose or vision but have not done the work to write it down and own it. In all the work that I do as a coach, positive psychologist, and business consultant, one thing is clear: knowing your values is critical to having an understanding of who you are and what you stand for.

If there is ever a time when something doesn't feel right, it is because it is not in alignment with who you are or with your values and beliefs. That discomfort can show itself in many ways; sometimes there will be a little discomfort, but other times there will be the proverbial flashing red light that you have no choice but to heed. If you have not articulated your intention and values, you may not be able to read the signs as they present themselves, and you may struggle unaware of *why* you feel resistance or unease. Resistance can be a helpful tool—it sends you a sub-conscious message of why you should either avoid or go for the thing that you are feeling resistance towards.

Your values show up in how you do everything. Have you ever considered how greatly your values determine *how* you live your life and *how* you feel about everything and everyone? When you live your life consistently in alignment with your values, you experience satisfaction with life. As a result, you will also experience peace, internally and externally, and your interactions with others (and yourself) will be more authentic and meaningful, and you will be fulfilled.

In order to really be able to be in tune with your values effectively, you need to know what your personal values are. On the whole, there is no right or wrong here, your values are *your* values, and they create the unique balance that is you. When you are not living in line with your values or are out of balance, you may end up with habits or actions that do not serve you or your aspirations. At the end of the day, your values describe what motivates you right now (short-term plan); they also enable you to define your hopes and intentions (longer-term plan).

We are looking at values as the first key element in discovering your true identity as your values influence your behaviors, actions, and decision making. They are the catalyst for choosing your project and, subsequently, how you connect with and implement it. A list of common values follows, but it's important to note that you may or may not find *your* values on this list.

Authenticity	Faith	Positivity
Achievement	Fame	Recognition
Adventure	Freedom	Reputation
Autonomy	Friendships	Respect
Balance	Fun	Responsibility
Beauty	Grace	Reverence
Boldness	Grit	Security
Buoyancy	Growth	Self-Esteem
Capability	Happiness	Self-Respect
Compassion	Honesty	Service
Challenge	Humor	Spirituality
Citizenship	Independence	Stability
Community	Influence	Strength
Competency	Justice	Success
Confidence	Kindness	Status
Contribution	Knowledge	Trustworthiness
Creativity	Leadership	Wealth
Curiosity	Learning	Wisdom
Determination	Love	
Dependability	Loyalty	*Insert your own*
Dignity	Meaningful Work	*values here*
Enthusiasm	Openness	………..
Esteem	Optimism	………..
Exploration	Peace	………..
Fairness	Pleasure	

List of values prepared as part of a crowd sourcing workshop within the RESULTS program.

RESULTS

Select the five values from the list above that resonate with you and try them on for size. Despite the practice of working to recognize one's personal values being more common, many people still have not taken the time to identify and articulate their values. Doing this for yourself is powerful, but then doing it *with* your family, friends, colleagues, and work teams really raises the positive impact of this work. Your values are important principles, beliefs, ways of behaving. They represent how you show up in life.

Another way to know your values is through the work of Richard Barrett's Values Centre. They have identified the top ten values of more than 500,000 people. They reported that the overall top ten values (in descending order) are: family, humor/fun, caring, respect, friendship, trust, enthusiasm, commitment, creativity, and continuous learning.[7] Barrett describes values as "the foundation of your culture… When your people thrive, your organization thrives." Your values determine how you live your life, how you manage your day, your attitude towards your personal growth, and your thoughts, words, and actions. The Values Centre offers a free assessment to help you articulate your values. You can find it at *www.valuescentre.com.* The assessment takes about 15 minutes, and they will email you a free report providing information that will help you identify your values and how they show up in your life. As with any assessment, you do not have to agree with the report. There is no right or wrong here. It is really an opportunity to reflect. Should you read things that you do not like, rather than focus on that, why not look at what lessons you can learn.

American actor, Matthew McConaughey's Oscar acceptance speech in 2014 is one of the most powerful articulations of how your values show up in your life. The official video has been viewed over 20 million times on YouTube alone.[8] His inspirational words follow:

> There are three things that I need each day. One, I need something to look up to, another to look forward to, and another is someone to chase.

First off, I want to thank God because that's who I look up to. He's graced my life with opportunities that I know are not of my hand or of any other human hand....

To my family is what I look forward to. To my father who I know is up there right now with a big pot of gumbo; he has a big lemon meringue pie over there... To you dad, you taught me how to be a man...

To my mother who's here tonight, who taught me and my two older brothers—demanded—that we respect ourselves. And in turn we learned we were better able to learn how to respect others. Thank you for that, Mama.

To my wife, Camilla, and my kids Levi, Vida and Mr. Stone (Livingstone), the courage you give me every time I walk through the door is unparalleled. You are the four people in my life that I want to make the proudest of me. Thank you.

And to my hero, that's who I chase. Now when I was 15 years old, I had a very important person in my life come to me and say, "Who's your hero?" And I said, "I don't know. I gotta think about that. Give me a couple of weeks." I come back two weeks later— this person comes up and says, "Who's your hero?" I said, "I thought about it. You know who it is?" I said, "It's me in 10 years."

So, I turned 25. Ten years later, that same person comes to me and goes, "So are you a hero?" And I was like, "Not even close. No, no, no." She said, "Why?" I said, "Because my hero's me at 35." So, you see every day, every week, every month, and every year of my life, my hero's always 10 years away. I'm never gonna be my hero. I'm not gonna attain that. I know I'm not, and that's just fine with me because that keeps me with somebody to keep on chasing.

So, to any of us, whatever those things are and whatever it is we look up to, whatever it is we look forward to and whoever it is we're chasing, to that I say, "Amen." To that I say, "Alright, alright, alright." And just keep living, huh? Thank you."

Matthew McConaughey, Oscars Speech, 2014, Los Angeles, USA[9]

I've shared this speech with you because it epitomizes how your values link with who you are. Have you ever thought about who your hero is? How do you connect with who that is for you, for your business, for your project, for your future? Many coaches, authors, and personalities in the personal growth industry talk about having a legacy and impact. I'd like to expand on that concept a little and invite you to ask yourself, "What do you want your great, grandchildren (or their generation) to remember you for, or how would they describe you?"

At the end of this chapter I will ask you to undertake a Self-Interview where you identify the guiding values that you want to have. Let's now look at the next piece of your evolution which is acknowledging your strengths.

Strengths

"Our job is to align our strengths so much so that our weaknesses become irrelevant."—Peter Drucker

Discovering your strengths can provide valuable insights when getting to know yourself better. It helps you to recognize that you have the answers inside to be your best. Knowing your strengths enables you to choose to do that which energizes you, thus allowing you to experience more joy in life. The innate traits and abilities you use in your daily life to complete your work, relate with others, and achieve your goals are your strengths.

Strengths-based work builds on what you are good at, making it possible for you to make progress on your projects. Having clarity on what it is that you want to achieve is a key part of strengths-based work.

There are a couple of downsides to strengths-based work. It could be that by focusing on your strengths you are over-exercising those specific muscles. It could also be that you spend time looking at areas which have not materialized as strengths for you making you spend more energy than is necessary there, ignoring what you are actually capable of. Regularly reviewing your relationship with your top five strengths will help you to address both of these potential shortcomings.

If I asked you what your strengths are, you may or may not be able to tell me—there are tools available to help with this. I advocate the use of the Values in Action Inventory of Strengths developed by positive psychology researchers Peterson, Park, and Seligman in 2004.[10] They describe "six universal virtues and 24 character strengths" and say that character strengths are the "process and mechanisms that lead to the virtues."[11] You can undertake the VIA Strengths Survey for free *(www.viacharacter.org)*. It's a simple, researched, and peer-reviewed tool to use to identify strengths based on your values which makes it the perfect next step in increasing your self-awareness in your RESULTS journey.

My hope for you is that once you know your strengths, you keep these capabilities in mind when working on your project or any other undertaking. In the workplace, a strengths-based approach has shown to bring about significant improvements in employee engagement and significantly increased productivity.[11] The RESULTS Method is in itself a strengths-based approach and when implemented in the right way it enables you to work not only on day-to-day performance, but also on areas that you want to develop including mindset areas such as lack of self-confidence or issues such as overusing certain strengths.

When you delve deeper into the strengths-based approach, you focus on the positive attributes rather than the negative, disagreeable ones, or those that require development. In life we tend to focus a lot on what needs to be improved and that is beneficial to some degree, but it only gets you to a certain point because when you focus your efforts and time on improving a deficit, you miss the opportunity to take greater advantage of your strengths. What if you were to play into your strengths more, and delegate the tasks that you don't enjoy or that don't fall within the scope of your strengths? This could save you time and unnecessary struggle. It also requires an awareness of your strengths and a willingness to make some decisions. And this is exactly what we will be doing right now. You can apply the strengths-based approach to leadership, work, home, study—pretty much any arena of your life.

Deficit Based	Strengths-Based (Appreciative Inquiry)
Identification of the problem (seeing) what is	Setting a context of appreciation of what can be
Analysis of Causes	Inquiry: Discovery Phase
"What's going on"	"Valuing the best of what is"
Proposed Solutions	Envisioning: Dream Phase
"Fix the problem at hand"	"What might be"
Action Planning	Dialoguing/Aligning: Design Phase "This is what will be"
"How to get it done"	
Problem Solving:	**Appreciative Inquiry:**
That the organization is a problem to be solved.	That the organization is a repository of strengths to be embraced.

Deficit Based v Strengths Based Theory of Change (Cooperrider, 2011) [13]

The strengths-based approach has its history in Appreciative Inquiry and Positive Psychology. When you know your strengths and you make them the foundation of your work practices and task choices, you actually build beneficial resilience and generate a self-image of skill and capability. By focusing on your strengths, as opposed to trying to develop some random skill which you may not even have, you are able to make better use of your time and further your progress. In addition, just by identifying your innate strengths and capitalizing on this new level of awareness, you start to develop the right environment for your RESULTS GPS (intention, identity, implementation, and integrity) to flourish and be located with precision.

Researchers have found six ways for building and using a strengths-based approach to self-realization: 'goal orientation, systematic assessment of strengths, methods and environment for goal attainment, hope-inducing relationship, meaningful choice, and the authority to choose'.[14] When you incorporate this approach into the process of getting to know yourself better, you increase your ability to create and be in alignment with your RESULTS plan, to get the results you desire, and to truly flourish.

Practicing a strengths-based approach to RESULTS requires:

- Completing an assessment to help you identify, assess, and start developing your strengths.
- Owning the results and deciding what to do with the information you have acquired. You are the expert on your own life, your strengths, and how to best use them. You know the resources you have and how you build hope and growth. The onus is on you to expand your choices so that you make the best of *all* your opportunities, rather than settle for a second-rate option.
- Becoming more goal oriented (you will see how important this later on).

- Finding available resources in your personal and professional environment—what is available to help you grow?
- Choosing the right method for you. Usually in coaching, the focus is on goal setting first and then using your strengths to support you. In the RESULTS Method, you use the knowledge of your strengths to gain a greater understanding of yourself and then utilize this insight as a basis for developing your vision, goals, and plan.
- Becoming optimistic. By identifying your strengths and making connections to other pieces of information you have gathered, you build hope for yourself, and that optimism ultimately translates into results!
- Having a community that will support you in your growth.

Please take a moment to discover your strengths as suggested above and start to think about how you can develop your natural traits so that you can then harness those to select the right projects for you and to continue chasing your hero.

Communication Styles

"But the truth is, we all have those things that we know about ourselves, and those things determine the outcomes of our life. And it comes when the pressure is on. You are going for that job interview. And if your personal truth is, I'm not as smart as these people, I'm not as good as these other applicants. This isn't me. That's gonna come out because 93 percent of your communications are nonverbal. So, your personal truth is going to scream who you really believe you are."
— Dr. Phil McGraw[15]

The best way to select the right project is to understand yourself. (Co-incidentally, it is also the best way to build better relationships.) One of the biggest challenges that human beings face aside from external oppression is the oppression we commit against ourselves by not learning to accept or fully love ourselves. Communication is the key to success in any relationship; it is a problem-solving tool that can provide you with helpful feedback and a safe space for sharing thoughts and feelings. Yet, many of us do not know how to communicate well and are not working to improve our communication skills. As a result, we end up losing real interpersonal connection—even losing ourselves. This loss of connection to yourself can lead to confusion, conflict, and a feeling of crisis.

It is for these reasons that I invite you to pay attention to your communication behavior and tone with yourself (and others), whilst also inviting you to look at the meaning of the words you use. A wonderful way to look at this is through the work of Gary Chapman. Although aimed at relationships, the five love languages have been used in a variety of situations including the workplace. They are a great tool to understand your personal communication preference, as well as that of others. Chapman's five love languages are:

- *Words of Affirmation*: the words you use to encourage or support others.
- *Quality Time*: undistracted and focused attention you give to others.
- *Receiving Gifts*: gifts given to demonstrate your affection and care of others.
- *Acts of Service*: actions speak louder than words when showing you care.
- *Physical Touch*: appropriate touches (a hug, a pat on the back, a kiss, etc.) to signal your affection.[16]

Each of these languages can be an effective means of communication, and every one of us uses all five of these love languages to some extent, but we each have a preference. While we all know that we communicate differently, Chapman's love languages are an easy-to-use reference that can enable us to understand ourselves and others better so that we can communicate with each other more effectively. Take a few minutes now, and go to

RESULTS

https://www.5lovelanguages.com/quizzes/ and complete the assessment. Then read the report to gain insight on your preferred love language and how you relate to others. The quiz should only take about 10 minutes and will give you feedback that could change the way you communicate in every relationship (including the one you have with yourself!)

In my work, I have found that using the love languages as a tool for communication has an immediate impact on all relationships. I know that the phrasing may make some uncomfortable, but the tool itself is very powerful. If you are feeling cynical, just trust me for a moment, put your cynicism aside, and take the test, research has been done to confirm the validity of the five love languages.[17] Try it out, and then decide. The insight you will gain has the potential to improve your personal and professional relationships. In fact, when I have used this assessment tool in corporate coaching settings, businesses have actually changed their reward packages to meet the priorities of individuals, rather than imposing more traditional rewards. For someone who values time, an additional half a day off work often means much more than a small financial bonus or a corporate gift.

Once you have taken the quiz and received the results of the assessment, you can use them to consider how you are communicating with yourself. Perhaps you worked on a project and told yourself that you would reward yourself in a particular way when it was completed. You may have:

- Completed the project and rewarded yourself but felt dissatisfied.
- Completed the project and rewarded yourself and felt good.
- Completed the project but decided you didn't deserve the reward.
- Did not complete the project and didn't get the reward.

Knowing who you are and what your love languages are will enable you to select the right form of appreciation to increase your excitement and improve your implementation. At the end of every stage of implementation, it is important to do something to recognize that you have reached a checkpoint—even if the reward is as simple as a 5-minute break, a pat on the back, a 2-minute celebration, or an affirmation.

My primary love languages are acts of service and quality time. What are yours? Once you know your communication style, you can gather it together with the insights you have gained from the Values Assessment, and VIA Strengths Survey results discussed earlier in this phase. Shortly you will put together your personal Johari Window—a tool used to help you understand your relationship with yourself and others more clearly. (You can take these acts of discovery even further by sharing these assessments and the results with your trusted family and friends. I guarantee it will open up conversations and understanding that you might not have otherwise had.)

Now take a moment to complete the RESULTS Who Am I? Template, you will add your vision later.

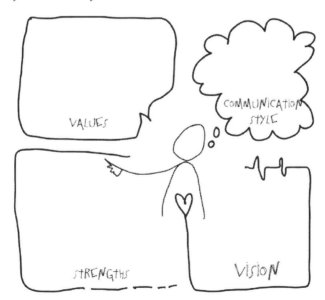

RESULTS 'Who am I?' Template

Getting Feedback

Always seek feedback, it is valuable to almost every human undertaking. Be open to hearing what people think about you.

Whatever form feedback takes, you have three choices as the recipient:

1. Ignore it—some feedback offers no benefit so don't waste your time or energy.
2. Listen to it—listening doesn't necessitate agreeing, you simply listen, say thank you, and then continue your journey.
3. Embrace it and learn from it—use the feedback as an opportunity to grow and improve.

By seeking feedback, you are inviting external opinions and listening to voices that would not otherwise be offered to you. Feedback is something you seek from people you trust.

Be prepared emotionally and practically to receive feedback. If it is negative, you are not obligated to accept it: remember your three choices. At the same time, decide not to get offended when someone gives you criticism that is difficult to hear. The word *negative* assigns a quality of being poor or bad, but on the contrary, it is an opportunity for you to make change. Rather than call this positive and negative, I prefer to use the plus- delta debriefing model.[18]

A *plus* is something that went well, or is good.

A *delta* is something that you want to change or improve. This approach invites a more useful response to feedback that you might have previously viewed as negative. Rather than it being something you shouldn't do, it's an indication to ask the question, "How do I improve?"

It is certain that the more feedback you get, the more you know what works and what does not work in your life. Others are able to point out what you cannot see (your blind spots) and being open to learn from those outside perspectives will result in your personal growth journey being accelerated. In the process of asking for and being given honest, valuable feedback, you will also strengthen the bonds of relationship with others because of the implications of the exchange: there is a mutual understanding of the trust you place in them to even ask for their input; they will realize your interest in improving yourself and your practices; and they will feel they are contributing to your effort to grow. It is an exchange that develops confidences, reciprocal respect, and understanding.

When it comes to feedback remember:

DO:	DON'T:
Be clear about the kind of feedback you want.	Restrict inquiries to your manager or family for feedback alone. Ask your friends, colleagues, and others.
Have your questions ready. Be prepared to ask for clarification or more specifics when they reply.	Restrict yourself to written inquiries and replies. Phone calls or virtual meetings can be more helpful because of the human touch. Feedback via email or text message can be misinterpreted.
Ask people whom you trust to be honest not hurtful.	Do not wait to set a designated meeting or conversation; ask the questions spontaneously and see what they say.
Ask in real time.	

Do and Don't of Feedback

RESULTS

There is no right or wrong here. Your single purpose at this point is to receive the information and note it. You can reflect on it later in your journal. And remember, if the asking for or working through the feedback is too difficult for you, then just skip this exercise for now. You can always come back to it when you are ready.

CEO-you Versus Employee-you

You have a choice to make: are you the employee in your life or the CEO?

CEO is the chief executive officer in business. They are the ones that set the strategy and direction that a business takes. I know many of you may not have a business nor an intention to have one, so please do not take this as an instruction for you to start a business against your will. For those of you who work in a corporate setting, I hope you will also rise to the challenge! When adopting the best kind of CEO-mindset you must be values-driven, understand where your gaps are, and then make longer-term plans while maintaining a drive for implementation.

You may have never understood that you have adopted an employee mindset, and that is fine, until now. Now that you have gained *this* insight, the key thing to do is to realize that going forward there is going to be a *CEO-you* and an *employee-you*. Learn to use each one when appropriate: allow the CEO to set the strategy, and then ensure that the employee shows up to do the work. The biggest challenge here is that much of the time the CEO shows up, and there are no employees doing the work!

This is often why the plans and dreams you have continued to be just plans and dreams instead of solid outcomes. When you have an employee mindset, you focus on the moment, and while this has some advantages, you can end up with many short-term plans and no long-term direction. The employee mindset is useful when it is time to do the work, but it does little for you when you are working on the strategy. So, remember you need both. In order to have an effective, efficient, effortless approach to the results you seek and the plan you create, you need to be both the CEO and the employee.

Whenever I have my personal planning days, I remind myself, "*Saiyyidah, time to step back now. It's CEO Saiyyidah here, and I am setting the strategy and creating the plan.*" This way the entire mindset and approach is different.

The two main steps to moving from an employee mindset to a CEO one are:

1. Create time to plan (later I show you how to take time out every three months and what to do in that time).
2. For each project you select, ask yourself, "How will this help my long-term vision and make my values come to life?"

Use your character strengths to move from one role to another. If you need to, buy yourself a little hat that says, "CEO" or find a spot in your house that is your CEO spot. Use that to be in the role that sets the direction.

Let's now look at the next piece of your evolution which is creating your Johari Window to clearly set out what you know about yourself and what you don't.

The Johari Window

There is a fundamental difference between who you think you are, who you are, and who others think you are.

RESULTS

That is why opening yourself up to knowing yourself better is crucial. There are psychometric tests you can take, therapy you can have, and retreats you can go on. I encourage you to explore all of these. But in order to move you forward right now, we are going to use one of the best tools I believe is available to help you increase your self-awareness.

Remember, *you* are the greatest project you will ever work on.

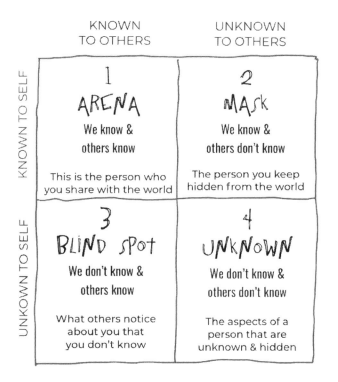

Johari Window

The Johari Window[19] is a classic tool for helping people understand a bit more about what they know about themselves, where their blind spots are, understand what others know that they might not, and to become aware of what others know that they also know. An interesting fact is that The Johari Window is called such because the creators thought that if they named it the Luft-Ingram model, according to their surnames, then it might become another tool that was not used much, but by combining their first names they came up with something memorable! Luft and Ingram created this method to study group dynamics with the premise that you can trust yourself and others more when you understand yourself and others more deeply. First, start by filling the quadrants in the Johari Window yourself. Then ask people who know you (and trust) to help you fill the gaps, and finally, you reflect on the information.

Of course, not everyone will want to ask others for feedback at this stage, so I would like to present another way of completing this which is for you to begin by completing the "known to self" sections and then leaving it until you do another cycle of the RESULTS Method. This gets you moving forward and removes any initial stress or anxiety of having to ask others for feedback. And, hey, if you're ready and willing to ask others for feedback now, that's great too. After all, this is your plan! Remember, we learn who we are in practice not in theory so start practicing.

As you can see from the Johari Window, the framework itself is quite simple, yet its completion requires some deep thought about who you are and what you know about yourself. Think of it like a window with four panes of glass— the clearer you can see through each pane the more effective you can be. The blind spot and unknown areas will always be there, but you can minimize them so you can increase self-awareness. It may be a case of the more you know the less you feel you know— that is certainly how I feel every time I complete a Johari Window! It is a simple way to put a mirror up to yourself and how you show up in the world. This information and increased awareness has a direct impact on you, your project selection, how you utilize your time, your leadership style, and the way you thrive and succeed with your plan and, pretty much anything you do.

To complete the exercise, you fill in the four boxes by describing your personality and what you know. Please either do this in your

RESULTS

RESULTS journal or use the ready-made handout available at *www.results.partners/bookresources*

1 - The Arena Quadrant

The Arena quadrant, or open area, is where there is vulnerability. It is where what you know about yourself is also known to others. It is no surprise that much of Brené Brown's work on shame and vulnerability uses the Roosevelt quote below.

> It is not the critic who counts; not the man who points out how the strong man stumbles, or where the doer of deeds could have done them better. The credit belongs to the man who is actually in the arena, whose face is marred by dust and sweat and blood; who strives valiantly; who errs, who comes short again and again, because there is no effort without error and shortcoming; but who does actually strive to do the deeds; who knows great enthusiasms, the great devotions; who spends himself in a worthy cause; who at the best knows in the end the triumph of high achievement, and who at the worst, if he fails, at least fails while daring greatly, so that his place shall never be with those cold and timid souls who neither know victory nor defeat. (*Theodore Roosevelt*)[20]

The Arena is like the pane of glass in the window through which people can see you. It is also an area where feedback is helpful in order to increase your awareness of the elements that really belong here and not in the hidden area. Every time I ask one of my private clients to complete the Johari Window and ask others for a 360-degree style feedback, they are amazed at what they thought was hidden but is known to others— particularly close friends, colleagues, and family members. The more you know here, the smaller your blind spot is.

2 - The Mask or Facade

This is the area that is perhaps the most obvious: you know it, and others do not. Facade is an architectural term meaning the front face of the building. Another definition says it is something that people put up when they are hiding something. Whilst I believe that to be true, I also think that many times people have an unintentional facade, that they are not aware of. That is, by not articulating certain things about themselves, they could appear to be putting up a facade to others.

Another way to think about this is authenticity. When you meet someone who appears as if they are being disingenuous or are hiding something, it can feel a bit awkward—that is when they are putting up a facade, even if they don't know it. Do not worry because most times having a facade is not intentional—we all do it sometimes. The key here is knowing that this occurs. Of course, there are situations when not sharing something is helpful—you will know when that is; for example, with someone you don't know well, when you are in a hurry, when you don't want to disclose personal information, etc.

To complete the Facade quadrant, place information about your attitudes, your behaviors, emotional intelligence, strengths, values, love languages, any psychometric or personality assessment that you have completed and not shared.

3 - The Blind Spot Quadrant

This is information that you are not aware of, but others do. You may think that you are behaving in a particular way, but it is apparent to others that you're not. Coaching is a very powerful tool to help you reduce those aspects falling into your blind spot and unknown quadrants. Feedback is also valuable here, as you might interpret things about yourself differently to others. Exposing yourself in this setting can be some of the hardest work to do in personal and professional growth as it requires humbleness and grace when receiving feedback that you might not relish. Yet, it is the best way to grow and make progress as it gives you information on how people perceive you, and it is a wonderful starting point for development. It will also help you develop confidence when people tell you about the gifts they see in you that you don't see. You will consider some of the information you receive as positive and some as negative. Some of the feedback may direct you to areas for improvement, and others may indicate strengths you did not even know you had! You will gain the most benefit if you adopt the understanding that in the end, it is all good—perceived positive or negative, feedback provides you with new information and new perspectives that serve as a jumping board to accelerate your growth and development.

In order to reduce your blind spot, and to find out information to put in this quadrant, you can ask people for feedback. The way you frame your question is important, but one thing is for sure, never simply ask, "What feedback do you have for me?" In all the times I have used this direct approach when asking for feedback, people have either refused or gone into a long monologue that, aside from not being helpful, was sometimes hurtful.

Ask specific, open-ended questions like the ones I ask you in the Self-Interview. In fact, at every phase you have an option to review your Johari window and add more information to it.

Work on creating an environment of feedback and self-discovery. When we do this as adults it can feel awkward and uncomfortable— that is where the growth is! These types of open and inquisitive exchanges will help you to explore more about who you are and opportunities to tap into your potential.

4 - The Unknown Quadrant

In this quadrant, the information is not known to you or others. There are other things which are unknown and will remain unknown until you become aware of them.

The unknown self can be interesting particularly when there is a lack of self-belief or inexperience. In these cases, there will be many skills, qualities, and abilities that are not known because they have not been explored or tested. By trying new things, you learn more about yourself. In addition, counselling or therapy is useful to expand your awareness of the known and unknown. I invite you to consider using coaching to help you discover your unknown talents, abilities, and opportunities.

#

Once you understand what you know about yourself and what you don't, and you have a general idea of your aspirations, you have a new problem: 'What do I do now?' This 'problem' can cause anxiety or uncertainty and you may deflect from the answer or avoid it; it can also make you feel excited and curious about the opportunity that presents itself.

Thinking that you will ever gain certainty over life, yourself, and your ambitions is the real problem here. Because let me tell you something, the only certainty in life is uncertainty. It may be a difficult tenet to accept, but once you do, then you will be in a solid place to embrace vulnerability and do the work that needs to be done to address the new problem—the problem of "What do I do now?"

Now that you have clarity on who you are (or at least a little more understanding), the next question of 'what do I do' is addressed in the next phase. you will create what I call, your Project3x3 and learn about goals and how to set them in a way that fits in with your RESULTS GPS and vision. Then, you will undertake a Reality Check™ to ensure that the three projects you have decided to work on are really what you want to do. But before that, I will show you how to create a compelling future vision, one that you are committed to as this will anchor you back every single day by visualising it.

Your future vision is an invitation to stand in the future and look back to now.

Future Vision

A greater self-awareness can come from external resources such as the free tools I have shared with you in this phase. (You may have wondered why I am suggesting tools that I have not created or amended, and that is a valid question. In short, I believe that if a tool is good then we should use it. There is no point in changing something that works or, as they say, reinventing the wheel.) By bringing together an awareness of your values, strengths, and communication styles, you have begun the work of establishing a strong foundation for the projects you select. You will continue to build your daily and long-term plans upon this solid foundation. Remember, these are tools that I use in my private coaching practice, they are research-based, and are effective. I know some of you will have heard about vision and visualisation before. I urge each and every one of you to look at these tools with a level of seriousness you may have previously avoided. Trust me, these tools are effective.[*]

Now it's time to start creating the vision of what you want your life to be. This will help you to strengthen and further develop your basis for selecting the projects that you take forward in the next quarter, year, and beyond. Your vision won't appear out of nowhere. It is something that you consciously create. You can choose to use one or both of two interventions to help create your future vision: the obituary exercise and compelling future vision.

---

[*] *When I had an idea for this book I thought, "It would be nice if my book was about 300 pages and had 25-30 images." As I do the final review before publication, I realize that, without planning it, this book is about 300 pages long and has 30 images! That is the power of visualisation in line with vision. It feels like a miracle.*

Begin with the end in mind.

Are you aware of the Nobel Peace Prize? It was established by Alfred Nobel. In 1888, Alfred's brother Ludvig Nobel died in Paris. At least one French newspaper believed that it was Alfred who had died, and they published his obituary. In that obituary, Alfred Nobel was referred to as the "merchant of death"[21] due to his work developing new types of explosives. It is said that upon reading his own obituary, Alfred Nobel changed the course of his life so that he would be remembered more for his humanitarian work and thus the creation of the Nobel Peace prize.

Writing your obituary can seem like a daunting task, but thinking sincerely about how you want to be remembered will have a profound impact on your approach to life. As Steven Covey would say, "You are beginning with the end in mind."[22]

Bronnie Ware's book, *The Top Five Regrets of the Dying,* is based on her palliative care work in Australia. She said that her patients consistently expressed the following:

1. "I wish I'd had the courage to live a life where I was true to myself, and not just lived up to other people's expectations."
2. "I wish I hadn't worked so hard."
3. "I wish I'd had the courage to express my feelings."
4. "I wish I'd stayed in better touch with my friends."
5. "I wish I'd let myself be happier."[23]

The common theme in these regrets is that they did not live intentionally. You are now going to work on creating your future vision so that you have no regrets and can live intentionally.

RESULTS

Obituary

I have encouraged thousands of people to write their own obituary because of the power of this exercise. You can find resources in the online tools accompanying this book to assist you if needed.

Once you are committed to writing your own obituary:

- Open your journal to a clean page or pull out a blank piece of paper, set an alarm for 20 minutes where you will not be interrupted.
- Write your name and a manner of death that you'd be happy with "*(your name)* died peacefully in her sleep, aged _____"
- Make a list of your main accomplishments.
- List the people you leave behind and those you will miss the most.
- List the people you have helped and whose lives you have impacted.
- Write about the kind of person you were, how you would like to be remembered, what you stood for and against.
- Write in a style that reflects the type of person you were.

Write until the timer goes off. If you feel emotional, allow those feelings to come. This is one of the most impactful positive psychology exercises I use—which is why I use it with care, and I share it with you mindful of how powerful and moving it can be. Reflecting on your life by writing your own obituary can be a positive experience for both you and your loved ones. One thing to remember is there is no wrong or right way to write your own obituary. Most importantly, it should sound like it's coming from you, so be sure to add some personality to your writing.

If you feel the obituary exercise might be too emotionally charged or overwhelming, then please complete the compelling future vision instead.

Compelling Future Vision

You have completed some really important work in this chapter and now you are ready to create your future vision. By valuing your future self, you are embodying a growth mindset. You are going to reverse engineer your life based on your compelling future vision.

Look at the summary page you have of your values, strengths, communication style, and the Johari Window. Which aspects leap out to you as you reflect upon the understanding you have gained? Write those down.

Owning your future self now will help you to determine the path to get there. Commit to one future self so that you have one path, not several. It's really important for you to live your values in your life. When you have a different image of your future self you say yes and no with more clarity. Describing that future self can be a challenge. Psychologist Dan Gilbert says,

> Most of us can remember who we were 10 years ago, but we find it hard to imagine who we're going to be, and then we mistakenly think that because it's hard to imagine, it's not likely to happen. Sorry, when people say, "I can't imagine that," they're usually talking about their own lack of imagination, and not about the unlikelihood of the event that they're describing. Human beings are works in progress that mistakenly think they're finished. The person you are right now is as transient, as fleeting and as temporary as all the people you've ever been. The one constant in our life is change.[24]

By articulating who you want to become, and writing it down, you are making a decision of who you actually want to be and reinforcing it. Now, I ask you to write a compelling future vision. You start by simply answering the questions below in your journal:

Imagine it is a year from today (write your journal entry as if it is the story of the future in the present moment).

- What are we celebrating? What do you see, feel, and experience when you look around at your life and realize that it is all beyond what you thought was possible?
- What obstacles did you need to overcome?
- Who did you have to become to overcome those obstacles?
- How do you feel about your ability to achieve even more?

Now, come back to this moment in time.

Ask yourself, based on your images of the future what do you need to start doing, stop doing, and continue doing?

Take 20 minutes today to do this exercise. Recognize how your values can enable you to identify the best possible version of yourself, make that person your hero, and then keep chasing your hero so that you keep growing and improving and making progress.

NOTE: It is really important to take a pause and do this exercise. No doubt you have had a request like this before, and perhaps have resisted. I want you to know that through writing your goals become clearer and your confidence increases. If you feel resistance towards it and want to skip it, ask if that is the reason why you might not have evolved as you would have liked in the past. By doing this activity you gain clarity on the outcome you are seeking, and the path *you* want to be on.

Visualization

As you think about your vision close your eyes. Take a couple of breaths, and imagine that each hour of your day is going better than your expectations. Visualize your progress: you are navigating the obstacles, getting through any challenges that arise, and achieving more than you ever have. Picture yourself at the end of the day full of joy, energetic, content, and pleased that the day has gone well. Imagine that your week has been full of tasks completed, priorities ticked off. See your month going even better than you can imagine, and then go forward to the end of three months when you are sitting to review what you have done, and you are in awe of your achievements! (As you go through the RESULTS phases and create your plans, take a few moments to visualise them each morning. It will pay dividends throughout your life).

Before you go to bed, spend a few minutes thinking about the next day. Remind yourself that it is strategically contributing to your dreams. You know you want your vision to become a reality so visualize your dreams, your projects fulfilled in a way that is greater than all of your imaginings combined. You've reached the goal that you went after!

Visualizing your dreams gives you the opportunity to reconnect with your goals every single day. It enables you to emotionally feel the possibility, it re-energizes you and revs up your motivation and desire to make it happen. When you nourish and nurture your excitement for the projects you are working on and your bigger ambitions, then you will keep going in tough times, feel optimistic, enthusiastic, and get more done!

Now take a moment to complete the RESULTS 'Who am I?' Template by adding your vision to your values, strengths, and communication style. Place this in a place where you will see it every day.

The insight you have gained in this chapter will help you know more about how you like to learn and how you make decisions. It will also give you a better understanding of what you don't know about yourself and an indication of areas needing further development. We all still have work to do. What will make you stand apart is the decision to include learning as part of how you live your daily life.

Self-Interview™

As stated earlier, the art of writing and journaling is a really important conversation with yourself. Of course, you can record a video or audio file, but writing is more effective. These Self-Interviews help you to reinforce the meaning and impact of your work here in RESULTS, so please do not skip past this.

Insight: What is your biggest insight from the **Evolve** phase?

Intention: When you explore your boldest hopes and highest aspirations, what is that you ultimately want to evolve to?

Identity: Why does your evolution really matter to you?

Implementation: What is one change you could make that would change your view of your future self?

What is the smallest or most immediate action you are willing to take?

Integrity: What can you now do to deepen your commitment to follow through?

WHAT DO I WORK ON?

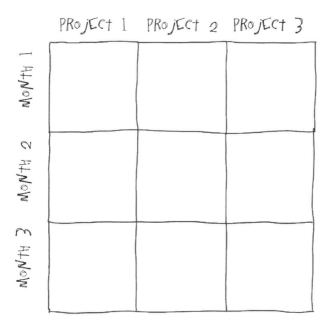

Before

CONFUSED

After

CLEAR

SELECT

"It's not enough to be busy, so were the ants. The question is, what are we busy about?"

Henry David Thoreau – (1817-1862)

RESULTS

You should consider changing jobs.

One sunny August day in 2016, just as I was closing my computer down for the day, I received a call. Adam, my accountant, was on the phone. Adam explained that he needed me to check some receipts and figures in order for him to be able to complete my tax return and company accounts.

"This is going to take you more than a few hours, Saiyyidah. I'm sorry," Adam apologized.

I really dislike crunching numbers but said, "If needs must, send it over and I'll get it done by the end of the week."

Adam briefed me, and I then spent the next two evenings working through numbers, checking receipts, and being bored but getting the task done. The next morning I emailed Adam and said I had completed the task. It was a thankless job and one that I was happy was over. Whilst I am happy to get involved when necessary, I really did not enjoy looking over numbers for a long period of time and am more than happy to pay Adam to handle the numbers side of my business.

A few hours later Adam called again. I thought, "Oh no, what now?"

Adam explained that he was really impressed at the speed and quality in which I managed to sort the files out; in fact, he was so impressed that he told me, "You should consider changing jobs and leaving coaching to become an accountant!" I laughed, and paused.

I replied, "Just because you are good at something doesn't mean you need to do it."

Adam didn't say anything.

"You still there Adam?" I asked.

"Yes, it's just I've never heard anything like that before."

Adam continued to reflect on this for a few weeks realizing that what you are working on so diligently can sometimes be a distraction from what you really want to do.

Occasionally you will be aware of it as I was above, but most of the time you do not know that you have given your most valuable resource (your time) to someone else's projects. This is why it is essential for you to be clear about what you are working on and how you are going to allocate your time.

What do I work on?

In life there are two kinds of people: those who know what they want to work on in life, and those who don't.

Having a plan gives you direction and enables you to remain focused on what you actually want to achieve. Even as a child there was a plan for you, you may not have known it, but your learning objectives at school were a plan so you knew what to work on. Sometimes it was clear, and other times it may have been more confused. The grades you received were your results. When you are seeking real results, you are looking for growth and development, and you need the processes in place to support you. But sometimes knowing what plans to make, what projects to choose and which to postpone is baffling. So how do you choose what to work on?

Do not allow another day to pass by in reaction mode. By taking control of how you structure your day, you give yourself the freedom of opportunity and a push forward in life. It is important to have clarity of your desired outcomes: what are you trying to improve, to make happen? What skills must you develop? What must you learn, and how? In order to implement a solid plan, you must have things scheduled in your calendar, and you must know how each item links back to your vision.

The widespread lockdowns caused by the pandemic in 2020 have given us a slightly different perspective of our calendars - days of the week blurred together so it was sometimes easy to lose track which day of the week it was. This loss of external structure had an unanticipated impact on many people: they became lost in a whirlwind of uncertainty and no direction.

Whilst I am driven by clear priorities that link back to my vision, I know that you may not be, just like I have not always been. Organization might not come easily to you, but there are still efforts you can make to anchor on to your goals and aspirations. Identify what kind of person you are in relation to your goals: do your goals move around a lot, or are they fixed? As you will see in this phase, you can learn to become goal oriented and do it in a way that suits you and your lifestyle. The issue is not whether or not you have goals; the issue is how you align to them. You will go through the Reality Check to help you assess whether the projects you have selected are, in fact, the right ones for you. You will also take a look at the right number of projects you should be engaging with at one time. I have seen many people take on too much or too little. Not finding the right balance often produces inadequate results. In the Capacity and Capability section you will find direction and guidance so you can reflect on your personal bandwidth and stage of life. Then at the end of this phase, I will show you how to create your Quarterly Action Plan and give you the tools and templates to do that.

So, let's go!

Project 3x3

You've done the work to reach beyond and find a way to develop a growth mindset. You've also completed the first version of your Johari Window, so you know more about yourself in a way that is transparent and easy to contemplate. Now is the time to start deciding what you will work on.

This is the next phase of the RESULTS Method. To help you gain certainty about the projects you select, I have created the Project3x3 model which basically means three projects with three priorities in three months.

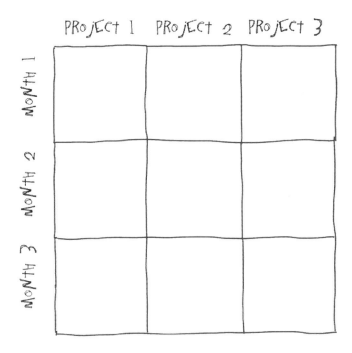

PROJECT 1   PROJECT 2   PROJECT 3

MONTH 1

MONTH 2

MONTH 3

Project3x3

Why three months?

In all the work I have done as a coach, leadership trainer, and as a member of some of the world's most elite mastermind groups, one thing is common—they all work in 90-day cycles. There must be a reason for this. I believe that a year-long plan is often too long a time in order to keep a realistic short-term view. It is possible for you to look ahead one month or even three, but a year is difficult for a lot of people— and most certainly will not give you the focus you desire until you know what you are doing for the next quarter, month, week, and day! A monthly plan may not be long enough to get a good look forward. You may find that you commit and exert yourself for the month, but once the time has passed you are unsure of what's next so you lose momentum and a few valuable days (or longer!) trying to figure it out. A weekly plan is just too short. It doesn't allow the space to set bigger goals; it is not enough time to get feedback; and keeping weekly plans without a bigger context is just too difficult to manage.

RESULTS

Conversely, a yearly plan will not sufficiently motivate you to take the steps you need in the first few months, you might get to the fourth or fifth month and then start to panic about what you need to get done in the seven or eight months remaining.

A Quarterly Action Plan, or 90-day plan, offers a more balanced perspective by giving you a look further forward in which you can devise a longer-term strategy, yet it is still short enough to have an imminent time limit that pushes and motivates you. The quarterly approach is not intimidating—it is far enough ahead for you to dream and close enough for you to execute and eliminate what might not work and replace it with what will. The Quarterly Action Plan sets out a path to progress that is achievable with some push and pull. It also gives you a chance to assess your results, re-align your goals, look at the systems you have set up, and make any necessary adjustments before you either take on new projects or start the next phase of your plan.

And of course, when you put four quarters together you get your Annual Power Plan. As you put together your Project3x3 you will discover and demonstrate a level of confidence and efficiency that you might not have even known was there! This is the start of developing your self-leadership and the creation of a systematic approach for implementation that will help you to realize your goals and the ability to set up weekly targets and measures.

The Project3x3 is particularly effective because it addresses the challenges of the one month and one-year plan approaches—the first constantly renewing and the second with too much time between reviews and both with timeframes that are ill-suited to efficiently measure the progress you are or are not making. By using the process and tools I share with you in this chapter you will create your Project3x3, and it will serve as the anchor for your future and for mapping out everything from the next year (or three or five) to the next month, week, day, and morning. It is an effective process that can be followed with ease and will enable you to move forward.

How does the Project3x3 work?

The Project3x3 is essentially a summary plan for a 90-day (approximately 13 week) period. The RESULTS Method offers you the opportunity to build in a two-day review, and a seven-day break at the end of each period (more about that in the **Succeed** phase). The 12 *working* weeks offer you a chance to either work in six, four, two, or one-week sprints.

When you have a great deal of clarity on your projects and are working by yourself, I favor a two-week sprint cycle as it gives you enough time to work, push, and then review, reset, and keep going.

A six-week cycle also creates a great deal of momentum and is great for providing direction for a team-based project where priorities and tasks are allocated clearly (more on that in the **Utilize**, **Lead**, and **Thrive** phases).

The key to effectively using any cycle is the rest and review interval. Plans focusing in on the 4-week month cycle can work, but after a while they can feel repetitive when not undertaken within the fold of a Project3x3 or an annual plan—you end up feeling that each month is a struggle. The two-week, four-week, and six-week cycle can all be used depending on the needs of your project and the team you have available. The review week incorporated into the Quarterly Action Plan and Project3x3 allows you time to pause and reset, and because it is a scheduled break, you remain emotionally, mentally and practically on-track to reach your goal—you don't feel like you've slipped or turned off course. This is huge when you consider the alternatives of burnout or boreout!

The Project3x3 is the axis of the RESULTS Methodology—get this one right and everything flows from there. From this vantage, you will plan your months, weeks, and days, and yes, even your year (or years) ahead. Don't worry if you feel unsure about the three projects you should work on, because the Reality Check (later in this chapter) will give you clarity and direction on that issue.

	PROJECT 1	PROJECT 2	PROJECT 3
MONTH 1	**PRIORITY 1** Deliverable 1 Deliverable 2 Deliverable 3 Deliverable 4	**PRIORITY 1** Deliverable 1 Deliverable 2 Deliverable 3 Deliverable 4	**PRIORITY 1** Deliverable 1 Deliverable 2 Deliverable 3 Deliverable 4
MONTH 2	**PRIORITY 2** Deliverable 1 Deliverable 2 Deliverable 3 Deliverable 4	**PRIORITY 2** Deliverable 1 Deliverable 2 Deliverable 3 Deliverable 4	**PRIORITY 2** Deliverable 1 Deliverable 2 Deliverable 3 Deliverable 4
MONTH 3	**PRIORITY 3** Deliverable 1 Deliverable 2 Deliverable 3 Deliverable 4	**PRIORITY 3** Deliverable 1 Deliverable 2 Deliverable 3 Deliverable 4	**PRIORITY 3** Deliverable 1 Deliverable 2 Deliverable 3 Deliverable 4

Project 3x3 Completed

Why three projects?

It's all about bandwidth and capacity. We all know that resource availability is finite. It is common sense that when those resources are stretched beyond capacity, a situation is created where something will fail. Likewise, if all available resources are not put to use, output will dwindle. So, there are negative results to the individual or the organization in either scenario, either by exceeding or falling short of resource capacity.

By working on more than three projects at a time you have too much to do—you're stretched beyond your capacity (unless of course you have the team and resources that can support you, and if that is the case, then you are operating more like the conductor than a member of the orchestra). If you only have one or two projects, then chances are that you are not working to your full potential, that you are falling short of putting your resources to use. I have seen instances when these one or two projects are too large in scope and so cause overwhelm. Taking on three projects or dividing larger projects into two or three elements that can be worked simultaneously enables you to work to your full potential without being overwhelmed.

The concept of the three projects is critical because it is the perfect number to prevent you from being bored out or burned out and allows you to link the three projects back to your vision. It keeps you focused without being suffocated. Three projects also enable you to have clarity on the specific outcomes you want for the projects, priorities and deliverables. It also supports you to have the capacity to plan things out in detail. As we get to the weekly rhythm you will find that you end up with a lot of unallocated time if you have less than three projects, and insufficient time if you have more than three. Trust me and trust this process: three projects, no more, no less.

Do I really need a Project3x3?

You might feel that you can work for more than three months without the need for a break, but I ask you to believe me when I say that it is difficult to do that over the long term. When you operate in three-month quarters, you create a rhythm for your life that enables you to create flourishing results where you succeed time and time again. I have seen even the world's most effective people burn out when they work focused for periods of longer than three months without a short reset and break. Some projects do take longer than three-months, and that is where it is important to have project goals that can be met

RESULTS

within the Project3x3. If you are defining your project beyond the three-month mark, you may find that you are unnecessarily extending how long it takes for you to get it done because you see a longer period in which to do it.

Overextending yourself causes other concerns as well. Burnout happens when you work consistently without a break. We want to avoid it at all costs, and that is why I urge you to work in three-month cycles. If you ever fall into a place where you forget to look at your plans for a few days, then take the time to pause and ask yourself what is happening; perhaps read the **Reach** and **Evolve** phases once again to re-ground yourself, and review your strengths, values, and communication styles. I know that when you are committed to your Project3x3 you will find a powerful determination, and you will move forward. We all have demands on us and can feel stress and pressure when we work hard consistently. I invite you not to work hard but to work efficiently. This is a key element of the RESULTS Method. Please remember that.

You cannot always be doing, but sometimes you are required to be. As humans, our effort and results will vary; there is no doubt in that, but consistency is key. Maintaining consistency is a superhuman requirement because human performance is variable. If at any point you notice that you are starting to burnout you need to have a break, this break is different from other rest periods and is required to avoid the full impact burnout may have on your plan and life and to alleviate fatigue.

Some say that if you want something done, you give it to a busy person. Their point has some validity because that busy person will tend to be more efficient, able to get more done, and have the know-how to squeeze something into their schedule. In comparison, sometimes someone who has a lot of spare time may not have the capacity to do anything because they have no motivation, and that means that even the most basic tasks can be a challenge.

Regardless of whether you use a cycle or a car to get you from A to B, you don't just do a weekly air and water check, you also have an annual safety check and will assess the tires every now and then. This systems examination is something you have to do for yourself too, and it occurs when you take a break. Without planned breaks, you will keep wanting to push and push and end up burning out. The same happens at the other end of the spectrum with bore out (we will talk about that later). Being clear that you are including the right things for you in your Project3x3, in this specific time, will help you to ensure that you are committed, consistent, and confident in your plan.

Notice how you are as you read this book, when you undertake every single one of your Project3x3s. With the Project 3x3 you set a strong foundation for how and what projects you select, and why each of them is important for you. Within a 90-day period you can test what is working for you, what you should change, and what you can do more of. These insights will all play a part when looking for feedback for your longer-term plans.

This is where you take a little time (10-20 minutes) to put down the book and do the work. So, wherever you are in your reading plan for today, I am officially telling you to stop reading for now, pick up a pen (or the keyboard) and do the work. Go back to the vision you created in the Evolve phase and visualize that. Is it still what you want? Make a list, journal, draw, scribble, take voice notes, as you wish, but once you come to the end of the time you allocate for this exercise, you will have identified some possible projects that can help you make your vision a reality.

Select three projects you will be taking forward at this stage. Of course, they won't be written in stone, so don't worry too much. Besides, you will have a further chance to refine during the Reality Check.

RESULTS

Remember, RESULTS require decisions, and they require you to make a commitment to yourself. In order to really get it done, you have to have clarity on what you will work on. The Project3x3 model incorporates all the critical success factors of a project. Eventually you will have four Project3x3s sketched out as part of your Annual Power Plan (longer projects can take space in more than one Project3x3, but please keep your goals and priorities for each Project3x3 clearly defined, with a specified end, please see page 178 to create your Annual Power Plan). Your projects will be at different stages, and that is fine, as long as the one you are working on now is scheduled out, you are good to move forward. When you create your plans and schedules in a manner that integrates with your aspirations and takes account of your day-to-day responsibilities, you will be setting a strong foundation to change your life in line with your overall vision. The point is that making this list will lead you in one of two directions: you will either feel motivated by your aspirations for life, or you will realize that you want more. Regardless, I advise you to reflect on your notes. Keep them—you can add to them over the course of the rest of your life.

Now look at your current circumstances and select the three projects you want to work on for the next three months. You are in charge so it can be pretty much anything you want. (But I'm still going to give you some do's and don'ts.)

Do:
- Write down all the projects you would like to work on for the next three months
- List them ALL, literally all (this list will help you when we come to the Reality Check later in this chapter).
- Ask yourself which of these are most important for you right now, all things considered. Which three projects will you work on?

Don't:
- Pick more than three because you have a set capacity for projects. (I know some of you will try and pick more or less than

three projects, but please, remember, trust me and trust the process! If you try to tackle more than three, you will find that your brain, energy, and time is unable to meet your expectations, and you will burnout before you even get started!)

- Pick less than three projects, you will find that you are bored out—you will have spare capacity which will very likely cause a lack of motivation even regarding the projects and tasks you want to see through. Trust me, I have seen this a million times.

At this stage do not try to be too detailed about your projects; we will come to that in due time. Remember that this is a process.

Examples:

Suzie is 34, living in a rented flat. She has selected *Couch-to-5k* (a nine-week running training),[1] launching a new business, and moving to a new house as her three projects.

Whether these three projects are good for her at this time, depends on what else Suzie is doing. If she also has a full-time job and or young kids, then taking on these three projects will be a challenge. In addition, "launching a new business" is very vague as a goal—Suzie's understanding of this could be very different to mine! If she is new to business, and this is her first venture, then it would be a real challenge to do.

I would encourage Suzie to keep the three projects but rephrase them like this:

Couch to 5k, decide which business to start and how to do it, and move to a new house (all SMARTER deliverables, more on that later in this phase).

#

RESULTS

Zak is 20 and living with his parents. He has selected finishing his thesis, reorganizing his room, and doesn't have a third project.

Depending on where Zak is in his thesis and what the deadline is, finishing his thesis is a great three-month goal. Re-organizing his room is something that could be done in a few weeks or a month at most, so perhaps this could be a smaller goal. I would advise Zak to think of something that would take two months to do after this one. And not having a third project is a problem. I'd encourage him to find something to do whether it be reading books he'd bought but not read, improving his health, prioritizing relationships, or leaning into his values, strengths, or love languages. All of these are valid projects and will give the motivation to do the others Zak has listed.

#

Helene is 63, living in a large house with one of her children and their family. She wants to run her business more efficiently, travel, and begin a structured program for personal development.

"Running a business more efficiently" is not a deliverable that you can measure. I would encourage Helene to start thinking about measures that she can use here so that when we get to the **Utilize** phase, she has a good starting point. The other two goals are a bit vague, and so I would encourage more specificity.

#

Jay is 31, living with his wife and 18-month-old son. His goals are to read 100 books a year, to pay off the mortgage, and to start a business now.

I would urge Jay to look longer term in respect to paying of the mortgage. He could look at his reading habits and realistically decide if he can read two books a week and start a new business. I would tell Jay to go back to his vision and see how his projects link in with that.

To be clear, it is not my place to suggest a plan for any of you. I am here to show you the process for how to do it. You are the owner of your vision and deliverables.

Previously we discussed the Stages of Change model. I want you to know that at every stage of your RESULTS journey you need to re-enroll yourself in your vision, values, and goals for life. In order to become the advocate and champion for your vision you need to (yes, need to) pour over your plans regularly. Spending a few minutes each day looking at your plans and visualizing them is spending a few minutes buying into your life.

So, back to your list. The key thing is to select three projects that you think will be right for you in your Project3x3 right now. Once you have picked your three projects and put them in the template available with the other online resources, then we can start expanding it.

Energy, Effort, and Effectiveness

Sometimes it becomes necessary to have a vulnerable conversation with yourself:

- Do I currently have enough energy, effort, and effectiveness to live a good quality of life?

- Do I have the energy, effort, and effectiveness I have always wanted in my life?

- Do I have the energy, effort, and effectiveness to be a good parent, colleague, friend?

- Do I have the kind of energy, effort, and effectiveness that people want to be around?

- Do I protect and cultivate my energy, effort, and effectiveness and use it wisely?

RESULTS

It is vital to understand that where you allocate your energy and effort is a huge factor affecting your ability to make progress in your specific plans and life in general. Spending your energy and effort unwisely most often results in burnout or boreout. So, if you are truly looking to achieve results, the energy, effort, and effectiveness you give to your projects must proportionately reflect that desire.

ENERGY + EFFORT + EFFECTIVENESS
= RESULTS

Energy is not just physical: it is also psychological, spiritual, emotional, and financial. It goes without saying, you need to have the physical energy that will enable you to take the physical action needed to move your plan forwards, but you also need these other energies too. I want you to strategically and purposefully care for your energy. Everything, and I mean *everything*, in your plan will be affected by the energy you create and send out to the world. It is possible for you to have such buoyant enthusiasm that you will retain effortless energy for your projects and life. And no, I am not talking about consuming those energy drinks on the market or increasing your caffeine intake! The solution is simply cultivating the right energy that you want to have in your life so that you can experience living more fully.

You can end up in a place where you recognize a desire to have more buoyant energy, even though the culture around you does not. In this situation, you will most probably also want to impact those around you with the kind of energy that they need—and probably want as well, even if they don't know it! In order to generate the energy you want, you need to be aware of the sources of energy.

Your **mental energy** is an invaluable source of energy. The self-talk that you activate generates the quality of your internal and external energy—the energy within you and the energy you put out to the world around you. Have you ever given serious thought to the kind of energy that you want to have and the energy that you want to share?

Brain scientist Dr Jill Bolte Taylor had a massive stroke at the age of 37 and wrote a book called *My Stroke of Insight*. Subsequently, she appeared on the Oprah Winfrey Show on October 21, 2008. She shared how despite not being able to speak or remember her own mother, she still felt the energy of the clinicians when they walked into her hospital room in. At the end of the interview Dr Taylor gave Oprah a sign which many people have copied and keep in their workspaces and homes. You can make your own on a sticky note or whiteboard. The sign reads: *Please take responsibility for the energy you bring into this space.*[2]

PLEASE TAKE RESPONSIBILITY FOR THE ENERGY YOU BRING INTO THIS SPACE

I believe that ***the psychological energy*** you give off relates to your stress, how much you have to do, and how you manage it. In short, the more you exceed your available bandwidth and capacity, the more stress you have. I always explain this by saying imagine you have a psychological reserve of 100 points. Let's say you allocate 30 points towards work, 30 to family and associated responsibilities, 30 points towards your self-care and health, 30 to your project, and 30 to your personal development. You can see that you have already committed yourself to giving 150 points, but you only have 100. You are trying to function at a deficit. You are over-stretched and will burnout. The other extreme is when you have a reserve of 100 points, and you allocate 30 to work, 20 to family and associated responsibilities, 0 to self-care, 5 to your project, and 5 to personal development. Here you have spare capacity of 40 points, and since you are not applying yourself sufficiently, you will bore out.

Knowing your psychological capacity is essential when it comes to allocating energy to your projects and life in general. Everything in our lives has a right of some form— even your body has a right over you in terms of eating well and exercising!

Your *emotional energy* shows itself in so many ways. There are moments when you are happy; other moments where your emotional energy is high, but you feel paralyzed which is why it is important to be aware of your own emotional energy and how you feel. This conversation is not about the *quantity* of your emotional energy; it is not even about reversing the charge of your negative emotions (fear, anger, disgust, sadness, rage, loneliness, melancholy, annoyance)[3] into positive ones (love, serenity, forgiveness, awe, joy, interest, hope, pride, amusement, inspiration).[4] This conversation is about managing your emotional energy or knowing *how* you want to *feel* during the day and making *that* feeling, that emotion happen.

There will be times when you are frustrated and irritated, it would be questionable if you were even human if you never felt these emotions. But managing these emotions means not allowing them to derail you, and that is the key point here. It is not a life situation or circumstance that takes you off course, it is usually your emotional response to that situation. I invite you to allow yourself to feel the so-called negative emotions, and I encourage you to build and develop the positive ones. This is about being a human and increasing achievement, not about becoming sterile!

Make it a practice to be aware of the emotions you feel. One way you can do this is by keeping an emotional diary or intentionally observing how you feel at different times of the day. Acknowledge your feelings, and if they necessitate action, act deliberately, responsibly, and with heedful intention. In this way, you can manage your emotional energy in an impactful way.

Your *spiritual energy* is both about your connection to your Creator (or what you believe in) as well as connecting to your soul. There are times in your life when your mind and body are operating in a particular way, and your soul will be crying out, calling for you to remember who you are, and demanding that you do something different. Sometimes, the strong messages your soul sends are ignored because you are busy being busy, rather than busy doing the thing that you are called to. When you know that your progress comes at the expense of your soul it can cause angst. Spiritual energy is not necessarily something that you will allocate to a project within your Project3x3, but it is something that will be present in the space outside your time blocks. To this end, it is important to know how it will serve you inside the times when you are working. This message may appear unconventional for the corporate world, yet understanding this energy has powerful implications. Whilst consulting and coaching with partners in international law firms and entrepreneurs, I have seen how the application of psychological and spiritual energy has turned negotiations from failing to succeeding and has enabled individuals to become more impactful and live with deep integrity.

I would encourage you to have a practice that allows you to connect to your psychological and spiritual energy every day whether that be meditation, stretching, Alexander Technique, breathing, priming, prayer, or whatever centering exercise works for you. Just keep a daily practice.

Your *financial energy* is not just about how much resource you have available, it is also about your attitude towards money. Many people do not have an abundance mentality, and they often become consumed in a mindset of lack when it comes to finances. Your life and projects will have a cost associated with them, rather than ignore it, do the work necessary for you to handle those finances.

RESULTS

It is okay for you to be in debt in the short term, so write that permission slip for yourself. However, what is not okay is for you to leave that short term undefined and to indebt yourself without a plan to get yourself out of that situation. Give yourself permission to be free of a monetary relationship centered around dependency or distrust; these are the dominate views society relates to financial energy. You know that you need money to be able to live, but why not imagine that these finances are a resource that exist for you, rather than against you? Trust that you will always have the financial capability or potential that you need in order for your results to become a reality. When you put the idea out there then you are able to manifest it. I appreciate that this sounds a bit far-fetched, but I know from personal experience and from hearing the experiences of other coaches worldwide, that visualizing and maintaining an attitude of prosperity will create a positive and enabling approach to your projects and plans. Insufficient finances will no longer be an excuse for something that prevents you from implementing on your projects because you will have adopted an attitude of "where there's a will, there's a way." In addition, you will no longer be making decisions based on your financial situation; I always say "Never make a decision based on money alone."

One final word of caution: having an attitude of prosperity and optimistic financial energy does not mean overextending yourself and burying yourself deep in debt. This confidence does not mean being unreasonable. Remember your energy is directly linked to your mindset, so an optimistic approach is, in large part, shifting from a concentration of lack to a recognition of abundance and ability.

Your *physical energy* plays a significant role in your ability to plan, implement, and flourish; after all, if you do not have the actual capacity to think and work on your projects, then it will be difficult to make the progress you seek. Physical energy is about ensuring that you have vibrancy, fire, and physical stamina. Your body is your sole source of physical energy, and so you must make it a priority to ensure that you eat well, sleep well, hydrate well, and take whatever measures you need to take care of yourself. This is neither the time nor the place so I won't advise you regarding what you should eat. You know what you like, and you probably have a pretty good education about what you should and should not eat (if you don't, please have a project in your Project3x3 to learn about nutrition and to improve your eating habits and steps you can take to increase your physical energy).

The last source of energy—something that may surprise you—is your ***project energy***. Your purpose, mission, and project are all sources of energy. They make you feel alive, generate vitality, and give you a reason to live; they motivate you to do more, to be better, and to feel incredible. Remember when you were at school and you completed reading a difficult book, or you finished an art project, or aced an exam? The sense of satisfaction that fills you when you have accomplished what you have set out to do is a source of energy; the very process that you used to complete that project is also a source of energy because of the small wins along the journey. In fact, each step, every bit of progress that you make on the way towards your goal is a source of energy and excitement. Projects that you love will take energy from you, and these types of projects return that energy to you by jumpstarting you as you work. You will feel alive. And that is the whole purpose of life, right? To feel alive and enjoy the experience of living. When you find your purpose and focus on the projects that you really want to work on, you will feel energized and inspirited—there is no doubt about that!

Effort

Effort is the key component to getting the results you seek. When you bring full intention and effort to your day, you are more likely to succeed. When you don't, it can feel as if you are just going through the motions and chances are you will work in a burst and then stop because you just don't feel the desire to continue. When people first start creating their plan, there is a huge amount of effort, but after a while this dwindles. In order to maintain momentum and continue through to completion, it is essential for you to have consistency in your effort.

A lot of people say that they work hard, yet sometimes I wonder what that means. Is the right work being done? Is their effort being put in the right place?

You need to have an edge to what you bring. When you know that, you bring your intention and focus to your current task, you increase your level of effort. It's the difference between the person who turns up to the gym class and spends their time and attention on the phone, and the one who is at the gym class, focusing and applying themselves mentally and physically to their workout, and they build up a sweat. You can spend the same amount of time, doing the same routine, and going through the same motions as someone who has no focus and intention, and you will do so much more because you have invested more effort. When you have the edge, you operate at a higher level. Giving your best effort requires that you prepare with your results in mind, and that you show up with discipline, focus, and intention. By including a determination to deliver at a higher level in your intention, you increase your chances of achieving your goal. You want to operate consistently. And you want to be your best as you chase your hero.

The right amount of effort will increase your self-esteem, confidence, and level of flourishing. It is incredibly powerful when you think about how your approach to effort makes such a difference. You can do this in three ways:

1. Be in a supportive community of like-minded people.

When you are in a community of people who will support you and your personal growth, then your effort naturally increases, this is because you are now part of a group. The conversations and support are life-giving for all involved. You want to be your best, and you want those around you to be at their best. When you put in your best effort, then you are able to show up more authentically for yourself and more deeply for others. Surrounding yourself with people who will help you to increase your effort is the foundation for building your support system, and a sound support system is profoundly influential to any individual's success. You can enroll people to support you in your goal or find others on their RESULTS journey. This support will increase your effort. One of the blessings of the virtual world is that it opens up your world to support that you would otherwise not have access to.

2. Allow your personal RESULTS GPS to always guide you.

One of the most powerful messages of RESULTS is to know your intention and to work consistently with the aim of becoming that hero you are chasing. This combination will deliver all the effort you need and more. As we work through RESULTS, you will learn to allocate your time effectively, develop strategic lists of tasks to complete, and perform a weekly, monthly, and a daily review. These techniques will be available to you; however, only you will know if you show up to do the work and take benefit from that feeling of satisfaction. It's up to you to decide what level of commitment and engagement you will bring to your work. You don't need to do everything, you need to do *something*.

When you choose to show up, why not show up with excellence?

3. Have one clear vision.

When you have one ultimate goal (your vision), and your projects fit in with that aspiration, then every action you take, and effort you put in, will also align with that goal. Having clarity on your one compelling future vision goal and then identifying the three projects you want to work on is the first step in distributing your effort appropriately. If you leave this point, then you will work but your work may not be as meaningful. Remember to look at your Vision, your Project3x3, Quarterly Action Plan, Weekly Rhythm, Monthly Moves, and Daily

Schedule every day—they will direct you and empower you to allocate your effort appropriately.

Effectiveness

You can work hard, or you can work effectively. It is not enough to simply allocate the right amount of time to your task to produce effective work; effectiveness is also driven by your one goal. If you are ineffective then it can often be better not to even do the task nor accept responsibility for it.

There will be some tasks that you know you do not enjoy and that you have little inclination to do. Discovering more about yourself during the **Evolve** phase ought to have enabled you to know which tasks are a good match for you to take on and which tasks you may want to delegate. (We will look at delegation more in the **Lead** phase). But before we move on let me give you some examples.

Unless you can find a motivation to connect you at a deeper level to these tasks, I would encourage you not to do them. I love cooking, but I do not enjoy the day-to-day of cooking. In order for me to be able to continue cooking on a daily basis, I have had to connect the act of cooking with the love for my family and those eating the food I prepare. That connection motivates me and adds purpose to the task. If I were to focus instead on the day-to-day repetition of the task, I really would not enjoy it at all, and perhaps not do it. I believe that we should not be doing anything we don't enjoy as it makes us less effective. In fact, those items are a distraction.

Think about the kind of things that you do not enjoy doing and reflect on what you will do with those as they are the tasks where you are likely to be less effective, unless you can link them to your values and purpose. We will expand on this in the **Lead** and **Thrive** phases.

Being effective requires you to do what I am sharing with you in RESULTS: **Reach** beyond your obstacles, **Evolve** into who you truly are and have a clear vision goal, **Select** the right projects for you to work on, **Utilize** your time, **Lead** yourself, and **Succeed** through flourishing. As you go through each phase you increase your effectiveness, enhance your organization, and do more of what you want to do which in turn enhances your experience of life.

Reality Check™

In selecting any project, it is important for you to truly care about it and ensure that it aligns with your one vision goal. I have seen that after going through the Reality Check, many people go back and change projects in their Project3x3. It is to their (and your) benefit to be open enough to recognize and admit that a particular project is not the best choice for whatever reason, and then to be willing to give yourself permission to adjust your Project3x3 accordingly. The bottom line is that if you don't care about it, have the bandwidth for it, or the general capacity for it, then you shouldn't do it. And it certainly shouldn't be part of your Project3x3. Spotting this now is better than realizing it at a later stage.

By saying no to projects that are not the best for you at this stage of life, you create the opportunity to say yes to others that really do mean something to you. You are able to focus on what matters to you not just in the present but to your long-term future.

Sometimes saying yes to the wrong projects can come from being a people pleaser. We've all been there and given in to please others, and there is no reason for shame. However, now that you have the RESULTS Method in front of you and you are aware of the self-defeating impact of saying yes and working on projects that you don't really care about in the long term, find the courage to say no. As you learn to say no to those ill-fitting projects, you will discover that your

RESULTS

connection to what you are working on significantly increases. You will experience exhilaration—you are all in! And that is what you want for any project you select—to be completely dedicated to it.

REALITY CHECK		Project	
	1	2	3
I am excited by this project today, and for the future.			
Do I have the ability to make decisions about this project myself, or by consulting others who support me in making a decision that is right for me today and in the future?			
I can see myself completing this, feeling good, and using it as a steppingstone for the future as I plan for it.			
This project allows me to use my strengths, and values in a way that aligns with who I am.			
Is this project important enough for me to make the sacrifices needed? A sacrifice that is worth making?			
In taking on this project do I have enough energy, effort, and focus for it?			
How much do I feel I can avoid being burnt-out or bored-out by this project?			

Reality Check™

But saying no is not enough. You have to learn *how* to say it. Your "no" has to be measured, not flippant. It has to be considered and deliberate. Say no being fully aware of the opportunities that are now available to you because you said no. By going back to your Project3x3 and then looking at the list of priorities you made at the start of this chapter, you will identify other items that are real projects for you to work on. If you do not see other project opportunities, then please go back and reflect on the vision you created and revisit your Johari

Window. It is possible that you may need to switch perspectives, consider longer or shorter-term views to help you gain clarity on the projects that are really important. For some people, this is the hardest exercise to do because you are making a decision to commit to three different projects that you will work on for the next three months.

Being outcome-focused comes easy for some and is more of a challenge for others. But either way, it is important that you reflect on the outcomes, as sometimes this can enable you to complete the Project3x3 with conviction.

Capacity and Capability Model™

Human beings are all different. We each have our own bespoke set of challenges and success. Due to our individual circumstances we each have a different capacity. Research shows that when you put people under pressure their ability to reason, rationalize, engage is reduced,[5] i.e. you are distracted by a secondary task when you are doing the main one which is often why it becomes difficult to work on your vision and goals.

The relationship between capacity and capability is really dear to my heart. I have seen several people put themselves under incredible amounts of stress for no reason other than comparison to others. If I could have one message to the world it would be that I want you to travel on your own journey, there is no need for you to compare yourself to someone else's speed of implementation, what they have and don't have, etc. All that does is cause you irritation and less success. The RESULTS Method demands that you create your own lifestyle, on your terms, to your capacity. The pace that is right for you is the pace that is right for you, it is that simple. The key to long term results is making sure that you enjoy the experience. Tough love moves the needle, but so does self-compassion (more on that in the **Thrive** phase).

RESULTS

Let me be crystal clear, you have the capability, but you may not have the capacity in terms of bandwidth, time, headspace, etc. That is not a judgement on who you are or what you aspire to. It is a plain statement of reality and when you allow yourself to accept this then you enable yourself to move forward at your pace to create the lifestyle you want.

A college graduate just starting out their career is in a different place than someone who is more established in their role. Similarly, someone at the start of a relationship is in a different phase of life than someone who has kids, possibly be divorced, or is looking at an empty nest. The current stage of your life has an impact on your overall bandwidth, psychological capacity, and the projects you are able to take on within a set period of time. It will impact whether you select a one-year, three to five-year, or even a ten-year plan. The Project3x3 is the critical feature or driving force in all of these plans because regardless of how far out you project your long-term plan, it is essential for you to know what you are doing in your immediate future (i.e. the next three months). The Project3x3 is effective because it summarizes your three projects, priorities (three for each project), and weekly deliverables, all in line with your vision (your one goal) so you can measure impact.

Nobel Prize winning Indian economist and philosopher Amartya Sen developed the Capability Approach. Sen quite rightly says that when evaluating well-being, the most important thing to consider is what people are actually able to be and do. In his research, he analyzes quality of life based on two concepts: functionings [*sic*] (which Sen says are the state of being and doing e.g. having shelter, being well-nourished); and capability (which is the set of "valuable functionings" [*sic*] that a person has access to.[6]

Considering this in conjunction with Abraham Maslow's Hierarchy of Needs[7] and the resources available enables you to clearly see the impact of capacity and capability on your quality of life and your ability to make progress. With this in mind I have created the Capacity and Capability Model.

The relationship between these elements is illustrated below:

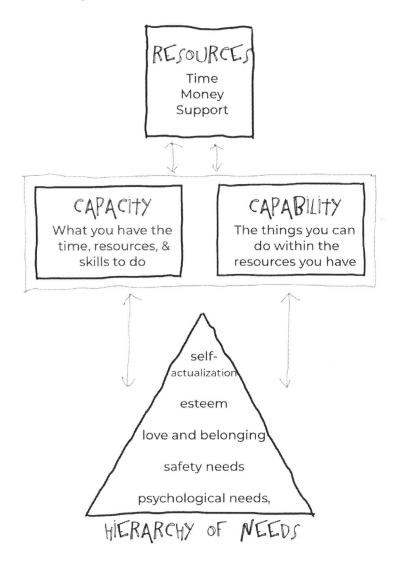

Capacity and Capability Model™

Let's look at your reading this book as an example. The resources are the book and the knowledge in it and your time. Your capacity is how much time you have to read and implement. Your capability is to purchase the book, read the book, and create a plan that you want to implement with the resources at your disposal. Both capacity and capability relate to the different elements of the Hierarchy of Needs in your RESULTS journey—sometimes it will be about self-actualization, other times about your psychological needs being met.

As you read this book and reflect on it and apply the learning you are moving towards flourishing. We all have a diverse capacity when it comes to capability, resource, utility, and well-being, therefore it is unreasonable to expect everyone to be on the same trajectory.

A lot of people say it's too late to start, or think they are too late. Please take this as a reminder that every experience you have had, and all the knowledge you have attained has perfectly led you to this place in your life. It is part of a bigger plan which we do not understand (you can call it God, the universe, fate, serendipity, or whatever description aligns with you). The point is that you are here because you can feel that there is something more for you to do and you are ready. I encourage you to trust that now is the right timing for you to take that next step, no matter how small. The issue is not your capability, it is your capacity. And when you work to your capacity, you make the right moves that fit into your life with integrity.

Now is a good point to pause and look at your life and responsibilities; you must become realistic about what you can and cannot take on. One of the reasons people get frustrated in life is that they do not consider the diverse capability and capacity they have—the focus is not on their personal quality of life. It is important for you to look at your quality of life and assess your capacity accordingly. I have deliberately not defined the different situations here as there are so many, but it is sufficient for you to assess your practical ability to take on projects in relation to your capacity to work on them without burning out.

Let me share a couple of scenarios with you:

Kara—divorced parent with three kids under twelve years of age, working full time.

Kara sounds like she has a pretty full life, and it is not that straightforward to bring new projects into the equation without knowing her values, strengths, love languages, and how much capacity she has. In the first cycle of the RESULTS Method, one of Kara's projects might be to work on organizing her current activities so that she can create additional capacity to work on other projects.

My recommendation for someone in this situation is to focus on a ten-year plan so that they don't try to do everything within a year and stress themselves to the point where they are unable to even meet their current responsibilities. However, if they have support and are able to delegate some tasks, then it may be possible to create the bandwidth they need to take on more projects. This is why the balance between capability and capacity is relative to your specific situation.

#

Kay—single person, working full-time, studying for a higher degree, aspiring to start a new business.

In this scenario I advise Kay to consider looking at a three to five-year plan so that she is able to look further ahead rather than limiting herself to the one-year plan that some might suggest. That said, a one-year plan might be useful if her immediate need is to get more organization in her life and work.

#

While there are always exceptions and extenuating circumstances, the following can give you a general idea when choosing which timeframe is most suitable for your long-term plan:

1-year plan	3 to 5-year plan	10-year plan
· New to personal development, · In transition, · A lot of options available.	· Moderate amount of responsibilities, · Settled at work and home, · Some experience with personal development work.	· A lot of immediate responsibilities, · Little support, · Provides support and assistance to others.

How to determine which long-term plan you choose.

Understanding your capacity is really about identifying what you can take on so you increase your chances of success, progress, and quality of life and well-being. The biggest reasons I have seen for people and companies not delivering on their plans is because:

1. They have taken on too much;
2. They have taken on too little;
3. They forgot about "business-as-usual."

Each of these scenarios has a negative impact on well-being because of disproportionate and faulty planning, but the RESULTS Method and its processes are designed to help you create a plan that balances your capability and capacity and enables you to work effectively. If you are mindful in following the guidance given throughout the book, you will be positioned to deliver on your plans and attain the results you seek.

Personal Priorities

A priority is something that you consider to be more important than other things. Your priorities are not your to-do-list. By primarily focusing on to-do-lists you are spending your time being busy without structure or an overall agenda, and moreover, it is very likely that you are not spending a great deal of time on what is truly important to you. Sometimes someone else's priorities might fall into your lap simply because you are available, and that takes you away from *your* priorities.

When you know your personal priorities, you can reclaim autonomy over how and where you focus your time, energy, and attention. Your calendar, plan, and the agenda for life are yours. It is important for you to know your priorities so that you can understand where you are allocating your personal resources. Sometimes we think we know our priorities, but we really don't. If I came up to you and asked you what your priorities are, would you be able to tell me without having to think about it? Would your answers be concise and full of conviction? Or would they be half-hearted guesses?

No matter whether you truly do have clarity on your priorities, or whether you need to sit and give the matter some good thought and contemplation, it is always a good exercise to take the time and make the effort to write your priorities down on a piece of paper. Give them a thorough thrice over and weigh them to see if these are the priorities you are really committed to and that are of the highest importance to you. Do your priorities align with your compelling future vision?

Goal Structure

One of the core components of having a plan is having a goal. It is important to understand what a goal is. The dictionary tells us a goal is "a purpose, or something that you want to achieve."[8] This understanding is useful as a basic definition, but a more sophisticated understanding of what qualifies as a goal is required for creating a plan that you will actually use. Research says goals are "reference values,"[9] "self-guides,"[10] "personal strivings,"[11] or "personal projects."[12] These definitions make it difficult to separate between the various aspects of a goal such as its aims, objectives, desires, or outcomes, and they also don't capture the true essence of the goal. We need goals to help us transition from where we are to where we want to be.

Yet, not all goals are the same. If you can believe it, over twenty types of goals have been identified. These include outcome goals, approach and avoidance goals, performance and learning goals, and higher and lower order goals, as well as the actual results which you aim to achieve! Outcome goals are actually the most common types of goals; they focus on achieving something by a particular point in time. Outcome goals tend to be harder to achieve, and it can be frustrating when you don't. Examples of this are reading 52 books a year, running a marathon in six hours, or earning $100k from your side hustle. These are very easily articulated and incredibly clear outcomes, but when something is far too much of a stretch then it welcomes refinement.

Priorities

Execution or performance goals focus on the act of actually getting it done. Later we will look at the Pomodoro method which can be seen as an execution goal, yet I prefer to use the term *priorities*. The advantage of priorities is that it breaks goals down. For example, rather than saying you want to read 52 books a year, a priority would be that you want to read for 25 minutes each day. All of a sudden, just by shifting your attention and breaking a large goal into smaller tasks, something that seems too big or too difficult becomes achievable. Priorities allow you to focus on the *behavior* that you need to achieve the result you want; you create a routine that aligns with the larger goal and vision rather than just *trying* to work on it and leaving the results to chance. Priorities enable you to create rituals (or habits, if you prefer) around your outcomes and encourage a feeling of satisfaction with the work you do. For example, reading for 20 minutes (even if you had planned to do it for 25) is still an achievement, even though you have only completed 80 percent of the task. When working within defined priorities, you will still acknowledge reading for 20 minutes as an achievement. And, let's say you happened to read for 30 minutes one day, from the perspective of a priority that overachievement could even be celebrated! The difference between saying, "I want to run a marathon," and "I want to run three times a week" and putting it in the calendar is the difference between setting an outcome goal and creating a priority.

Pablo Picasso summed it up nicely when he said, "Our goals can only be reached through a vehicle of a plan— in which we must fervently believe— and upon which we must vigorously act. There is no other route to success."[13]

From Vision Goal to Project Goals

Having clarity when writing the goal for your project is one of the hardest things to do when it comes to project management. Governments, international organizations, and individuals struggle with gaining this clarity. Yet, one day you might end up like Usain Bolt, eight-times Olympic champion. When he was younger, he was not a keen runner, but he realized that he wanted to get his mom a new washing machine and could see that running would help him to get that.

> That's how it started out, to help my parents. My mother always washed and when she finished washing her fingers sometimes blistered and stuff like that...I wanted to buy my mother a washing machine…. …the next thing for me was to get my father a vehicle because he had a bike but he used to use the company van and then he got redundant, so he had no van it was just a bike. And then I wanted to help him pay off the loan off the house that we were living in. (*Usain Bolt, 2016*)[14]

Bolt's goals were very clear and kept evolving as he achieved them. They always fit in with a goal which may not have been articulated so clearly—to help his family. When you first decide to set a goal, target, or aspiration for your life you might think that that's it—that once you've achieved that goal, you're finished. As you can see from Bolt's story, project goals are ever evolving, but they align with your one big goal—your compelling future vision. There are so many examples of where you set a goal, meet it, and then set a new goal. That is what Matthew McConaughey's story about chasing your best self demonstrates.

Another example for us to consider is Jose Mourinho. Mourinho's first managerial type role was as the translator for Bobby Robson who was the FC Porto team manager at the time. After Robson left Mourinho was appointed as manager and he led the team from almost being demoted to winning the Portuguese league. My perception is that this experience gave Mourinho confidence in his ability, and it could be that it was the point when Mourinho saw his clear vision. In the Netflix series *The Coaches Playbook*, he says "For me, since the beginning of my career, I had a dream which was to win the championship in the three biggest leagues in Europe. So, I did England, and since I did Italy that night, I knew that I have to try to do it in Spain too. So I decided I was going to Real Madrid the next day, for the new job."[15] He also won there.

This achievement is something that has never been done before with such pinpoint precision: three championships, in the three biggest leagues in the world, with three different teams. His next key role was as manager of Manchester United where he was sacked, and in 2019 Mourinho became manager for Tottenham Hotspur. He is yet to win a trophy again. Without talking to him I could not know for certain, but my hypothesis is that once he completed his clear, compelling vision, he may not have set another one, and hence is now experiencing reduced circumstances.

#

Goals are the fundamental first step in making your projects a reality. They help you to plan for the future and play an important role in moving you from where you are now to where you want to be. Clear goals are your destination: it's the difference between saying you want to travel from London to the USA (unclear) and you saying you want to travel from London to sit on the Hollywood sign in Los Angeles, USA (very specific).

In the world of positive psychology, coaching, high performance, and project management much has been written about goals and goal setting. I agree with Professor Edwin Locke a leading researcher and pioneer in goal setting theory when he said "Every person's life depends on the process of choosing goals to pursue; if you remain passive you are not going to thrive as a human being."[16] The moment you have a clear goal you find an impulse building within, ready to take you places. A clear goal has the power to activate someone suffering from stagnation into someone wanting progress and movement forward, and that is where momentum comes from. If a goal does not motivate you (or you have too many goals), then you will not do anything.

Locke's research found that sometimes goal setting can cause stress and anxiety; and that if there is a conflict between two or more goals, then the performance in each project or goal can be undermined.[17] The RESULTS Method provides you with the tools to ensure that you have processes in place to mitigate potential stress, anxiety and conflict associated with goal setting. This is why you have a clear compelling future vision goal and three project goals that everything else focuses around. We have done the groundbreaking work needed to understand your values, strengths, and RESULTS GPS and then created (and visualized) your vision goal; and selected the three projects and performed the Reality Check. In the **Lead** phase we will look at your awareness of your role as a leader and how it relates to you, your responsibilities, and projects.

RESULTS

One can have very clearly set, beautifully illustrated goals which have taken a while to create and articulate. Yet, if the person writing them does not feel *fired up,* then they certainly will not be *ready to go* when it is time to take action. This feeling of being "fired up and ready to go" is pivotal to the success of your personal projects, just as it was to Barak Obama in his presidential campaign in June 2007.[18] Obama had arrived in Greenwood, South Carolina for a campaign meeting. He needed early support from this state in order to succeed in his clearly articulated vision goal of becoming the first African American President of the United States. He attended this meeting feeling tired and exhausted. To top it off, it was raining, and when he entered the room there were only about twenty people there. It took him about ninety minutes to get there and would take another ninety to get back. Everyone was a little damp because of the rain, and they didn't seem to be very happy to be there. Reflecting back on this incident, Obama said the following:

> I have a job to do. I'm running for President, I shake their hand, I say, "How do you do, what do you do, nice to meet you." Suddenly I hear this voice should out behind me: "Fired up?" And I almost jumped out of my shoes. But everybody else acts like this is normal, and they all say, "Fired up!" And then I hear this voice: "Ready to go?" And the people around me, they just say, "Ready to go!" I don't know what's going on. So, I look behind me, and there's this little woman there. She's about 5'2", 5'3", she's maybe fifty, sixty years old. And she looks like she's dressed for church. She's got a big church hat. (Laughter.) And she's just grinning at me, just smiling. And she points at me, and she says "Fired up?" (*Barak Obama, 2016*)

For the next five minutes she keeps saying, "Fired up, ready to go." and people start joining in. By the end of the meeting everyone is "Fired up, ready to go." Obama could have not heard Edith Childs, been disconnected from his goal, and the whole thing could have been a flop. But that did not happen, and that phrase became one of Obama's go-to phrases of his campaign in 2008.[19]

#

You make a decision for what is meaningful in your life, and any project you select should have goals set that motivate you to achieve and succeed. Bear in mind that the crucial issue in goal setting is not selecting goals according to your ability or knowledge, it is selecting project goals that align with your compelling future vision goal and intention, identity, integrity, and implementation. (If you are still not clear on any of these or would like a refresh, please go back and review.)

There is a significant amount of research and plenty of experience to show that having goals increases your motivation and satisfaction. Think about young children: when they are unable to crawl, their goal is to crawl; when they are unable to walk, their goal is to walk; and when they are unable to run, their goal is to run. As they pass through these stages, children feel motivated by each success, and even when they fall, they don't hesitate to get up and try again because they are not familiar with the negative, societal, and psychologically-damaging weight of blame and condemnation: "You failed, and you'll fail again." At that time early in your life, you just believed that you could do it and would do it; you overcame adversity (you may have even fallen down the stairs a few times), but you did it. When you faced a challenge, you found a way to overcome it. You had no idea that those strategies existed, but you found them. And here you are today—navigating obstacles and challenges as you make your plan a reality and continue to build your confidence and efficacy, just as you did when you were learning to walk.

The same rule applies in your life now; the only difference is that some people do not set project goals that align with their compelling future vision goal, intention, identity, and integrity. When you participate in a learning opportunity like this, you plan for the future and are goal-oriented. You pause to reflect on the skills you have and what you want to develop. In this environment, under these conditions, you are working on improving your subjective well-being, which is a fancy way of saying you are working on becoming happier, and the process of planning actually increases your control over achievements and your future self.

Minimum, Target, Outrageous

Imagine this scenario, you have set a project goal to increase your income by 20 percent. If six months later you manage 15 percent, are you disappointed and unexcited? Does missing your target by 5 percent take away from the joy of the 15 percent increase? How do you overcome this?

Raymond Aaron developed the MTO Technique.™ MTO stands for minimum, target, and outrageous.

Aaron says: Minimum is defined as "what you can be counted on to achieve based on your past performance". Not on your hopes. But on the reality of your actual past achievements.

Target is the "stretch", that which is slightly beyond what you know you can accomplish.

Outrageous, in this context, means "what you know you cannot achieve."[20]

Perhaps internally you knew that 20 percent salary increase was too much and that becomes your outrageous goal. You will celebrate on another level when you get it! But meeting the target goal still merits a celebration. Even the minimum goal is still considered an achievement and allows you to celebrate if you get there. When you permit that excitement and joy, it allows you to stay present, focus, and enjoy every step of your progress. There is no disappointment if you increase five percent, that additional five percent is still a gain but without a proper perspective, you devalue it.

Linking your project goals and impact measures to MTO results in you being able to enjoy the outcome regardless. It gives you something to aim for and pushes you forward. This helps you to create progress, more progress than yesterday. It is the incremental progress of the day that helps you get RESULTS.

Minimum	Target	Outrageous
Write 500 words	Write 1500 words	Write 2500 words
Lose ½ lb.	Lose 1 lb.	Lose 2lb
Read 10 pages of a book	Read 15 pages	Read 20 pages
$2000/month income	$5000/month	$7000/month

Example MTO's

You aim for the target, and you celebrate the minimum if that is what you achieve (rather than experience the disappointment you might experience without the MTO approach).

Setting Goals

Much research has been done in the area of how goal setting should be undertaken; and you, no doubt, have your own personal experiences

RESULTS

of how goal setting has worked for you. Call it a dream, aspiration, desire, goal… whatever you want to call it is fine, for as Shakespeare's Juliet declares, "A rose by any other name would smell as sweet!"[21] This is your journey with the RESULTS Method, so please use the words and language that fit for you!

Regardless of the different names we could use for goal setting, Locke identifies five key principles for successful goal setting. These principles are commitment, clarity, challenge, complexity, and feedback.[22]

Commitment describes how attached you actually are to the goal and how determined you are to attain it despite the challenges you will face. You know that when you have total commitment to something, nothing will get in your way, or if it does, you will work to navigate around it.

Clarity is essential in articulating your goal. If a goal is vague (as in "I want to be more confident"), then it is of little value. You need to be able to *visualize* what a goal looks like and to define it in a way that is precise, so you know exactly when it has been achieved. If the goal cannot be broken down or measured, then it will not be effective.

Challenge is important in goal setting. Having a goal that is too easy or too difficult will not activate your subconscious to support you to make it happen. In fact, it is very likely that you will just ignore the goal completely. You may also end up frustrated with yourself because you've set a goal that you have no likelihood of achieving.

A good goal should be something that pushes you, but it is neither easy pickings, nor out of reach, but rather, it is on the boundary of your limits. You saw the differences between minimum, target, and outrageous goals, and you now understand why target goals are always a good aim to have as they can be more motivational.

Complexity should be avoided when choosing your goals. When a goal has many layers, it is important to break it down. Goals that are too complex will just overwhelm you and make you feel discouraged and unmotivated. As you write down a goal, if you feel that there is too much involved in making it happen, then stop and review it. Break the goal into smaller chunks or tasks so that it is something you can visualize. We all feel disheartened by goals that are too complicated, but when you break it down, and it becomes achievable then you will feel rejuvenated!

This is a key reason why I ask you to create the vision goal and have three related project goals. Removing the complexity enhances your implementation.

Feedback refers to getting others' input and perspectives. By establishing a system for receiving advice from others, you immediately increase the effectiveness of the goal, and reduce the effort that you have to put in. By using the resources that we give you in RESULTS, you create your own personal feedback system. Then, if you find, for whatever reason, that you are not on target, rather than abandoning the plan and project all together, you can use the feedback to identify what needs adjusting so that you can keep making progress. Sometimes the need to pause and take one step back will keep you on target, just like small navigational adjustments keep a pilot on course. The adjustments facilitated by feedback minimize your goal abandonment rate and keep you moving forward.

Neglecting your goals.

Goal neglect is something that too often happens when you have not done the prerequisite work. Essentially you set yourself a goal or task, but despite the fact that it is understood and important, you still ignore it. Goal neglect happens when you do not pay enough attention to the importance of a goal, and instead, focus your attention on another goal or task (often spending time being busy doing nothing of real substance). This mismatch of your goal or task results in a discrepancy between the actions required of you and what you actually do. Human beings are goal-oriented, but our behavior, thoughts, feelings, and physical actions are shaped and given direction by the purpose and meaning our goals hold for us. Your behavior is shaped and directed by the goals and values which are inside your immediate conscious awareness. It is your values that give direction, meaning, and purpose to the goals and actions. If you have misidentified your compelling future vision goal or project goals you may not have the proper direction, meaning, or purpose to achieve those goals. This understanding will help you avoid misdirection in the future. And remember as you evolve as a person, your compelling future vision will grow as you grow.

RESULTS Process

Now that you have a better understanding of how to set goals, write out your vision goal, your three projects and three priorities in the next illustration's template which is available in the online resources.

By linking your priorities and project goals with your well-defined, precisely articulated values and vision goal you are more likely to commit. Making clear links between your values, goals, and specific actions will help you to define the small steps you need to take to implement. Linking your goals with your values means you *will* take action.

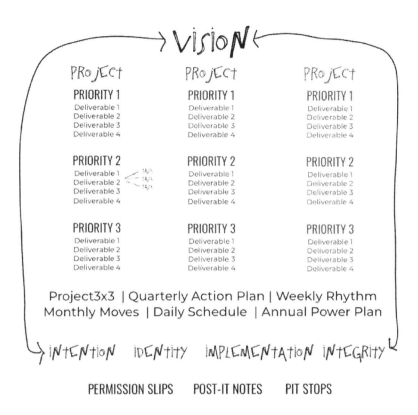

The RESULTS Process

Visualizing your values, goals, and action steps provides you with a useful and motivating way to look at your plan as it links your day-to-day activities with the core of who you are.

SMARTER

Regardless of what system you use to articulate your goals, it is important to keep your goals SMARTER—this is an adaptation of the SMART concept created by George Doran.[23] Whilst the idea represented by SMART is useful, it also underplays the work, determination, and effort required in order to make it effective. I believe that occasionally SMART has helped to people create shiny plans that they then put in their desk drawers and ignore (I know because I've done this in the past). A clear understanding and knowledge of application will make any concept useful, rather than academic. Practical goal setting is far more than the simplistic SMART acronym implies, but it provides an excellent foundation to build upon. So, we go from SMART goal setting to SMARTER goal setting.

SMARTER stands for **S**pecific, **M**eaningful, **A**chievable, **R**elevant, **T**ime Bound, **E**valuate, **R**eset.

Specific: The more specific you are about your goals, the more able you will be to actualize them. Being specific makes your goal measurable. It is important to be specific when stating your goals in order for you to *own* the goal—not just in your heart or mind but viscerally, so that it becomes part of your identity. When the vision and project goal is not specific or clear, there is no real aim. When the statement of the goal is obscure, so is the target, and your chances of meeting that goal decrease. Being specific gives fuel to take the necessary actions and increases the likelihood of these goals becoming a reality.

Meaningful: Your goals should have meaning to you and you should have a meaningful connection with your goals. Otherwise, the incentive to follow through is superficial, and as you just don't own it as much, you are less likely to do the work to make it a reality. For example, if your goal is to have an increased income, it is essential to know that isn't really the income you desire, rather the goal is what that income will provide, as per Usain Bolt's story earlier. Having more money is not as meaningful as knowing you can create an increased sense of security for your family with that money.

Achievable: Recall the discussion related to minimum, target, outrageous goals. You want your goals to be more than just achievable—you want goals that push you to strive so that you can exercise your full potential. Aim for something that is a bit of a stretch further, this way even if you are off target, you will still have met your lower target.

Relevant: How relevant is the goal you are setting for your life right now, all things considered? Some things you desire are better suited to the longer term and other things you need to do sooner rather than later. Your aspirations should be in line with what you want out of life; they should carry echoes of your strengths and values. If your goal is inconsistent with your strengths and values, then it will be harder to achieve, or at the very least, will mean a more frustrating and complicated journey.

Time Bound: Boundaries are essential as we will see in the **Utilize** phase. The one boundary that tends to slip out of control even more than the financial one is the boundary of time. By setting (non-negotiable) dates for when you want to achieve your goals, you are making yourself accountable to yourself, setting a clearer target, and increasing your ability to make and measure progress.

Evaluate: Make time for daily, weekly, monthly, and quarterly evaluations so that you can see what you have done well and assess what needs improvement or adjustment. This is an important part of the process and not to be ignored. If you really want to improve your ability to take an effective self-evaluation, keep a journal of how you are making progress; your entries will prove to be priceless as you come to your evaluations.

Reset: This is the part of the RESULTS Method where you review where you are, how it has gone, what you've learned, and then reflect on how you can improve for the next iteration. Resetting is a key component of the plan cycle. In the **Succeed** phase of RESULTS you will cover this aspect in more detail.

Priming Goals

Alex Stajkovic, of the University of Wisconsin, relates an experiment. He explains that a sales company CEO would send out a motivational email every Monday to his employees; it was a way of creating confidence in the workforce and setting the weekly targets. In the experiment, half the employees received a slightly different email—twelve achievement related words were inserted into the email. These boosted emails were randomly assigned, and the control group got the email without the achievement words. The words were simply words like win, compete, accomplish, etc. The purpose of the experiment was to see the impact that these words would have on the results of those employees. Just five days later (actually it varied one day to five days), those who read the email with the additional 12 words performed significantly better than those who didn't. The goal priming by the CEO had little or no impact on cost, yet it increased objectively measured performance effectiveness by 15 percent and efficiency by 35 percent over a five-day workweek. The individuals were totally unaware of what was happening—the goal to achieve had been set in their subconscious.[24] "Goal priming" such as this has been done with pictures, words, and even complex marketing campaigns to test if this subconscious incentive really does work. Each and every time, even the skeptics agreed that goal priming is effective.

You are living according to goals, whether you have established them or not, and whether you are aware of having established them. Considering all the published scientific evidence, I can confidently tell you that:

- You have a much better chance at everything and anything if you are in control or have agency over your own life.
- The quality of your decisions is directly related to the quality and quantity of the information that guides them.

- The more abstract and transcendent the top goal (the compelling future vision you created) is, the more flexibility you have at the lower levels of the goal structure hierarchy.
- You decide to be the master of your fate and the captain of your ship, or you outsource it.

With that in mind, I want you to think about the goals you have selected and the words that you use with yourself. Simply take those goals and edit them to add in achievement words. I appreciate that you may be skeptical, but I urge you to try it out and see what happens. Achievement words that were used in the experiment above included prevail, accomplish, compete, strive, thrive, triumphed, achieve, mastered, win, success, gain, and attain.[25]

Quarterly Action Plan

The creation of your Quarterly Plan is one of the biggest gifts you will ever give yourself. Preparation is key. So now that you know the three projects you are working on (that align with your compelling future vision goal), you are in the running to get it done! A quarter actually has thirteen weeks. The last week is blocked off for two major components in your RESULTS cycle: two days to review and reset where you reflect and create your next quarterly plan, and seven days for a break before you start implementing your new plan. You can find agendas for the two-day retreat in the **Succeed** phase and with the online resources.

Your Quarterly Plan is written on one page. I have learned from working with hundreds of individuals and companies that in the hustle and bustle of day-to-day life you need to be able to look at your plan and absorb it in one moment. When your plan is two, six, or twelve pages long you just won't use it. When it is a one-page plan, you can look at it every single day. Every. Day.

RESULTS

Your Quarterly Plan includes your vision statement, the values relating to each project. Your Monthly Moves, and your Weekly Rhythm support the Quarterly Plan. It might be incomplete at this stage, but that is okay because you will expand on your Quarterly Plan in the next few chapters. One thing to note is that your plan is both fixed and flexible. It is fixed in that your Project3x3 is now set, and you know the overall outcomes you are aiming for. By thinking and imagining you have come up with a destination, allow yourself the curiosity to be flexible when obstacles come your way or you go off on a tangent. I believe that everything happens for a reason, and there is balance in all that you do. Some things will go faster than you wish, others slower.

As you become more familiar with creating your Project3x3, you will also know how you work and where you have contingency built in allowing for flexibility. This is your plan. You are the one that owns it. Remember, you can change or end projects at any time. If you do end a project, ensure that you have a strong reason for it; we'll cover more about that in the **Lead** phase. For now, I urge you to make some decisions and stick to your Project3x3 so that we can move onto the **Utilize** phase and start looking at how you will make the best of your time.

Annual Power Plan

Once you have created your first Quarterly Action Plan you have the ability to map out your year. There is no need for it to be complete. Having an indication of what you want to achieve by this time next year is the key. Even if all you do the first time is put in projects and broad goals for what you want to achieve in each quarter that is enough. You will be able to add to it each time you review your Annual Power Plan in the **Succeed** phase every quarter.

The RESULTS Annual Power Plan

You can look at your Annual Power Plan as something that gives you short to medium term direction. Remember, it is ok for it to be incomplete as long as the first Project3x3 is 90 percent there. If completing your Annual Power Plan feels like too much right now feel free to leave this for now and come back to it when you are in the **Succeed** phase.

Self-Interview

Insight: What is your biggest insight from this phase?

Intention: When you explore your boldest hopes and highest aspirations, what is that you ultimately want from your projects?

Identity: Why does selecting the right projects really matter to you?

Implementation: What is the smallest or most immediate action you are willing to take?

Integrity: What can you do to deepen your commitment to follow through?

HOW DO i GET it DONE?

Before

UNORGANIZED

After

FOCUSED

UTILIZE

"I try to do the right thing at the right time. They may just be little things, but usually they make the difference between winning and losing."

Kareem Abdul-Jabbar

RESULTS

The university options will inevitably be reduced unless…

Let me introduce you to Mike. He is 16 and is currently studying for his A levels at college. Like all other students in England, due to Covid-19, he was unable to sit his GCSE exams in summer 2020 and was given center-assessed grades. Mike was homeschooled for some of his subjects, including German and Sociology, and the authorities decided that in his situation no grades would be awarded, and therefore those students affected would need to sit exams. Mike received his college grades and decided that he would sit the papers for mathematics at the next sitting.

In the time leading up to the exams Mike was reluctant to engage with what was required of him for his mathematics GCSE and was spending a lot of time and effort focusing on sociology (a subject in which he was a very strong candidate). The offer of additional support from college and home did not persuade Mike to study the mathematics.

RESULTS

This makes me wonder: why, as human beings, do we choose to engage with the easier project? Why do we exert additional (and often unnecessary) effort into the project that needs the least attention, and effectively ignore the more demanding projects until they scream at us like a toddler having a tantrum? There will be some elements of your projects that you do not enjoy, that is a given. The question to ask is how much do you want to deliver on your vision? If you want to achieve the best results, then you must dig deep within and find a way of connecting to the parts that are a key part of your vision and that only you can do.

Mike's vision is to be a lawyer. He is a smart student. If he doesn't put in the required effort for the mathematics exam then the university options available to him will inevitably be reduced. A student that meets Harvard and Oxford criteria on everything else should be able to suck it up, but sometimes they just can't. This is a problem that many of us face. Keeping a strong connection with our bigger vision and values will give us that added support when we need to do the things that we do not want to do—it moves us from being unorganized to focused.

#

So, now that you have identified your personal values, drawn upon those values to select your three impactful projects, and with the guidance of the SMARTER approach, defined your priorities within each project, you are probably asking, "Okay. Now, how do I get it done?"

In the **Utilize** phase of RESULTS you will focus on recognizing and managing the different blocks of available time, learn the BART system, gain clarity on how you measure the outcome of your action, how to achieve in alignment with who you are, and create the first pass of your weekly plan.

How do you get it done?

Managing your time, most particularly your week, is the most critical aspect of you making your plan a reality. Humans, by our very nature, tend to have distorted perceptions of time, and this makes managing that time a challenge. Karl von Vierdort's time perception theory identifies a very interesting aspect of our estimation of time. It says that "retrospectively, 'short' intervals of time tend to be overestimated, and 'long' intervals of time tend to be underestimated."[1] What that means is that when we are thinking in shorter terms, we think we have more time than we actually do, and as a result, we often fall into the trap of overcommitting ourselves. We think we can accomplish more in a day or week than is within our reasonable capacity because we assume the day or week is longer than it is, that we can get more done in an hour that we actually can over time. The end result is burnout. The opposite is true of our long-term perception. We tend to view the long term as shorter than it is and therefore fail to take advantage of it. We assume there is insufficient time to accomplish anything significant. The result is boreout and not meeting our true potential (we will come back to this when we consider the Planning Fallacy later).

So, what is the answer to this dilemma?

One part of the solution is having a real understanding of your personal bandwidth and recognizing the difference between capacity and capability. The second part of the solution is utilizing a planner. As you will come to see, at this stage it doesn't matter if you use an electronic or printed planner—the key is using one. I personally would urge you to use both, but more about that later.

Identifying the different blocks of time available to you is critical to your progress. It is not possible to simply delineate lots of identical time blocks in your planner and expect everything to fall into place. You need to be deliberate in choosing how you use your available time and which priorities you allocate time blocks.

Ensure that you schedule specific blocks of time for learning, free time, self-care, your projects, and your responsibilities. If you spend most of your time at home, I advocate having virtual meetings, or phone calls, with friends or colleagues every day. Human connection is highly conducive to making you feel empowered, motivated, and confident that you are able to make the progress you need. These "check-ins" strengthen your support system; they will give you a daily boost, help keep you focused and help you to build self-compassion. And when those inevitable setbacks and unexpected obstacles do show up, these connections will help you remain calm, keep your sanity, find a way to navigate through, allow you to "get it off your chest," and push forward.

Time Blocks

Time management is something the majority of the world's population struggles with. From the kid at school, to the CEOs of the world's largest companies, everyone wants to know how to manage their time more effectively. Now that you have a clear idea of the projects you want to work on and the logistics associated with them, learning how to manage your time effectively is the next step in getting it done. We all realize that not knowing how to take control of our time is one of the leading causes of stress. According to psychologist Russ Newman, PhD, JD, and APA executive director for professional practice, high levels of stress "can have long-term health consequences, ranging from fatigue to obesity and heart disease."[2] Yet, the answer is rather simple: work in intervals where you have no distractions or disruptions, then have a break, and repeat.

The process of work and rest is not just one that works on a practical level; it has also been researched by Professor Alejandro Lleras and Dr Atsunori Ariga. They found that their subjects' performance decreased when they worked in periods of 50 minutes or more, and the same subjects were more productive when they worked the same amount of time with two short, intervening distractions.[3] Before we return to this, I would like to give you a broader context of how to break down the available time.

Time blocking increases your productivity and focus. A byproduct of using time blocks is that it reduces guilt and anxiety and increases the joy and satisfaction you experience in daily life because you are getting it done!

The Ten Impactful Time Blocks

1 quarter/3 months/100 days	2 hours
1 month	1 hour
1 week	25 minutes
1 day	10 minutes
½ day	1 minute

The Ten Time Blocks

Over the course of my personal and coaching experiences, and in my studies regarding time management, I have found that there are ten different time blocks that can be applied to impactful planning and scheduling. It is important to have clarity on how you will use these blocks in your schedule and the planning system that you are creating for your life.

RESULTS

1 Quarter/3 Months

> 'It's supposed to be hard. If it was easy everyone would do it.'
> — Jimmy Dugan, A League of Their Own.

The Project3x3 is the anchor of all your planning. We have discussed the details and significance of the Project3x3 previously, and you can go back and review this vital connection in the **Select** phase of RESULTS if needed. Review the process for creating the goals and priorities of your Project3x3 at any time if needed (remember the first time you are reading this you can create a 100 Day Plan, as suggested on page 25).

Once you know the three projects you will be working on, find three priorities within each project that will move you closer to its completion, and your vision. Then break each of these priorities down into steps and identify four deliverables that will help you reach that monthly priority. You will end up with twelve deliverables per project; these deliverables and any associated tasks must be scheduled when planning your week. As you read this it may sound overwhelming, but don't overthink the process. As you use the RESULTS Process for the first time, do not worry if you have less than 12 deliverables. Just start with what you have, and then at the end of every week, review your deliverables to see what additional items you are now aware of. The first time you work on a project you will inevitably find new things to add to your schedule. That certainly happened for me when I planned to write this book.

You might take it for granted that three months is 12 weeks, but in case you haven't ever realized it, let me be the one to tell you that it is actually 13 weeks. I love this play that the calendar has with us because it gifts us a week to review, reset, and revitalize our plans before we start the next quarter. I strongly encourage you to identify one or two planning days every quarter and then take a week off (more about that in the **Succeed** phase). Plan a get-away and take a break if you can

(Covid-19 safely, of course!). If you can't travel anywhere, have a staycation where you take a few days living like a tourist even though you are at home—go places, eat out, have fun. And if you are unable to leave your home, find films to watch, get food deliveries, create a spa at home, read books that you've not looked at since you bought them, do whatever it takes for you to have a break. The aim of the break is to reward yourself for the hard work you've been putting in, to detach yourself from work, and to go through a real reset. If you keep going without a break and take no resets, you will burn out. All the research verifies this inevitable reality, and I suspect your personal experience tells you that too. You need time for you to recover.

30 Days/1 Month

I love a 30-day challenge! But I don't like the word challenge, the dictionary says challenge is "the situation of being faced with something that needs great mental or physical effort in order to be done successfully and therefore tests a person's ability."[4] There is a time and place for competition. Yes, I want you to be in competition with your best self. But I don't want you to subconsciously feel that the competition is putting you off.

Feeling engaged and committed to your vision and projects is critical to you and your progress. I invite you to view your year as an opportunity for 12 different life-changing, ritual-forming, skill-building 30-day moves! Reflecting on the work you completed in previous phases, think right now about what you want to achieve—just make a list. Write everything down that you'd love to do in terms of the following:

Skills. What do you want to learn by this time next year? Challenge yourself to do more than just learn the basics. Going beyond the basics is the difference between learning a few words in Italian and being able to go to an Italian restaurant and order a meal in Italian.

RESULTS

When I ask what you want to get skilled up in, what makes you excited? Write that down. (If you don't have a journal, feel free to write it in the margins of the book or as a note in your Kindle).

Being strategic about your calendar helps move what you want to do from becoming a hobby to becoming a skill.

Health. Where do you want to be in terms of your next level of health? Consider your health from a holistic perspective—your emotional, physical, spiritual, and psychological well-being. What would you need to do to have better health in any of these areas? You have one year ahead of you, so dream as big as you want!

Experiences. The year 2020 resulted in many experiences being cancelled for people. That doesn't mean you abandon all hope of new experiences that will make you feel alive. In 2019, I decided to "do new things," and joined a Brazilian Ju Jitsu class. It was one of the most mindful experiences of my life! Due to Covid-19 all classes were cancelled, but I still have the memory and hope to start again one day. Schedule time in your calendar to do new activities that bring you joy. It can be as simple as taking half a day and going for a long walk in a country park or joining a new class.

Monthly Moves. The Project3x3 gives you three personal project goals to aim for and within each project goal you have three priorities for each month. These priorities are strategic moves along the path towards reaching your project goals. In the RESULTS Method, we call these your Monthly Moves. You will find these moves will give you direction and motivation, especially if you create a little scorecard (Kanban board) to record your daily progress. I appreciate that this might sound childish to some, but I know it is as effective for the 45-year-old CEO whose scorecard is hidden in their desk as it is for the five-year-old whose scorecard is stuck to the fridge! Templates for the Kanban board can be found online along with your other RESULTS resources.

Identify strategic moves in three areas of your life: personal, relationship, and professional. Link the moves to your values, strengths, and communication styles.

These personal challenges could be leaning into a value—how do you become more grateful this month?

The personal challenges can strengthen relationships—how can you express love and care to someone every day?

A personal challenge can improve your professional knowledge or positioning—what podcast or book could you read? What course could you complete?

1 Week

A week gives you enough time to monitor what is going on for you. By planning and reviewing weekly, it gives you the opportunity to renew your weekly priority commitments whilst still being able to react to current changes in an optimal, timely manner. Weekly planning and review sessions allows you to be tactical in your planning, and by assessing where you are in comparison to your deliverables, you can make sensible, well-considered adjustments that will enable you to get better and better results. We all know that it can sometimes feel like we are living in chaos. Your weekly rhythm empowers you to bring order and organization to the chaos. It also gives you the chance to look at a slightly bigger picture than the day-to-day focus allows so that you can plan precisely and then adjust as and when needed.

Reminding yourself of your bigger goals and connecting to their importance daily and weekly will re-anchor you as to why they are important. Knowing how you are performing on a weekly basis will enable you to check in on how your values and strengths are showing up in your life. It will also enable you to see how much self-care you are practicing in terms of being true and supportive in your self-communication.

Creating a weekly rhythm also gives you the chance to record varying time blocks in your schedule so that when life does happen, which it inevitably will, you are able to adjust and navigate back to your plan, rather than wonder how you lost the day, or ask where you messed up, or even wonder why you bother. When you look at your plan on a weekly basis then you do not get lost in the to-do list busyness which keeps you occupied but not actively pursuing the business of making your plans real.

In terms of planning the week, you need to make a decision as to whether you will do it by the clock and say 9 a.m. this and 10 a.m. that, or whether you will work out the blocks of time you have in each day and leave the specific times fairly loose and work according to how the day pans out. Both approaches have their pros and cons, and I am including them here because as a result of the 2020 coronavirus and lockdown, many of us have experienced a different view of time. Given that the wider routines of school, leaving the house to go to work, and set times for activities was significantly reduced, you may want to build in flexibility in how you approach the day, and that is what the latter approach offers you.

We will discuss the different types of time blocks further as we continue breaking down the **Utilize** phase, but before we do, we need to pause to consider the overview of your week. I prefer to approach the week with the following fixed blocks of time:

Review. At the same time every week, sit down with your schedule for 20 minutes and look at what is coming up in the next seven days and reflect on the previous seven days. Ask yourself what went well and what you learned from those successes? What are you grateful for? What did you enjoy? What will you do differently in the next seven days? Make any necessary adjustments.

Visualize having an incredible week by running through each activity and anticipating that it will go better than you can even imagine. That's it.

And take the opportunity to decide, delete, or delegate anything (as per the Eisenhower Matrix) that is no longer required.

White space. You need time to think, reflect, and pause. I know you have the capacity to be a superhero, but all the superheroes we know need time in their day to pause too. We have been programmed into thinking that downtime is wasted time, it is often difficult to pause without feeling guilty, so I want you to build in blocks of time in your schedule for doing nothing. This is not working time, not time for meetings, cleaning, or reading emails. It's time to stop and do nothing. When you have these times, it gives you the scheduled time and the written permission to relax. If you are a stressed out parent or executive reading this and you don't believe you can do this, then know that not putting white space (or empty blocks) in your calendar is a contributing factor to *why* you are so stressed out and often feel like you are drowning. It is these blocks that truly enable you to take back more control of your life. See this time as the rest days in between exercise— an invaluable and necessary part of the process! Start with 10 minutes of white space a day and build on that.

And for bonus points, build in at least one of these white space times with the people you live with (or friends or family), a time when you have nothing significant planned and can just spend quality time with each other, with nothing planned, and no phones around!

Contingency/catch up time. As von Vierdort's theory on time perception shows us, it is natural to be more optimistic about what you can do in each time block than what reality actually permits. We all do this: I do this! But we can easily mitigate this tendency by including blocks of catch-up time so you have a scheduled opportunity to make more progress in areas where you feel necessary. Having a couple of contingency times in your weekly schedule alleviates many points of stress and allows you to be more relaxed because you know that there is time for you to carry on or finish things off. Just a small word of warning: the availability of contingency time blocks should not become an excuse for procrastination! Otherwise, instead of working in your favor, these opportunities to catch up will be working against you.

Sleep. Sleep falls at the opposite end of the activity spectrum, yet it is equally as important to put into your schedule. By knowing what time you go to sleep, you will know what time you will wake up. I utilize the timer on my smart watch to wake me up, and I also use it to remind me to start my nighttime routine and go to bed. If I didn't have the nighttime timer, I would get a lot less sleep and inevitably wake up late or unrested. My whole day could go wrong because I started it in the wrong way, I am sure the same happens for you occasionally. If you need to adjust your sleep times because you have an activity later or earlier than usual you can make the adjustment, but it is widely agreed that a consistent sleeping schedule has the most benefit overall. Failure to consider sleep as a daily, scheduled activity is why 80 percent of people are sleep deprived.[5]

Exercise. Once you've got your main blocks of time recorded in your planner, you owe it to yourself to add in time blocks for exercise. When you don't plan some form of physical exercise on a weekly basis, it is because you haven't prioritized it. Not prioritizing your physical health translates into failing to position yourself to fully activate your being in delivering on your plans. It does not matter what exercise you choose to do (see **Lead** phase), doing some form of physical movement is critical to waking your entire being and reducing lethargy.

Once you have scheduled in your weekly time blocks, the next thing to do is to look at each day. But before we do that, I want to introduce you to the Pomodoro technique.

The Pomodoro Technique

The Pomodoro technique was created by Francesco Cirillo in the late 1980s.[6] He called it Pomodoro (meaning *tomato* in Italian) after the tomato-shaped, kitchen timer he used to plan his work when he was a university student. The concept is a bona fide example of the power of simplicity. When working on any task, a series of Pomodoro sessions can enable you to make progress and break the task into manageable increments. A Pomodoro refers to the 25-minute block of time designated for a single sprint of concentrated work. Working for 25 minutes seems a lot easier than working for an hour or more, and the brief session trains your brain to concentrate on the task at hand for short periods of time. The Pomodoro technique helps you to consistently make progress, avoid unmeetable deadlines, or feel as if you are constantly chasing your tail. This technique has even been proven to improve attention span and concentration. The idea of working in short sprints makes you more effective and committed, and the five-minute break in between sessions enables you to reset your motivation and drive, take a break, and stay creative.

To run a pomodoro, you simply:

1. Choose the task you will work on.
2. Set a timer for 25 minutes.
3. Work on the task until the timer rings, then stop the task.
4. Take a short break (five minutes is enough).
5. If you do more than four Pomodoros in one sitting, take a longer break of 15 to 30 minutes after the fourth one.

You will be amazed at what you can accomplish in these short intervals of time. In fact, most of this book was written in 25-minute Pomodoro sessions. My 5-minute breaks consisted of getting a drink, sending an email, catching up with the family, or a quick breathing exercise or meditation. I used some of the 15-30-minute breaks to reset, have lunch, go for a walk, or sit with family.

The biggest challenge with the Pomodoro technique is dealing with distractions, but the technique itself is also the solution for dealing with them. Nothing is so urgent that it cannot wait 25 minutes, and if it absolutely cannot, then pause the timer, go and deal with the emergency and start again. If someone calls, and it is not urgent you can always say, "I'm in the middle of a meeting, I can get back to you in 10 minutes" (or however much time is left on the Pomodoro).

The numerous benefits of the Pomodoro technique include:

- Eliminating the habit of multi-tasking.
- Focusing on the task at hand.
- Getting more things done because the short session creates a sense of urgency.
- Making tendencies of perfectionism inconvenient and therefore more likely ignored.
- Building higher levels of willpower and concentration.
- Decreasing stress levels because you're doing one thing at a time.

I suggest you start each Pomodoro with an exercise that disconnects you from what you were doing before. This *trigger* will put you in the frame of mind to make progress on the task that is in front of you. It is the trigger that prompts you to change your behavior.

A trigger can be of varied length. If you only have a minute, you can use box breathing (a technique of deep, purposeful breathing), do a one-minute meditation, recite a positive affirmation, or anything you choose. The key is to have a trigger. If you have a few more minutes available, you could use a trigger of closing your eyes and meditating for five minutes or listening to a motivational talk or song that will get you in the mood for what you are about to do. As you take these five minutes, be aware of the opportunity to transition, reset, and disconnect so you are fully ready for the 25 minutes of work ahead of you. If you are doing additional 25-minute Pomodoro sessions, take a five-minute break, then reset the timer and repeat.

Now that you are familiar with the Pomodoro technique, let's jump back in!

1 Day

In planning your days, you will most likely schedule different time blocks depending on the day. You know that your weekend days will look different from the weekdays. As we reflect back on 2020 and on lockdown in particular, one of the reasons why many people experienced anxiety is because each day was the same, and 100+ days of the same with no demarcation for rest or work makes it difficult to maintain joy and well-being.

Determine which days will be your working days and which will be your rest days. You can have as many working or rest days as you want, but I recommend four to five working days and two to three rest days.

These planned Pomodoro sessions are times in which you do your work. If practical, you could use some of them to prepare for the work you will do and use others to actually do the work. You could even allocate some to doing your research.

½ Day

Half a day is two two-hour Pomodoro sessions. This is a good time block to use for more substantial tasks e.g. planning your Monthly Moves, work, study, rest! It is essential that when you work solidly for half a day (2 x 2-hour Pomodoros) that you take a substantial break between this and whatever you are doing next. The sixty-minute lunch break seems to be a myth these days, but it is a good delineator between blocks of time and overall makes your day more effective. In productivity studies, it has been found that the average office worker working an eight hour day is in reality productive for only two hours and 53 minutes.[7] In my opinion, the only difference between working three hours and eight hours a day is the effective use of time blocks and the BART method I outline later in this phase.

Use ½ day periods for longer tasks and think about them as the equivalent of your full working day. Go into it with the intention that you will be fully present and engaged in that time.

2 Hours

Two-hour Pomodoro sessions are best for breaking down a big project. Use these time blocks to work on the larger deliverables attributed to your project priorities (the projects selected in your Project3x3). Have four tasks ready to do and then do them in the four 25-minute sessions. If any specific task is bigger than your available sessions, it is not a problem to use multiple sessions for that task (see ½ Day above). The two-hour sessions are suitable for the longer, more time-consuming tasks. I use my two-hour session to write or do research. I would not use it for shorter activities such as answering emails or using social media for work.

1 Hour

This can be a great session to have scheduled every day so that you can make progress on bigger projects. If you schedule a one-hour session every day, realize that a break every six days to reset will give you optimum results. I know some people like to work in streaks, but unless you are feeling really confident in your plan and have a strong handle on it, I would recommend you take a day off every week. This is one of my own biggest areas of resistance, so I know the temptations of working in streaks. I have worked 100-day streaks in the past and then burned out and essentially made no progress for several months. Don't think that just because you're being smart and doing it every day for a long period of time that you will go faster, it will not, and if anything, it will slow you down. More often than not, streaking becomes a real-life manifestation of Aesop's fable of *The Tortoise and the Hare*. Remember, sometimes it is better to pace yourself in order to cross the finish line faster.

25 Minutes

This is the designated time block for the classic pomodoro—a single 25-minute working period. You set a timer and work non-stop for 25 minutes. If you have a single Pomodoro session, it is essential that you not take a break and avoid all distractions. It may take a bit of time to train yourself, but it is worth it. During lockdown in 2020, I created what we called the "Cousins' Family Zoom Meeting." At the start of lockdown, we would meet online to maintain a daily connection with people outside our immediate families.

About six weeks into lockdown, one of the younger cousins suggested that we have a homework club, and we turned the Cousins' Family Zoom meeting into a daily homework club which consisted of two Pomodoro sessions with a five-minute break. The only instructions given were to come with a task that you can work on for 25 minutes. It could be homework, reading a book, watching a lesson for school, anything that they could concentrate on. As the group on the call included children aged from four to fourteen, I also added, "You can't unmute yourself unless it is an emergency. If you need to go to the toilet or get a drink of water ask the adult in your home, but other than that no disruptions." At the time of writing, these homework club meetings have been happening five days a week for nine weeks and are planned to continue until the children return to school. I share this experience with you so that you can see how with a bit of repetition, you can have personal sessions like this that are effective and give you solid progress towards your goal.

RESULTS

At the end of the day, it is the small steps that enable you to climb a mountain. And it is having a process, doing the planning and preparation that enables you to take the first step in your practice.

10 Minutes

Have at least three 10-minute Pomodoros in your daily schedule. Use one in the morning preparing for the day. This is not for catching up on email or social media; it is specifically for looking at your schedule, verifying what you need to get done, reviewing your Eisenhower Matrix (more on this later), and checking in with anything that might derail you during the day. Spend a couple of minutes imagining that your day goes as well and that you are ready for whatever the day brings. Imagine any challenges you may face and then think about how you will overcome them.

Keep a 10-minute Pomodoro for the end of the day when you check over your schedule for the next day and ensure that your working time blocks are allocated with tasks that will enable you to make the progress you are seeking and not just keep you busy. Use this time to tidy up your desk or workspace and tidy up your mind. Take a quick moment to shuffle things around if necessary. Do a quick assessment of what went well for you and what you will do differently tomorrow. Then you can go to bed knowing you've done a great job.

Tips Regarding Pomodoro

Being an advocate for and having used Pomodoro for much of my life, my clients and I have come up with some helpful advice on how to use this technique:

1. **Breaks are a must**. When the timer goes off, you must stop and take a break. You might be mid-sentence or just have one quick thing to finish, if it will take you less than a minute or two then go ahead and complete it, but it if will take longer than a few minutes you must

obligate yourself to pause. I guarantee that if you honor the process, you will reap the most benefit. If you need to leave a task, leave it in a state fit for you to return to. Take your 5-minute break, and then come back and set another 25-minute Pomodoro. To avoid breaks becoming longer (remember, it's human nature to overestimate time in the short term), set a timer for those too. Do something simple such as get a drink of water, a hot drink, stretch, or go to the bathroom. What you do doesn't matter as long as you take your break.

2. **Allocate appropriate tasks to the Pomodoro.** The reason I encourage you to have a variety of time limited Pomodoros in your week (25 minutes, 1 hour, 2 hours) is so that you can allocate the time according to the complexity of the task. For example, a task that requires a lower level of concentration or focus could be completed in one hour; something more complex may require two hours to generate a feeling of substantial progress being made (writing is a perfect example); and less complex tasks are probably best in a single or double 25 minute time period.

3. **Partial Pomodoro.** True Pomodoro aficionados will be horrified when I suggest utilizing partial Pomodoros, but I think that the reality of our lives makes these very helpful. If you have a 10-minute task, there is no point in putting it off or taking any longer than needs be! I would go as far as saying if you have 5-minute tasks, these also count as a partial pomodoro, although anything less than that would be a real push to even measure! That said, if you start a 25-minute Pomodoro and end up going to deal with something else (life does happen) then that Pomodoro is not complete until you go back and complete the time—another version of the partial Pomodoro. Ultimately, making progress is the key point here, and Pomodoro sessions of any timeframe will add up. At the end of the day you are in charge of your schedule, so utilize the time blocks and Pomodoro times that work for you. Set out what you can do in a day and a week, and then get the work done.

RESULTS

4. **Pomodoro allocation.** A good aim for those starting with the technique is to schedule three 10-minute Pomodoros and two 25-minute Pomodoros a day, and one 2-hour Pomodoro during the week. As you progress through your Project3x3 and become more accustomed to the Pomodoro technique, you will adjust these times according to your needs.

There are different ways you can utilize your weekly Pomodoros. Tasks are allocated to the different Pomodoro times depending on complexity and amount of time for completion. Some people bundle their 25-minute tasks together into a 2-hour Pomodoro; others choose to allocate a bigger task to that time. You do what works for you. One thing I have found effective for managing social media in my personal and professional life is to reserve a 25-minute Pomodoro daily for this task. I divide that time by allowing five minutes each for twitter, LinkedIn, Facebook, Instagram, and my public Facebook page. If there is a follow up message or action as a result of my postings, I put that on my action items list and review that twice a week.

You can find examples of how people allocate their time blocks in the online community.

Batch

Grouping, or batching similar tasks is also an incredibly effective way of working. By putting together similar tasks and undertaking them in the same time block you are more efficient in your day, week, and month. By now you have an idea of the priorities you have for the week and the tasks that result from the priorities. Group the tasks and then undertake them in the same time period rather than scatter them throughout the day or week.

For example, important phone calls or emails can be done in one sitting. As I write this book, I have been batching the writing, the research, the edits into separate time blocks. It means that the set-up of the task only happens once rather than multiple times. For example, for the research, I only need to open the relevant sites once. In addition, the mind is ready to tackle that particular task.

Batch working is particularly useful for items that require more set up than day-to-day tasks. I recommend you try it for writing, video filming, chores, etc. It can be applied to tasks that you find repetitive as well as ones that require more use of your capability. Try it out!

Multi-tasking

"To be everywhere is to be nowhere" – Seneca.[8]

I cannot leave this section on time blocks without saying something about multi-tasking as it creates a lot of debate. The term multi-tasking was originally used to describe how a computer microprocessor can process many tasks at the same time. So, the question remains, if computers can multi-task, can humans? Do computers even actually multitask? In order for a single processor to process tasks it actually has to *time share* the processor, meaning that only one task can be processed at a time, but these tasks are alternated multiple times per second. In reality, a single-core processor or a multi-core processor is actually only performing one task at a time, even if it is only for a split second.

We might think that we are able to do more than one thing at the same time, but research shows that when you attempt to perform different tasks simultaneously, you are not as effective. Sure, you can watch TV and read a book at the same time, but do you understand what is happening in both? You will pick up bits from both, not fully enjoy either, and miss elements of the TV program you are watching or details in the book you are reading. Your comprehension is impaired because you are not truly capable of giving your full attention to either task. Even when you listen to an audiobook while performing another

RESULTS

task, it is hard to capture the full essence of what you are listening to. It can be argued that there are a few physical tasks which leave you sufficient brain capacity available to listen to an audiobook with focus, but these are exceptions—tasks such as travelling, exercising, or doing housework.

Our brains were not designed for multi-tasking. Even when switching from task to task, your brain needs time (even if only minimal) to reset and pick up the alternate task. Bouncing back and forth from one activity to another relies on a part of your brain called Broadmann's Area 10. People who appear to be great at multi-tasking are really just activating this area of their brain and juggling multiple tasks. As the computer, rather than multi-tasking they are simply moving quickly from one task to another. This is called *serial-tasking* and is not only tiring but is also not the best use of your attention and focus. Our brains are adapting to the increased stimulation that technology brings, but they are not evolving.

(I'd like to digress briefly to point out that even with our brains ability to adapt, we are still suffering from numerous negative complications related to the sudden surge of technology—physical, mental, and emotional complications. As responsible humans, I strongly recommend that we increase our awareness of the impact technology has in our lives and put measures in place so that our sleep, focus, progress, health, and relationships are not impacted negatively by technology, but are rather enhanced by it. For example, there is a case to be made for how video games enhance attention, hand-eye coordination, and visual and spatial problem-solving capabilities, but conversely, playing video games late into the night impacts sleep quality and overall effectiveness.)

In the end, people are losing 2.1 hours a day just getting from one task to another. Some studies have shown that your effectiveness decreases by as much as 40 percent when you multi-task![9]

The answer to our need to accomplish multiple tasks in a specified time and our inclinations to multi-task is the Pomodoro. If a task you are doing is mundane or easy (e.g. cooking and cleaning the kitchen at the same time) then multi-tasking can be done, but if you have a task that requires a different level of focus, care, and attention it is better to avoid multi-tasking in order to get the best results and make the most progress. You can recognize the tasks and areas of your life that require your concentration. Rather than tell you not to multi-task, I will instead urge you to consider how multi-tasking affects your efficiency and effectiveness in the important tasks in your life.

Calendar

You can achieve a great deal of growth just by using your calendar more effectively. You will progress each month by using your calendar to record everything from logistical tasks to planning what you want to accomplish, experience, and achieve. By using your calendar, you will give your life direction—just like a map on a road trip. The personal calendar is a powerful, yet underused tool. Start using your calendar by occupying it with time blocks for your activities, the things you are doing, and appointments you have. As you become more experienced with its use, you may find that you use your physical calendar slightly differently to the electronic calendar on your phone.

One additional practical tip for you to consider in terms of using a calendar that I personally found helpful is to create a family calendar. As an extended family we have one with key school dates for the kids, any holidays or key events marked. I also share my calendar with my husband, and vice versa, so that we can each see important meetings and time blocks in the other person's planner. These days arranging quality time with your family can be a logistical challenge, but by sharing your calendar with key people you remove much of the WhatsApp or email Ping-Pong for arranging events.

RESULTS

I have many tools that I recommend for diaries and calendars and I regularly update the list, so rather than recommend tools here please go to the online RESULTS resources *www.results.partners/bookresources* and you will find a list that has been updated in the last six months.

Calendars and planners will help you to manage yourself more effectively. They prevent you from overcommitting and under-committing your time. It will give you focus on your bigger picture plans as well as the small details of what you are doing today.

BART

Another useful tool to help you maximize the effort, energy, and effectiveness of your time blocks is the BART system. Zachary Gabriel Green and René J. Molenkamp explained the significance of the BART model based on identifying the Boundaries, Authority, Roles, and Tasks as it is applied to group learning.[10] The BART system is frequently applied in the corporate world, and it can be equally beneficial as a framework for considering personal and professional projects. Once you have understood this concept, I think you will remember it for life. Day-to-day life often presents us with deadlines, due dates, and uncompromisable timelines. Sometimes, not meeting these limits or exceeding these boundaries can have detrimental consequences. If you have ever had the misfortune of missing a train or plane, you know that you are faced with either cancelling your trip or paying heavy costs to change your ticket. Not all missed deadlines carry severe consequences, but even so, you will find BART to be a trusted companion when it comes to planning and reflecting.

Boundaries

Boundaries are comprised of the physical, psychological, and time limitations of a task. Depending on the specific task or circumstances, these boundaries can be either flexible or non-negotiable. Maintaining clarity over which boundaries are adjustable and which are not is essential.

Time boundaries are set by the amount of time allotted or defined for a specific task. For example, an effective meeting must have a clear starting and end time, and its participants must understand these time boundaries.

Culturally in the West, we tend to expect meetings to start and end on time; This is not the case globally. When meetings run off focus, they fluctuate in time and then the boundary is lost. It is crucial for you to think about how you relate to time boundaries: what habits or perspectives have you noticed and even adopted by observing friends or the culture of wider society? How can you value your time boundaries so that you maintain clarity of their importance and then actively protect them? Respecting time boundaries is particularly important when you use the Pomodoro technique.

Physical boundaries relate to where you are carrying out or doing the work of a particular task and how you keep focus in those physical surroundings. One of the techniques I learned that enables me to work anywhere is to create a trigger in relation to my physical boundary. For example, like most people, I do work in a coffee shop or café at times. In terms of physical boundaries, I restrict my laptop to work or studying; I do not use it for virtual socializing (I do that on my smart phone). The act of me opening my laptop and turning it on is the trigger that puts me in my *workspace*. That psychological trigger creates a physical trigger so I can sit and do productive work pretty much anywhere. Many people will say that they are flexible and can work anywhere, but if you don't set that physical boundary you will not be as effective. Another technique is to carry a small token (stone, flower, card, anything you like) and associate that with the boundary of your work so that whenever the object is in front of you, you make a mental shift into a working environment.

RESULTS

Psychological boundaries are all about knowing what specific task you are working on within set time boundaries and keeping yourself focused, it is the boundary you create in your mind. Respecting the psychological boundary means not working on anything else and not allowing yourself to get distracted when you are implementing a task.

When utilizing BART's boundaries element to improve your energy, effort, and effectiveness, ask yourself the following:

- What is the specific time boundary I am using for my work session?
- What are the physical boundaries of the space I am in? How will the space impact my effectiveness? What is the right room for me to complete this particular activity?
- What psychological boundaries can I set up to sustain my concentration levels and keep from being sidetracked?
- Am I sticking to the boundaries I have set or am I crossing the lines?

Authority

Being clear on the authority you have over any given task will enable you to know what you are in control of, what elements require getting permission, and what you might need further information about.

You can gain a better understanding of your authority in a task by asking yourself:

- How effective am I in giving myself authority—or the confidence—to take ownership of my task?
- Who do I need to support me in this?
- What other roles are required in order to complete the task and make progress?

If you feel any sense of nervousness about doing the task remember to lean into that resistance. Do not surrender your power over to the thoughts in your mind that might be holding you back (we addressed this in the **Reach** phase). Remind yourself of your values and strengths and your aims for the project. Give yourself permission.

Roles

Other than tasks that you are monitoring, it is your role to do the tasks and to ensure that they are done well, remember that. For tasks that you have delegated, you are still responsible for checking in and monitoring how they are progressing (more on that when we discuss the **Lead** phase). To put it bluntly, this is your plan, and you need to act like it. So, take charge of your plan and do the work to get the results that you seek.

Task

Knowing precisely what tasks need to be done and when, is absolutely fundamental if you are going to bring the appropriate energy, effort, and effectiveness to complete those tasks. In the work you have done planning your Project3x3, identifying your priorities, and establishing your weekly deliverables, you have a clear agenda outlining your work tasks not only for the quarter and week-by-week, but also the tasks that need to be done day by day.

When gaining clarity on the task in front of you, remember to ask yourself:

- What am I trying to accomplish in the Pomodoro ahead?
- How ready am I to work on the task?
- What can I do to focus completely on the task?

Use the BART system to analyze the tasks you have set for the Pomodoro session, and you will find each time you sit for another session it is more effective. Once you have used this methodology a few times, you will see that you only need a few seconds to mentally go through the system, and you will keep making progress.

Measuring Growth

As Jim Doerr and Larry Page say, "We need to measure what matters."[11] In RESULTS, your vision and goals are measured by the progress you make.

That leads us to ask the questions: What constitutes progress? How do you measure it effectively? Do you measure impact? Financial return on investment? Personal freedom? How you feel?

There are so many possible answers, and each and every one of us has a different view on what progress is and isn't and how it should be measured. As a project manager, I have tried and tested many of the measurement systems available. You may be aware of The Disciples of Execution (based on the book of the same name by Chris McChesney, Jim Huling, and Sean Covey), Objective & Key Results (as popularized by Google and the basis for Doerr's book *Measure What Matters*), the Balanced Scorecard (proposed by Robert Kaplan and David Norton in 1992 Harvard Business Review), and Key Performance Indicators (suggested to date back to the Chinese Wei Dynasty in the 3rd Century).

They all work very well. However, in RESULTS you are measuring more than just impact and actions completed; you are measuring personal and professional growth in line with your overall vision. It is for that reason that I like to use the Kanban system. Kanban was developed by Taiichi Ohno, an engineer at Toyota, the Japanese car manufacturer. The system takes its name from the cards that track production within a factory.[12]

I like the simplicity of Kanban and its flexibility to be used for more complex projects. In my experience, I have found that individuals and organizations can do everything right in terms of linking what they work on to their goals and values, but if there is one area where they fall down, it is in measuring their progress. Measuring your progress on tasks may not be the most exciting aspect of RESULTS, so let's take a slightly different perspective on this element by considering every task you undertake and complete as a step forward in your personal growth as it aligns with your vision.

Kanban enables you to visualize your work and manage your workload, so what you measure gets improved. Literally, visualizing your work allows you to see the tasks ahead, what you are currently doing, and the progress you have made. It also allows you to consider your capacity: can you take on more or are you overloaded?

Create a Kanban board like this:

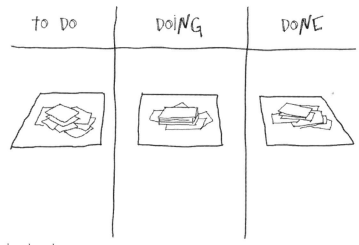

Kanban board

Using sticky notes, or cards, write out the tasks you will be doing throughout the week. You can also use a whiteboard to do this. Each day (preferably in your daily morning prep 10-minute Pomodoro) look at this task list and allocate the tasks. Ideally, you only work on one task at a time (batched, if appropriate). This will help you to have more focus, so you can get more done. As you complete each task move it into the done pile. That simple move will provide you with personal satisfaction, visually show you that you are able to get it done, and give you the motivation to keep working. Remember, you are your personal CEO—you are the one setting the strategies and directions to move your progress forward.

Applying the Kanban Principles to RESULTS:

- Start with what you need to do today/this week. Don't try and Kanban your entire life or any more than one week ahead.
- Plan for incremental change, not huge sudden ones: Kanban only works when you have done the work that leads up to this point.
- Use the BART principles and respect them. Enough said.
- Apply necessary leadership (more on that in the **Lead** phase).

Avoid Complexity and Oversimplification

If you end up with so much information to measure that you need an assistant to appraise it, you've reached a point that defeats the entire purpose of what we are doing and that requires rethinking. If your measures are either nonexistent or too simple you end up with no solid idea of how you are progressing. Putting measures in place can seem like something that is holding you back because you want to focus on progress, but the measures are critical to your progress. Here are my recommendations for effectively measuring your to-do, doing, and done tasks to best serve your RESULTS Process:

- Focus on a small number of weekly critical priorities and know your Monthly Moves in relation to your Quarterly Action Plan and Vision. This will enable you to have a focused understanding on what (and why) you are tracking. This will help you organize yourself and your project and make it easier to reflect back.

- Ensure that you have review points in your Weekly Rhythm, Monthly Moves, and Daily Schedule. By creating a ritual related to exploring and understanding your measures, you help you to identify areas where you can improve or enhance.
- When you see a consistent pattern in your progress, explore what new information that gives you. Are you on track? What needs to change? Is there anything that needs to be done differently?

The one-degree shift

You can bring precision into your plan by the use of a 1-degree shift. The 1-degree shift can make or break a plan. I also like the 0.01 refinement used in Formula 1 racing. I had the privilege to go into the Paddock at the British and Malaysian Grand Prix races a couple of times. At the time all the teams used Pirelli tires and most used Mercedes engines. So, where did the innovation come from? What was the difference? It was the one-degree shift or the 0.01 refinement, that literally would make or break a race for teams. It was in the small details, and they are the private details we were not given access to. You can use this 1-degree shift or 0.01 refinement for your project by asking yourself what small adjustment can you make to improve the outcome and experience? I used the 1-degree shift when it came to write this book. By taking a 5-minute break after 25 minutes of writing the quality of my writing improved and the break enabled me to write for longer periods.

Now, one other insightful factor I observed was that teams whose drivers had a good chance of winning came across as more confident; knowledge of their track record, their ability, etc. made them walk on air. Whereas the teams who were not in the top 10 were participating in the race, but they appeared to have a different energy—it appeared that they were there to have fun. You are here to make progress and have fun, not just one or the other.

There are two key lessons: create a plan that you are committed to and identify your 1-degree shift or 0.01 refinement. Take these steps with the confidence and knowledge that you will win. Because to come second place in your life is to work on someone else's agenda without doing it deliberately.

Align and Achieve

You have achieved in your life. I know you have. Achievement is not the issue. You're able to fight the urge to stop and abandon your project. You keep going despite the challenges, adversity, and all the hassle that life throws your way. So, yes, I know that achievement is not the issue. The big challenge is living life where your achievements are in alignment with your values and aspirations.

Burnout, boreout, and losing the commitment and desire are a reality even for the ambitious. People may perceive you as confident and in control, while you may think of yourself as lost in chaos, unable to slog through the thoughts in your mind long enough to feel you are able to keep making progress. I know you have achieved many times in your life, but you might have forgotten. You might be unsure of what to focus on or how to believe that you will be able to achieve again. In the past, you may not have had an operating system, but now with RESULTS, you know exactly what to do. You are capable of more than you can imagine, so do not allow your self-expectations to cause you to live in fear of falling behind or settling without striving.

Working hard is not the issue. The issue is achieving alignment with who you are. It goes without saying that the Covid-19 pandemic and the year 2020 have sent us a huge reality check. Many have now gone back to assessing what is really important for them. The time when things were predictable and ran as expected are gone. The only thing that is certain is uncertainty. Stress now comes not from knowing that you know, but rather from living in the unknown.

Yet the expectations of what you are capable of may not have changed. I believe that when you have expectations, then all that will happen is that your exceptions will fail you so set high standards instead. How about giving up your expectations and try waking up in the morning and feeling joy just for the gift of breath you have?

As someone who has been lucky enough to have a good set of achievements (qualified as an architect, became a director in local government, coach, trainer of coaches), I still sometimes feel as if I have not aligned with my achievements meaning that I downplay the joy I feel when I think about them. I have had coaching, therapy, read books, listened to motivational programs, undertaken courses, been to multiple personal development courses, and am still working on this. Doing the internal work as set out in this book has helped me to focus on my strengths and values and have clarity on what I want from life. As soon as I found that focus and clarity, then I started to experience more moments when I was able to enjoy my achievements. Reflecting on this, I recognize, even more, the importance of doing the work of the **Evolve** phase because clearly distinguishing and acknowledging your strengths and values and who you are is key to your success. After this my advice to you is to consider how you can take your achievements and associate them with your identity.

It is one thing to focus on your achievement and be grateful for it, but when your achievement is aligned with your values and strengths, your satisfaction will move up to a completely different level! Comparing the two feelings is comparing something superficial with something that reaches the soul.

Alignment is created by having rituals that you practice every day rather than a set of habits that you create and struggle to keep up. Many people advocate habits—there are good and bad habits that need to be deciphered, and when you're in habit mode, your effort can feel like hard work. On the other hand, rituals are practices that are embedded in your life and driven by purpose and intention—we will dive deeper into this later for more discussion on this distinction. It is a very subtle distinction that can make all the difference to your getting it done.

The relative issue is not making achievement after achievement, it is setting goals, having a schedule and system that is inherently linked to your values and strengths, that you are fully invested in, and that gives you the momentum to excel each and every day. Remember, just because you are good at something doesn't mean you have to do it. Your achievements, rather than just being for the sake of achievement, should be about your personal growth, your satisfaction with life, and your overall experience of life so that you live in a manner that is thriving, flourishing, and where you feel fully alive.

Weekly Rhythm (Part 1)

As you reach the end of the **Utilize** phase, you will have created your Weekly Rhythm. There is now a process of testing it to see if it works for you. You do this by implementing your weekly plan. Be sure to print out the templates provided for you in the online resources, complete them, and put them in a place where you will look at them every single day. You will not obtain the results you are seeking by simply creating a great plan and then ignoring it. You must look at your plan every day, imagine how your life will be when it becomes a reality, and you see it as part of your short and long-term growth and development. And then, you must implement!

You will learn more about flourishing in the **Succeed** phase, but for now I want you to know that these few minutes you spend each day focusing on your plans and imagining what you want to achieve in your life are as important as your plan's creation. In all the years I have been doing this work, I have realized that the people who create plans and put them on their shelf have a significantly lower chance of making the kind of progress that they deserve. It is not because they are not skilled or unmotivated, it is because they haven't found the method that feeds their momentum and that constantly reminds them of the direction that they want their lives to go.

HOURS	SUNDAY	MONDAY	TUESDAY	WEDNESDAY	THURSDAY	FRIDAY	SATURDAY
6—7 AM							
7—8 AM							
8—9 AM							
9—10 AM							
10—11 AM							
11—12 PM							
12—1 PM							
1—2 PM							
2—3 PM							
3—4 PM							
4—5 PM							
5—6 PM							
6—7 PM							
7—8 PM							
8—9 PM							
9—10 PM							

An example Weekly Rhythm Template

When you have that daily reminder of your dreams, what you want to achieve, what visions you are working to make reality then you have the motivation and drive to get it done.

So, if you haven't already done so, download the templates and use them to create your Weekly Rhythm.

It is now time for you to move to the next phase of RESULTS!

Self-Interview

Insight: What is your biggest insight from the Utilize phase?

Intention: When you explore your boldest hopes and highest aspirations, what is that you ultimately want to do with your time?

Identity: Why does utilizing your time and resources really matter to you?

Implementation: What is the smallest or most immediate action you are willing to take?

Integrity: What can you do to deepen your commitment to follow through?

HOW DO I FOLLOW THROUGH?

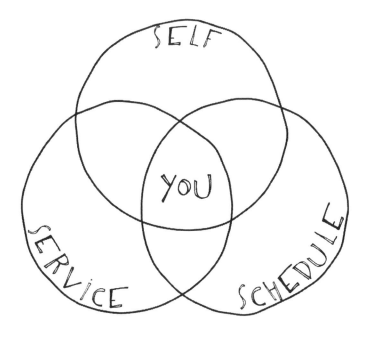

Before
AVOIDING

After
IMPACTING

LEAD

"When one man (or woman), for whatever reason, has the opportunity to lead an extraordinary life, he has no right to keep it to himself."

Jacques Yves Cousteau -- (1910-1997)

RESULTS

I was safe and loved, but not happy

"How can you leave your kids and go to work?" an acquaintance asked me in a very busy period of my life. "My kids are safe, happy, and loved where they are. That is how I go to work. If they were not, then I would not be able to focus on my job," I replied reflectively. In that period of my life I was an assistant director, my kids were three and five years old, and my life was full, if not slightly brimming over the edge. One day as I was driving back from work, I realized that whilst I was safe and loved, I wasn't happy.

At that time, I was not well-versed in personal growth and the need for self-care (which I call self-leadership). This meant that I was giving and giving, without really taking time to replenish. Looking back at that time, I now know that I was on the verge of burnout and was in denial about it.

Through the work I have done (hiring coaches, taking courses, undergoing therapy) I realize that in order to flourish as a leader, you need to have a handle on self-leadership, service leadership, and schedule leadership. By taking stock of what was happening in my own life, I was able to identify a method of increasing my well-being and effectiveness and help others to do the same. This is why leadership *is* for people like you and me—it is for everybody.

Leadership is not just for people with a fancy title or an executive office. Leadership happens in a wide variety of contexts, in both our public and private lives. Being a leader requires you to follow through and commit to the plan that you have created. It is about managing your energy and resources so you can meet the needs of your day-to-day agenda and look forward to creating a life pursuing excellence as you strive towards a goal of living your values and truth. These days the badge of leadership seems difficult to accept but someone in your life is looking at you as a leader: it could be your kids, your friends, or a neighbor you don't really know.

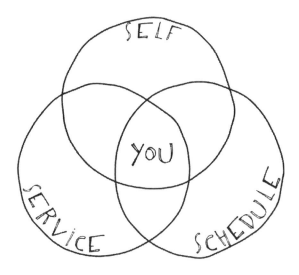

The RESULTS Leadership Model™

When you embrace leadership, you make a responsible choice towards one of the biggest challenges you will face. It also has some of the biggest and most satisfying rewards. As Warren Bennis, a pioneer in modern leadership studies, said, "Leadership is the wise use of power. Power is the capacity to translate intention into reality and sustain it."[1]

Leadership involves fulfilling the rights and obligations you have to those people or activities for which you have assumed a role of leadership—including your own personal leadership. Done with intention and care, leading can be very fulfilling in all its guises: self-leadership, service leadership, and schedule leadership.

When you set the intention to follow through on your plan and get the results you seek, you are required to take the lead. The plan you have created in the previous phases of RESULTS is the vision you have for your life; it is the dream you want to make reality, and it is a very powerful tool. Your RESULTS plan is an invaluable asset, and spending time developing, aligning, and renewing your plan is an excellent example of you leading—picking up that scepter of authority and commanding—with that plan in mind. If you are able, share your plan with people who will support you. If you have not yet gathered a supportive circle around you, then look at the online resources available and take the immediate step of joining the RESULTS community where we have people from all over the world supporting each other. Remember to lead with your values at front and center.

I have seen so many people let themselves down when it comes to leadership, not because they don't have the skills, but because they don't believe in themselves. If you are wondering how *you* can be an effective leader, I ask that you stop doubting yourself and your capabilities and go back to the Showstoppers section to refresh yourself on strategies for dealing with internal challenges.

Self-leadership

Self-leadership requires two things: self-care and a set of plans for the direction you want to take in life. Under stress, or when people are *busy*, they sometimes forget to take proper care of themselves or will abuse certain activities. This is the person you may know who—under the guise or misconception that they are taking care of themselves—

over-exercises, studies too much, or spends excessive and unbalanced amounts of energy *self-caring*. On the other hand, you might also know the person who abandons exercise, eats fast food, sleeps for only a few hours a night and burns themselves into the ground. For many, this disproportionate focus becomes a contributing factor leading to burnout.

When it comes to having a plan and delivering on any project or activity that you have undertaken, you want to ensure that you take care of yourself. Failing to do so will make you ineffective and may misalign any success you do manage to achieve in respect to your values and who you are. Not taking care of yourself ultimately contributes to unsustainable working conditions.

It is critical to the success of any plan that you know what your personal logistics are. In some ways, almost everything in the RESULTS Process falls under the functions of self-leadership, but there are some very specific areas of your personal care that I advise you to dedicate particular effort and care: sleep, hydration, exercise, fuel, and rest.

Sleep

Research shows that the average person needs eight hours of sleep a night.[2] Of course, it is possible for you to survive on four hours of sleep a night, but RESULTS is not about survival, it is about striving for excellence and that necessitates getting the right quality and quantity of sleep. Relying on four hours of sleep each night would require a significant effort from you in terms of diet, supplements, and how you structured your day, and may still result in you experiencing some of the side effects of sleep deprivation: increased propensity to heart disease, diabetes, obesity, high blood pressure, and general low-level exhaustion. In addition, lack of sleep can result in a 30% increase in anxiety levels—good quality deep sleep "decreases anxiety overnight by reorganizing the connections in the brain."[3]

Taking charge of your sleep will give you a generous payback. It will enable you to increase your level of focus, improve how you feel during the day, brighten your general mood, enhance your ability to get the right things done, and curb the need for firefighting. Waking up well in the morning really starts the night before.

Identify the time you want to sleep and take a moment to set an alarm on your watch or phone to remind you that it's time to start your nighttime routine. I recommend utilizing a countdown to my clients. For example, if you want to sleep at 10 p.m. so you can wake up at 6 a.m. then your first *nighttime routine* alarm goes off at 7 p.m. Stop eating two and a half to three hours before you go to sleep to allow your body the time it needs to digest the food so it is able to rest as you sleep. This next alarm is also a signal to stop working or thinking about work. If you have chores to do around the house, aim to get those done 90 minutes before your scheduled sleep time. I appreciate that this may not be as simple as it sounds but remember some things can be left for the next day. For many of you, the hardest thing I will ask you to do as a part of your sleep routine is to *put* your phone to its own bed (somewhere outside the room you sleep in), not *take* it to bed. Stop looking at all electronic devices an hour (or more) before your sleep time. Your brain needs to know that it is time to wind down, and the light from electronic devices activates the mind and prevents you from sleeping. In the time before you sleep have a shower or bath, journal, read, meditate, or anything that keeps you away from food, work, and electronic devices.

Keep a worry journal. Professor Matthew Walker, a neuroscience and sleep researcher, recommends keeping a worry journal. Simply write a list of the things you are anxious about. This gets anxious or agonizing thoughts out of your mind and cuts the time it takes you to get to sleep by half. By keeping such a journal you also reduce the number of times you toss and turn during the night.[4] If you hit the pillow concerned about all the things you need to do tomorrow, or have other anxious thoughts running through your head, you're likely to find sleep elusive.

In today's busy world, I appreciate that some of the specifics of this routine will be difficult, but that is what leaders do, they accept and meet the challenge for the sake of attaining their desired results. (If you find the particulars of the nighttime routine challenging consider making mastering the routine one of your Monthly Moves.)

The room you sleep in should ideally be around 60–65 degrees Fahrenheit (16–18 degrees Celsius),[5] and keep the heating off unless it is the middle of winter. I know in some countries cooling your room is a challenge if you don't have air conditioning, so I urge you to do what you can. In addition to keeping your room cool, keep it dark. You can buy blackout blinds or get light-blocking eye masks to wear when you are sleeping (I use these all the time when I travel; they are a real gift in terms of improving the quality of your sleep). Lastly, one tip that really helps is to do a quick body scan where you lie in bed, eyes closed, focus on your breath and allow yourself to connect back with who you are. A little gratitude or forgiveness at the end of the body scan will also get you ready for sleep.

Hydration

The water percentage in the human body varies from 45–75 percent. Your brain is made of 80–85 percent water.[6] Researchers at the Physiology Lab, Georgia Institute of Technology found that even a mild level of dehydration affects the ability to focus and decision making in athletes; it impacts reasoning, mental mathematics, and proofreading.[7] A simple way to know if you are dehydrated is to look at the color of your urine: if it is dark it means your kidneys are working harder to get the water to where it needs to be in the body, and if it is a light color you are doing fine. Most people are not drinking enough. In order to drink more you can do any (preferably all) of the following:

- Get a nice (reusable) bottle that you like and keep it full of water and with you wherever you are.
- Drink a glass of water before each meal.
- Add a (non-sugar, non-chemical) flavoring, such as lemon or mint, to your water.
- Drink hot lemon and honey instead of coffee as you wake up (note: I know this is not easy for coffee drinkers like me, so I have the hot lemon and honey every other day and enjoy my coffee. Remember, you do you!).
- Keep track of how much water you are drinking each day.

Exercise

Exercising will help you get more out of the time you put into your plan. You will feel happier, more alive, and more focused. Research shows exercise has a positive impact on you physically, emotionally, and psychologically.[8] Rather than spend space in this book telling you all the different types of exercise that are available, I would like to encourage you to incorporate the following in your week:

30-minutes of walking outside. Every day take this chance to reconnect with nature and re-ground yourself, even if you are in a city! Spending time outside will de-stress you and give you a break to unwind. Something I recommend to my clients is to think about a problem or a challenge they are facing and aim to have a resolution by the time the walk is finished. You'll be amazed at what happens!

Strength training. Do something twice a week to build or maintain muscle strength.

Cardio. Find an activity that gets your heart pumping faster and do that two to three times a week.

Stretching. As you get older you will find that you are naturally less flexible. Pick a form of stretching that you can do for 10 minutes a day and add that to your routine, you could do this as one of your Pomodoros. You'll be amazed by the amount of joy you feel when you have a little more mobility in your body.

I know that the list above might feel somewhat overwhelming. There is no expectation to do it all overnight. What is essential is that you are on a journey with a solid intention to add these physical disciplines to your life. If you are already doing them, ask yourself where you can improve and how can you make your exercise schedule even more effective.

Fuel aka Food

What you eat and when you eat it has impact on you. I am not going to suggest you follow a particular type of diet nor will I advocate certain foods. If you are reading this book you are smart enough to know what you should and shouldn't be eating. What I will remind you is to be aware that the foods you consume have a direct impact not just on your physical energy but also on your psychological and emotional energies.

With that in mind, I do want to encourage you to eat a diet that is mainly vegetable based, with a good amount of protein, and balanced in carbohydrates. Most people can get the vitamins that they need from the food they eat if they plan their meals correctly; that said, I am not here to give you medical advice. What I do want to do is draw your attention to what you are consuming.

Vitamin D. I have a special space here for vitamin D, as deficiency in this particular vitamin has been described as a global health problem,[9] and also, the symptoms of low vitamin D can prevent you from being the leader that you are capable of being. Symptoms include: fatigue, mild depression, mood change, muscle weakness, and bone pain. When I lived in Egypt, in the 40-degree sun, I, ironically experienced the first three symptoms due to vitamin D deficiency and required supplements.

The UK's Public Health England advises every adult to take a Vitamin D supplement, and the Canadian government advises the same.

None of what I have said above constitutes medical advice. I would urge you to speak to your own health professionals to get the specific advice that you need.

Rest

In order to implement your Project3x3 powerfully, it is important to build times into your schedule for planned rest. If you keep working and implementing at your optimum, then you can burnout. Build in times for rest. I would suggest that you have a daily, weekly, monthly, and quarterly rest, we will explore this in more detail in the **Succeed** phase. The objective and duration of each is different.

The daily rest could be a meditation, cup of tea, or chat with friends.

The weekly rest could be going out for a few hours or doing an activity that brings you joy and relaxation.

The monthly rest could be a day off and doing something with family or friends.

The quarterly rest is wonderful because—as I have mentioned previously—the quarter actually has 13 weeks, so you work on implementing your plan for 12 weeks and take five to seven days off before the next quarter comes in.

Summary

Remember people in your circle are watching you, you are a role model to someone even when you don't realize it. When it comes to self-leadership, I invite you to think about your daily plan: when do you exercise, eat, and rest? What do you eat and drink? And, what are other things you must manage? As we continue through this phase, you will start to have a better picture of your responsibilities and that understanding will culminate in reviewing your weekly plan and creating a daily plan.

Service Leadership

Taking leadership of the multitude of responsibilities you are likely to have can take over your entire life. These responsibilities can be related to your parents, work, kids, house, and even your pets if you have any! The bottom line is that if you are responsible for it then you must factor in how you will manage it. I know you might read this and think it sounds unrealistic, but I know that these are the things that can throw you off track if not considered in advance. Know where your boundaries are and whose support you can enlist to assist you with some of these elements.

Responsibilities associated with service-leadership can be broken down into six categories: immediate family and those you live with, extended family, friends, work colleagues, community, and finally, others. I will take you through each one, so you know what to consider and how to be aware of each category.

Immediate Family and Those You Live with

If you live with your children, regardless of their age, you will have some responsibilities towards them. Even adult children have ongoing demands, and you have a subconscious sense of responsibility towards them. With younger children your responsibilities are clearer in that they have needs that you must see are fulfilled. These responsibilities will have an impact on how you structure your day. For example, in the morning you might not be thinking about the evening meal (assuming the evening meal is your responsibility), but as the day goes on that task slowly creeps up in the hierarchy of importance. And if food is not ready come the time for your evening meal, then there can be problems! You may also find yourself responsible for chasing your children (again, regardless of age) to put things away, do their homework, and do their chores, etc. This all takes time and energy, so it demands your consideration.

By ensuring you are clear on the tasks that relate to the responsibilities within your home and allocating time for them in your schedule, you can manage them more effectively. Scheduling time facilitates these responsibilities being met, and so then they no longer seem a barrier to your progress. When people work from home, they tend to think that they will be more efficient overall because they can work and put on the washing machine at the same time. Whilst this might be true in the honeymoon period of working from home, in the long term the responsibilities of work and home become blurred. You will burnout quickly because with no boundary between work and home, you end up unable to switch off.

When it comes to managing your logistics within the household, I would also suggest that you are clear on the logistics for others. Be clear on the tasks that others are responsible for and communicate that to them so you provide clarity and more accurate delegation of the task to the responsible individual. In the short term it might take longer, but in the long term it will reap dividends because you will have more time (as you are doing less), more mental bandwidth (you are worrying about others and their tasks less), and you will be making others responsible for their logistics, which in turn will also reduce their stress levels because they know what they need to do, when, and why.

For your tasks, I would suggest that you download Google Tasks (or a similar app) on your phone and add anything you are responsible for there; that way, when you've added it once, you no longer have to keep reminding yourself because Google tasks and your weekly schedule will do it for you. I don't really like the word tasks for this because we use it as a to-do list and this is more of a reminder, but the app calls it that, and so will we.

Extended Family

This may be something that you have not considered before, but if you have extended family then you have some responsibility towards them. These responsibilities may not show up in actual time, but they are there in your subconscious. Someone creating and following a plan, who is clear on their values, ethics, and morals will want to ensure that they are the best version of themselves for their extended family too. That said, do ensure you have clear boundaries in place for members of your extended family that may need them. Without question, this includes ensuring that every relationship's need is met and handled with ease and flow.

Be clear which members of your extended family warrant that you should be in touch with more regularly. Are there gifts or cards that you want to send to them or phone calls you want to make? Are there people you want to message regularly? Having these connections organized means that you do not spend psychological bandwidth thinking about it or fretting because you have forgotten—it also means that you are a better relative!

Just as you created tasks above for your responsibilities to members of your household, now create tasks for key important dates for extended family.

Taking the time to do this will save you the complications that arise when you do not take the time to contact individuals in your extended family. It will also bring you a great deal of satisfaction and joy knowing that your family feels loved, cared for, and that whilst you are able to show your appreciation for them, they also appreciate you and what you do for them.

I know for me, when I handle my extended family relationships in a good and effective way, I sleep better at night because I know that I am doing what I can to support and provide a highlight for someone else. Plus, it always feels good when you are doing what brings out the best version of yourself.

Friends

There are different types of contact when it comes to friends. We all have several social media "friends" or contacts that we have never met or had any live face-to-face interactions with. Those are not the people I am referring to here. In this context, friends are real people that you know, with whom you have developed some form of a relationship, virtual or in person. Friendships do require management. It might be difficult to read, but it is true. Firstly, I would encourage you to think about your friends in categories: long-term friends, growth friends, and light-touch friends. This distinction will help you to be a better friend all round.

Long-term friends are those you have known for a while, but you don't have to be in touch with regularly. Sometimes relationships have run their course, and now you can look back at that time with joy and warmth. Other times relationships with long-term friends need more care and attention.

Growth and learning friends are those who inspire you and support you in your journey of development. You can find people in this category virtually as well as locally. You will be amazed to know I have some growth and learning friends that I met online over eight years ago, and we still have not physically met!

Light-touch friends are those with whom you once had a more regular relationship, but you are now in touch with just every now and then.

RESULTS

These distinctions are important because they will help you to be a better friend in the long run and not feel guilty about not having contacted someone. People won't feel that they are off your radar, and you will feel more in control of this part of your logistics.

In your tasks, put in a reminder to contact people around a certain date, or you could have a task that reads, "Send a message to someone I haven't been in touch with for a while."

There are different ways to be in touch with friends: you can send a voicemail via WhatsApp or a similar tool, record a quick video message and send that, send a card in the post with a note of appreciation, or any other simple, yet thoughtful gesture that you can do with ease.

I encourage you to put this in your schedule because it is these simple things that we tend to delay or forget when we are busy, but they make a huge amount of difference to the lives of others and— whether you know it or not—to your own sense of satisfaction with life.

Work Colleagues

Depending on whether you are employed or not, this may nor may not relate to you. If you volunteer or have a working relationship with people, then this applies. Open communication, praise, and support are the keys to managing your responsibilities towards work colleagues. To be clear, we are not referring now to the actual tasks of work itself, but instead, we are concerned with how you can be a good friend or support to those that you work with. You can do this with words of encouragement and support, helping out if someone is stuck (and by this I do not mean taking on their work!), or maybe taking a break with someone providing a safe space for them to talk though something that is happening at work.

Even the virtual world can provide a great space to download and relax with work colleagues. It is as simple as agreeing you will take a break at the same time and have a drink and snack over Zoom or Skype. That said, the current pandemic has seen everyone conducting almost every interaction over Zoom to the point that people are now starting to get *Zoomed out*, so don't neglect the old-fashioned option of picking up the phone and speaking to a colleague. Small actions like this build a lot of depth in a relationship and can also mean that you will find the support you need when you want to get some feedback on an idea or just talk something through.

You will know the people who you want to be in contact with regularly, perhaps make a little list in your schedule and if you've not been in touch with them over the course of the month make a special time just to get in touch with them.

Community

Your responsibility towards your community will depend on how you manifest your service to community. How much do you volunteer? What groups are you involved in? What interests do you have? This is an area that tends to be an add-on in most people's calendars. Rather than have it on the periphery, I invite you to adopt a planned approach to this.

Identify the community work or projects you want to be involved in, know how much time (or money) you can give, and what tasks you can do. Have precision over how you will help and then put that on your schedule. When you don't do this, you will either miss opportunities to help in your community or you will do nothing. I believe that we all have a responsibility to the locality in which we live, and we should try and do something within our capacity to contribute to the society around us. If you have a lot going on, and your Project 3x3 is such that your bandwidth is full, it's okay to have less in this category than you aspire to, just be aware of it.

RESULTS

Other

There will no doubt be some other responsibilities you have which are not included in your personal or project logistics. This category is a catch-all for anything that you have on your mind which doesn't fit in anywhere else. If it is something you think you should do, and it will improve your life, then be aware of it even if you are not currently doing anything in relation to it. Ignoring these items could be the thing that takes up more mental space than is necessary, especially if you have cleared up space elsewhere by having a good plan for the other categories above.

How to Put It into Practice

Make an initial list of all the people that fall into these categories. Think about how you want to communicate with them and handle your responsibilities, and then schedule it either by using an app or by adding it to your schedule. As you compile this list, you will recognize people you don't want to contact as regularly, and others that are not necessary to include on the list because you have a deeper relationship with them doesn't require being *constructed* like this (I would still put them on my list in just in case I forget someone!). You do what feels right for you. Do not feel obliged to contact anyone you do not want to, and if you are able to naturally have a regular relationship with key people in your life then do not feel obligated to write their names down either.

I have found taking this approach to my responsibilities has made my service leadership better and has made me feel like a better family member, colleague, and friend. The RESULTS Method has enabled me to free up space in my head that I would not have otherwise had and create deeper connections in my heart. It might seem calculated to you, and it is, but that means that I am able to maintain a deeper relationship with people that are important to me, not worry that I've missed someone, and do it with ease and flow.

Knowing that this part of your life is taken care of means you then have the right quality of space for leading your projects without worrying if your personal responsibilities are taken care of. That in itself is a game changer.

Schedule Leadership

"Ultimately, leadership is not about glorious, crowning acts. It's about keeping your team focused on a goal and motivated to do their best to achieve it, especially when the stakes are high and the consequences really matter."—Chris Hadfield, Astronaut

There is a difference between being a project *manager* and being a project *leader*. As a project manager, you are responsible for implementing, doing the actual work, and overseeing all the parts of your project: you are a leader of your schedule. As a project leader, you have a more strategic role: you create the vision and communicate it to others and set the culture of the project as a whole. You could say that the project manager is the employee while the project leader is the CEO.

Accepting this dual leadership role has its challenges as projects are never the same. Despite your innate strengths and abilities, you will still feel stretched and pushed and pulled. True schedule leadership requires you to develop new skills and learning—sometimes in areas that you did not even know existed!

No longer avoiding this leadership role requires self-management and paying particular attention to the guidelines I provided for self-leadership and service-leadership is essential. Chances are if these two areas are not appropriately handled then you will find schedule leadership more challenging because taking adequate care of yourself and the things you are responsible for is a prerequisite to being able to concentrate on additional projects.

RESULTS

In RESULTS, schedule leadership requires that you wear two hats: project manager (doing the work or overseeing it) and project leader (setting the vision and having the strategic overview). Day-to-day project manager tasks will be organized by the plans you have created and are implementing, so I won't go into more detail on that here (go back to the **Select** and **Utilize** phases for more detail if needed). The key question I want to address now is how do you lead a project effectively?

In my experience, having worked on projects from small-scale home extensions to $500 million regeneration schemes, I believe that the essence of effective project leadership is consistency. No matter the size of your project you need:

- Clear intention
- Well-articulated vision
- The right team
- Capacity and desire to implement
- Ability to problem solve
- Tenacity to keep going
- Metrics to measure
- Communication skills
- Project ownership

Ultimately, schedule leadership is you deciding to take an idea and turn it into reality. It applies to anything that involves multiple levels of planning and implementing —going on holiday, starting a business, changing careers, getting married, going shopping are all projects on some level. I'm sure you have made firm decisions in your life, and this demonstrates that you already have the leadership skills within you; all that remains is for you to make the committed decision that you will be the project leader of your life and your projects.

If you are having any doubts, I have one statement and one suggestion for you.

The statement: if you are on this page of the book, you have all the makings of an effective leader, and I am here to support you.

The suggestion: go back and review how to overcome the self-doubt, and then **Reach** beyond that doubt and hesitation, navigate past that self-erected barrier, pick up the torch, and run!

Let's move onward!

There are three concepts that will give you insights to make you a more effective schedule leader. Let's discuss these now.

The Pareto Principle

The Pareto Principle (named after Vilfredo Pareto) indicates that 80 percent of your results will come from 20 percent of your activities.[10] In other words, 80 percent of your results comes from 20 percent of your efforts, or 80 percent of your outcome will come from 20 percent of your input, etc. The 80:20 rule can be applied to almost any situation and understanding this concept will help you to lead and take ownership of how you follow through on your Daily Schedule, Weekly Rhythm, Monthly Plan, and Project3x3.

Given that the Pareto Principle suggests that out of a list of 10 items, two will be worth more than the other eight put together, it is especially striking that most people tend to procrastinate on the top 10 or 20 percent of items that, in fact, have the most valuable and important effect on their overall results. They leave or delay the most impactful items on their list and keep themselves busy with the 80 percent that contributes very little to their vision or project aims or that comes easily to them (remember Mike and his GCSEs?).

If you understand the profundity of Pareto's Principle, you will recognize that you don't have to do everything, just the 20 percent that will give you 80 percent of the results. Applying Pareto's Principle even further, you could ask yourself what is the 20 percent of the 20 percent—these are the tasks that you can't delegate to anyone else, that you can't train anyone else for, that *you* must be the one to get them done.

As a schedule leader, focus your time and resources on either the top 20 percent or, at the very least, the top 20 percent of the 20 percent.

Parkinson's Law

Parkinson's Law states, "Work expands to fill the time available for its completion."[11] You probably already know this to be true! This means that if you give yourself a week to complete a two-hour task, then the task will increase in (perceived) complexity and over time become more overwhelming, to the point it will eventually fill the week. The task itself may not fill the extra time with more work, but the stress and tension created about having to get it done will. By allocating the right amount of time to a task, you gain back more time, and the task will reduce in complexity to its natural state.

Planning Fallacy

Remember when you were at school and you had an essay that was due in a month? You had submitted essays before and written them in 10 days, so you felt as if you had plenty of time. Yet, as the submission date got closer and closer, you realized that you needed more time. Then you rushed, didn't get it done in time, or had to ask for an extension. Researchers Daniel Kahneman and Amos Tversky named this the Planning Fallacy, and it affects everyone! At some level we all have a bias towards optimism concerning our own abilities, but when it comes to our capabilities, we do not always assess those accurately!

Kahneman and Tversky said, "Scientists and writers are prone to underestimating the time required to complete a project, even when they have considerable experience of past failures to live up to planned schedules."[12] A false sense of confidence means that sometimes you will over-believe in your ability. When you plan a project there is a focus on outcomes rather than risks that need to be mitigated against.

Being aware of this concept is not enough to stop it from happening[13] in your projects. You can overcome the planning fallacy with a three-part strategy:

1. Set intentions for your goals; be clear about when you will you start and finish.
2. Specify when (put it in your calendar!) and where you will implement the actions.
3. Visualise yourself following through on your plan.

Research shows most people will only do the first and chances are, even if you know to do the second and third, you are not consistent in doing them. When you actually allocate time in your calendar and visualise implementing your plan, you tend to be more realistic in your goal setting. This does not mean you reduce what you can do, in fact it means you get more done because you are being more effective.

Deep Work

Day to day, much of our time is allocated to tasks that do not create much new value or tasks that are easy to replicate and are often performed while distracted. Cal Newport, author of *Deep Work*, calls this "shallow work." He encourages us to strive to limit shallow work and train ourselves to maximize our potential by focusing on "deep work." Deep work is work that creates value and, unlike shallow work, is hard to replicate, pushes your cognitive capabilities to their limit, and is best performed free from distractions. Newport says, "The ability to

RESULTS

perform deep work is becoming increasingly rare at exactly the same time it is becoming increasingly valuable. The few who cultivate this skill, and then make it the core of their working life, will thrive."[14]

Deep work enables leadership in all areas of your life, and it is a concept that can enable you to be effective and thrive. I suggest that when you work deeply you can also play deeply and really enjoy your time off!

I know that now you are wondering how you can work deeply so you can put this concept to work in your life. There are a number of active steps you can take to make deep work a part of your work ethic, but it comes down to setting some boundaries and following up with discipline.

Remove Distractions

The workplace, home workspace, coffee shop, and library can all be equally distracting if you are unable to focus. Distractions are everywhere and given the complexity of life there is little you can do to remove all distractions. But what you can do is optimize your three environments and develop a mindset of readiness to work. One way to develop this mindset is by creating a mental trigger that removes the distractions. I mentioned a particularly useful ritual in our discussion about setting up boundaries in the **Utilize** phase; I shared that I have associated opening my laptop as the trigger of opening office and getting ready to work. As I type in the password it becomes time to start work. This trigger has helped me to work all over the world—busy airports, empty hotel conference rooms, coffee shops, at my dining room table during lockdown, and countless other places. (If you have noise cancelling headphones, use them. They are an effective tool for eliminating external distractions.)

Don't Work Alone

Always working alone can be a lonely experience, even for introverts. In 2020, research started to look at the impact of working from home over the long term, and it will be interesting to read a systematic review of that in years to come. What we currently know is that working alone long-term is a lonely and isolating experience. We all have a need for human connection and interaction with others. If you are based at home, consider joining a virtual co-working space (the online resources give you some ideas for this option). Knowing that others are working with you even though they are not sharing the same physical space and are working on something completely different is very motivating. (Do you recall the Cousins' Zoom Homework Club?)

Implement Like You Are Getting Paid for It

During deep work, *focus on the critical.* Utilize the BART method so you have a clear set of goals to maximize your deep work. Ideally, these goals should feel challenging and perhaps even a little bit intimidating!

Utilize your impact measures to evaluate your effectiveness.

Keep track of how many hours you work deeply per day. Take note if there are specific times during the day that you tend to work more deeply than others. Decide which time blocks you allocate for deep work and strive to meet your personal benchmark every time. Approach this with curiosity so it is fun. The motivation to improve by creating self-accountability is powerful when done appropriately. During your weekly review, quickly assess your performance and evaluate how you can improve.

Rest Time

Time away from work is very beneficial. It enables you to switch off, reflect, and avoid burnout or boreout. You only have so much capacity for work which is why I encourage you to work in Pomodoro sessions with breaks. Studies show that you can focus deeply for three to four hours a day,[15] so when you do your best during deep work while working on the most important work (i.e. that 20 percent), you are not missing out when not working deeply during the rest of the day.

Take advantage of your built-in periods of rest during the day, week, month, and quarter. (We've already discussed how and when to build in these crucial times during the **Utilize** and **Lead** phases—specifically when we spoke about Time Blocks and Self-Leadership.) These essential built-in periods of rest are opportunities for you to recover and get ready for more deep work. I know I keep repeating it but it is important!

Create a shutdown routine at a specific time of the day. Take 30 minutes to complete and close out any ongoing tasks. A shutdown routine will enable you to stop working at the same time every day and prepare for the next day.

Deep Rest

I consider deep rest to be thoughtful rest. It is time to go into your thoughts, ponder and reflect, and just think about, and do, nothing. Such time is a real treat! So schedule it in.

Meditate on problems. Train your mind to focus on a particular problem or question while you are occupied physically but not mentally. With practice, you will be able to explore a problem in your head, consequently sharpening your concentration and strengthening your distraction-resisting muscles. I keep a list of problems and questions that I save for when I take my walks or do chores around the house. I am always in awe of the ideas I come up with when I use these times that I am physically busy to brainstorm and mentally solve the items on my list!

Social Media

In one way or another, most of us spend the majority of our time online. Whilst it is very useful, the internet is also a big distraction and gets in the way of deep work. Restricting your access to electronic devices is hard—your smartphone addiction has a similar effect on your brain as drug addiction[16] producing dopamine and endorphins. Know that if you have not set self-imposed rules for social media, there could be a significant negative impact on your Project3x3 and your overall results. If the time you spend on social media is not contributing positively to the energy and effort and effectiveness equation, then it is time to bring it in check!

Use the ideas below to keep your social media time within bounds:

Use social media like a craftsperson uses their tools. If it supports your project, then use it. Identify the main factors that determine success for your professional and personal life and use social media tools only if the positives outweigh the negatives. Remember your compelling future vision.

Apply the Pareto Principle. Identify the 20 percent of the activities that generate 80 percent of your results. How does the use of social media impact your current results? How long are you spending on social media, and does it contribute to the completion of your goals?

If it doesn't help you succeed, quit. After considering social media in regard to the previous two points, do you still need to use it as much as you do? If it doesn't help you achieve your goals, quit it, or significantly reduce it.

Set hard deadlines. Allocate a specific time block for internet entertainment—it is not the same internet time spent on research or work. Put thought into your recreation time by spending time doing things intentionally.

If you've allotted 20 minutes to use the internet, only use it for 20 minutes. You must learn to be very disciplined in this matter because without discipline, 20 minutes easily turns into two hours or more. The ability to resist distractions will give you more energy and focus generally. We've all experienced the Netflix/social media hangover!

Specify When You Are Available: Stop surrendering to other people's agenda! Set rules for when you will deal with email and remember that you do not need to respond to everything, reply immediately, or accept responsibilities that others are allocating to you. When replying to emails or messages make your communication specific and assertive (remember the more specific you are, the less likely you will receive additional emails requesting clarification or further information), offer solutions when you can, and remember you don't have to reply. If replying takes more time and effort than you are willing to give, consider whether the issue really requires your response.

Allocate specific time blocks for when you will check and reply to emails.

In order to work deeply only take on matters that are specific and necessary for you to address.

The Eisenhower Matrix

"What is important is seldom urgent and what is urgent is seldom important." —Dwight D. Eisenhower (1890 – 1969)

The Eisenhower Matrix[17] was created by American President Dwight Eisenhower and is a widely used model for prioritizing and dealing with tasks. It is also commonly known as the Do, Decide,

Delegate or Delete model and the Urgent and Important Matrix. The simplicity and power of the framework is second-to-none in terms of helping you to take leadership over what you work on. You have probably already used a version of it, but understanding it in more detail will help you to more strategically apply it. This process enables you to make decisions about what to do every day, week, and month. Spending a few minutes taking your tasks through the matrix can save you time, effort, and resource allocation and can give you the ability to focus on your actual responsibilities.

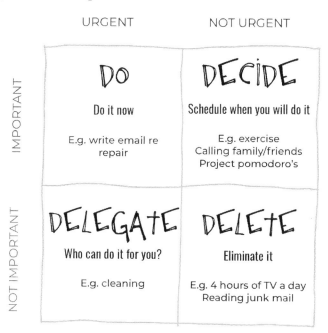

The Eisenhower Matrix

If you don't allocate enough time when planning the tasks in the decide quadrant (important/non urgent) they will eventually become urgent or they will end up not being done. An example I like to use here is making dinner. When I review my task list in the morning, often one of the items is cooking dinner. I could decide to get takeout food and delete the task altogether or I could delegate the task and give someone else the responsibility to make dinner that day. If I do not delete or delegate the task, then I remain responsible for it and because it is still the morning, it will be a decide task (non-urgent but important). If I do not decide what I will prepare for dinner, then as the day progresses, this task becomes an increasingly urgent and important task. If I have gotten caught up with other tasks and have done nothing to prepare dinner, then in the evening it moves to a "do it now" task, and I need to address it immediately. If I continue to ignore that task and it is not done, then I end up with an unhappy and hungry family, and no one wants one of those!

Making dinner is an easy example to apply to the Eisenhower Matrix because everyone can relate and it can populate any of the four action quadrants depending on the circumstances. The same can apply for any domestic task, studies, work tasks, and pretty much any other responsibility you might have. I suggest that you put a couple of tasks from your own life through this framework to see what happens when you don't do the task. Understanding this model at a visceral level will help you to be able to use it effectively and make it part of your personal planning system.

Delete

If it doesn't need to be done delete it. It is that simple.

Delegate

Pass it to someone else to take care of it.

Communicate what you want done. Be particularly attentive to relating the specifics of the final results so they know exactly what you want. Make sure that there is an understanding of boundaries, end results, and timeline. Also tell them why you have chosen them. "I've chosen you because you are really good at…" Verify that they understand, and then they are more likely to accept responsibility and be able to follow through.

Create an environment for open communication so if there is an issue, they can come to you straight away and seek direction or guidance. Delegate to people who are reliable. Build in a realistic deadline, not a false one.

You have a lot of tasks that require attention so delegate if you can. If it can't be delegated, can it be deferred? Deferring a task means moving it to the important, not urgent action field for scheduling.

Decide

Tasks on your list that are not deleted or delegated must be scheduled. But first you should decide whether or not the task is urgent and how important it is.

- We often judge importance based on our impulse and thinking, "I should do this first." Instead try this:

- Rank each item with an urgency score from 5 to 1 (5 being it must be done first)—the discipline here is that you can't give every task a 5.

- Give each a 5 to 1 for level of importance. Truly important tasks will be associated with your projects or values.

Then urgent x important = priority.

Anything with a high number should be moved to the first box to be done. Other tasks should be addressed during your evening 10-minute Pomodoro session to be scheduled on your calendar.

Do

Implementation is in your hands! Give everything a slot in your calendar, or a time in your day so that it gets done.

Weekly Rhythm (Part 2)

Emboldened with the new information you have learned throughout this phase, you are now going to review the weekly plan you put together during the **Utilize** phase. So, take out the weekly plan that you created and start allocating time blocks to self-leadership, service-leadership, and schedule leadership. Having gone through Eisenhower's Matrix and clarified which tasks are urgent and which are important and having considered the Pareto Principle and identified the things only *you* can do, you should have gained additional clarity on what you are actually responsible for. You know that none of these things will happen unless they are in your calendar—if it is not scheduled, it is not happening!

If you want to re-prioritize time blocks, then this is the time to do that.

As you come to the end of this chapter, look at your weekly plan and ask yourself if this is something you can commit to. If it is—excellent! If it is not, then review and review until you are able and ready to start visualising it and making it a reality. Remember the two differences that make people follow through on their plans: 1—putting it in your calendar and 2—visualising it.

Act on Your Schedule.

Once you know *what you are doing, when,* and *for how long,* you'll need to act on your schedule. You have made a commitment to yourself so it's up to you to follow through on your promise.

Start tonight by optimizing your sleep routine, and then in the morning start with your first time block. Begin and end at the set time. Then go through the rest of your day until you reach the end of the day's schedule

This may seem like the easiest step in the time blocking process—you've laid out the ground rules, and now you just need to follow them. Acting on your schedule will only become simple once you figure out whether your time blocks work in real life, and you review this at the end of every week.

Test and Revise

As you start working on your time blocks, it's best to keep track of your time expectations or perceptions versus the reality as you go through each time blocks. This way you'll know which, if any, time blocks are too short or too long, and you'll be able to revise them for the future. For example, if you block all your tasks with 25-minute and 2-hour blocks, but your review tells you that this works only about 80 percent of instances, and some of the tasks actually take much more or less time than you allocated, you might then try moving those over to different time slots in an effort to use your time blocks more effectively.

In addition to completing your weekly plan, now is a good time to start looking at your daily schedule.

Daily Schedule

Your daily schedule has more detail than the weekly plan. It contains all the information you personally need in order to follow through. Sometimes nothing else is required, but other times you need more accuracy to help implementation. When you look at your schedule you will know. The day planner that I use looks like the image below, you can find a template for it at *www.results.partners/bookresources*

RESULTS Method Day Planner

I AM	TASKS	PROJECT 1	PROJECT 2	PROJECT 3	HOURS	TODAY	TOMORROW
I am...	1				6 AM - 7 AM		
I am...	2				7 AM - 8 AM		
I am...	3				8 AM - 9 AM		
I am...		AFFIRMATIONS			9 AM - 10 AM		
I am...	I can				10 AM - 11 AM		
I am...	I am				11 AM - 12 PM		
I am...	I will				12 PM - 1 PM		
I am...	I do				1 PM - 2 PM		
I am...		TO DO			2 PM - 3 PM		
I am...	1				3 PM - 4 PM		
I am...	2				4 PM - 5 PM		
I am...	3				5 PM - 6 PM		
I am...	4				6 PM - 7 PM		
I am...	5				7 PM - 8 PM		
I am...		TODAY'S PRIORITIES			8 PM - 9 PM		
I am...	1				9 PM - 10 PM		
I am...	2						
I am...	3						

The RESULTS Daily Planner

As a project manager and positive psychologist, I believe the day starts the night before. Your morning and evening routines are critical to the success of your day. You can go back and review the sections on self-leadership if necessary, to optimize these routines. You will also develop your A.M./P.M. plan when we go over the next phase.

Theme Days

Some individuals will theme the days of their week: they choose one day for calls, another for meetings, and another for desk-based work. If this is something that you think you want to test, then take a few weeks and reschedule your time blocks based on the themes that you have for the day. This way you fully immerse yourself in one type of activity and you have all the tools and materials you need for this type of task.

If you don't want to theme your days, you could theme certain parts of the week. For example, I use Friday evening as a review of the week that just finished and what I have scheduled on the following week. I specifically chose Friday evening so that I know I do not have to think about this over the weekend, and I am bouncing, ready to go on Monday morning—after my Sunday night review of the next day's schedule of course! I know some choose a Sunday to do their weekly review, and it doesn't matter which day you choose, as long as you have a weekly review scheduled in your calendar.

There are also some themes that only need to be done on a monthly basis, and you will learn about those in the next phase—**Thrive**.

Self-Interview

Insight: What is your biggest insight after reading the **Lead** phase?

Intention: When you explore your boldest hopes and highest aspirations, what is it that you ultimately want by leading?

Identity: Why does your work on leadership really matter to you?

Implementation: What is the smallest or most immediate action you are willing to take to lead?

Integrity: What can you do to deepen your commitment to follow through?

HOW DO I DEAL WITH OBSTACLES?

PEOPLE

PHYSICAL

ENVIRONMENTS

PSYCHOLOGICAL

Before
SPORADIC

After
CONSISTENT

THRIVE

"My mission in life is not merely to survive, but to thrive; and to do so with some passion, some compassion, some humor, and some style."

Maya Angelou 1951–2014

RESULTS

Make sure you are clipped in.

When I was 16, I had the privilege to spend two weeks on a tall ship (picture an old fashioned ship with masts and sails) that sailed from Southampton in England, to St Malo in France and then back to Plymouth in England as part of a London Police initiative to take city kids onto the sea. We would work four hours on, four hours off in shifts. One night we were all called on deck. As I woke from what semblance of peaceful slumber I could manage and grabbed my kit, I could feel the ship was not stable under my feet. Going up on deck made me even more anxious. I could feel the effect of severe sea sickness as the force 8 gale winds hit the boat, which, to me, felt like it was on its side. "Make sure you are clipped in!" the 2nd Officer yelled to us as we got up on deck. He kept repeating it. We were each allocated very clear roles about how to keep the boat safe and us alive through the storm. "Clip in!" the 2nd Officer kept reminding us.

One wave was particularly huge, and the ship was now really listing. I knew not to panic, for I had clipped in. I decided that the only time I would panic was if I were actually in the sea! From the corner of my eye, I could see my friend Sally was not clipped in. "Clip in!" I yelled at her. She either ignored me or couldn't hear me; I did not know which "Clip in!" I yelled again.

"Keep an eye on my post," I told Helen. I went over to Sally to tell her to clip in. Sally was shocked. She had thought she was safe, but her clip had missed the metal safety bar when she attempted to clip in. In that moment I learned a lesson that still serves me today—you yourself have to *clip in* first and then you can make sure your colleagues are clipped in. If they are not, you will not be able to work on the priority at hand.

#

There are two primary types of obstacles that you need to navigate in order to move from sporadic results to consistent ones: internal obstacles can sabotage progress and external obstacles can stand in the way of progress.

External obstacles are obstacles that do not come from you or within you. For example, if you want to start a business but you don't have the funds to make the financial investments necessary to get it off the ground, that is a real-world obstacle; it is a fact that stands in the way of you moving forward. If you have the mindset that says you don't know where to raise the funding, then it is also an internal obstacle.

Internal obstacles usually relate to how you are thinking or feeling—they involve emotions. Fear, insecurity, lack of self-belief, and imposter syndrome are all examples of internal obstacles that can sabotage your efforts to make progress despite there being little or no external obstacles. If progress could be achieved despite the internal or external obstacles, everyone would make it. Yet, even when you have a great deal of clarity about your vision and a well-mapped plan to reach your destination, obstacles will still come up. This is why knowing how to navigate past the obstacles and through the unexpected is required.

The next two phases focus on how you can thrive by overcoming internal and external obstacles so that you thrive and succeed in the short and long term.

In this phase, we will look at how you thrive while pursuing your goals. The Oxford English Dictionary definition of thrive is "to prosper and flourish." Thriving is a state where you experience more open and creative thinking, richer connections with others, better performance, and more positive emotions. You reap the benefits of ongoing personal growth and fulfilment as you thrive. You make effective use of your strengths and feel a greater sense of well-being and purpose. As you thrive, you have higher levels of resilience and resourcefulness, lower levels of stress, better health, and even a longer life span.

Shawn Achor, author of *The Happiness Advantage*, analyzed 200+ scientific studies on happiness and concluded that: "[Happy employees] have higher levels of productivity, produce higher sales, perform better in leadership positions, and receive higher performance ratings and higher pay. They also enjoy more job security and are less likely to take sick days, to quit, or become burned out."[1]

Navigation

Imagine you are driving from where you are now, to somewhere about 50 miles away. Before you start your journey you have prepared everything you need: your car is ready; you have fuel; you've checked the air, oil, and tires; there are snacks and water in the car; you know who you are traveling with; you've checked the route for traffic jams; and you know the weather is going to be fine. You have done everything you can to get you to your destination with ease and flow. You leave in perfect weather, on time, and you are in a great mood.

Then 20 miles into the journey you see red lines in your route map, and the traffic ahead is at a standstill. You are stuck in eight miles of traffic, and there is no way out. What do you do? You might miss that important meeting you are heading to. You start to panic. You didn't plan for this. It's not fair. It always happens to you. Why you? Why now? Why? Why? Why?

Then you pause for a moment and start to think of all the ways around this. When could you turn off the road and take another route? Could part of the meeting you are attending in an hour be held virtually on your phone, in the car? How else could you overcome the obstacle? Unexpected traffic jams are not the only obstacles you might face when travelling. Other travel related difficulties could include the plane being late, the flight being cancelled, the luggage getting lost. These are all dilemmas that need to be overcome because there is nothing you can do to change them.

One thing I know about my own experience is that growth is defined by the obstacles you overcome. I don't know what your current personal external obstacles are or have been in the past, but there are some universal themes that happen as a result of those obstacles: resilience, grace, strategy, a desire for consistency.

When you're striving to achieve anything worthwhile in life, you will run into obstacles, challenges, and failures. If the process of achieving these worthwhile things were easy, everybody would do it—making them not so worthy achievements in the first place.

Just because they are inevitable doesn't make running into these obstacles any easier. Doubts, fears, and insecurities arise, and you start to question if your striving was a good idea in the first place. Nevertheless, you should embrace the obstacles that come your way. If nothing else, appreciate them as fuel necessary to prompt your growth and achieve your most ambitious goals.

Although it doesn't seem like it at the time, your challenges are catalysts that will force you to either rise to the occasion or leave the playing field. When you *choose* the former, you'll learn new skills and gain valuable experience and wisdom. In other words, it makes you better equipped to achieve the goals you desire. And that's exactly why you should embrace the obstacles, failures, and challenges that come your way.

How Do You Overcome Obstacles?

Pause and reset. If we look at the individuals and companies that were able to pivot successfully in 2020, they are the ones that paused, assessed the situation with the information that they had available, and then decided what next steps they would take. They became comfortable with the certainty of uncertainty. They decided not having all the answers was ok. And they dealt with the circumstances that were dealt to them and adapted.

So, when you face the difficulties and the unknown is in front of you, don't have a knee-jerk reaction. Instead, take the time to carefully assess the obstacle and understand all its aspects. From there, review your plan and amend it with revised goals and deadlines if necessary. If additional support is needed and you have the capacity to bring that in, do that as well. Take the measures available to you to go around, jump over, or tunnel under the barrier that has sprung up in the middle of your path. The willingness to adapt will help you to stay on course, avoid derailment, stand strong against the whispers of self-doubt, and enable you to stay on course, even if the path is slightly different from the one you had originally charted.

Obstacles do not only challenge you to rethink your goals and strategy, but they also help you discover unknown skills and new possibilities for your work and life. You may end up with a completely unexpected new job or opportunity! Meeting the challenge obstacles bring requires you to separate yourself from the past and to be open to unexplored opportunities.

RESULTS

Obstacles are a part of every journey, but they don't have to result in defeat. Managing life knowing that challenge and obstacles are part of it will allow you to turn even the most frustrating obstacles into new opportunities.

Managing Impatience

When faced with obstacles, it's easy to get caught up in an emotional whirlwind. Yet negative thinking and anxiety can weaken any motivation to work toward important goals. Not only that, but the stress and upset exhaust you by using up valuable energy of various types. Yet, by adopting a calm and relaxed attitude in the face of challenge, you set yourself on a course to conquer it. It is easy to become impatient and wish it away, but when you think like that, you are unable to see the new opportunities that are being made available to you. Do whatever it takes to remain calm and focused. Summon your values, strengths, and communication styles to serve you now that your mettle is being tested.

Three Environments

The constitution of the World Health Organization reads, "Health is a state of complete physical, mental and social well-being and not merely the absence of disease or infirmity."[2] With this in mind, we will approach our mission to thrive from a holistic perspective. That said, your physical, psychological and people environments play a key part in this. By mastering these three areas you will be in a strong place to continuously build on all the great work and reflections you have done so far and overcome obstacles as they come your way.

The Three Environments

People

Our relationships with others are central to our experience and quality of life. Human beings were created with an innate need to get to know one another, even the introverts amongst us! People have a huge impact on your ability to thrive.

"People will be most likely to thrive with well-functioning close relationships that serve different support functions," with those functions dependent on whether or not we're currently facing adversity in life.[3] I believe that to some degree, post-2020 we are all facing adversity in one way or another, the privilege of living without hardship has gone. Human interaction doesn't only provide us with support, but it also enables us to cope with stress or adversity better. Researchers Brooke Feeney and Nancy Collins also found that the right people environment can help us in our efforts to learn, grow, achieve goals, cultivate new talents, and find purpose and meaning in life. They noted "Relationships can permit a person to thrive, but unfortunately we know relatively little about how relationships promote or hinder thriving."[4]

People can make you feel happy and loved. Many relationships fail because someone is not thinking about the other, and they are focused on their own selfish bubble. Be thoughtful, kind, and understanding of the other, and make the effort to communicate your care and concern. You need to step outside your own bubble of need—which can be hard.

Think about how you show up when you or others are frustrated, annoyed, irritated? How do you want to be? It might take a little while for you to get up, but you have to get yourself together for your project, your loves, and yourself. By consciously choosing the energy that you create and being aware of how it impacts you and your environments, you will have a fundamental impact on your ability to increase progress in your projects.

If people around you are negative or not the kind you'd want to choose, then don't fall in line with them. Create a new level and support them to rise up. You owe this to yourself and to your higher purpose to go that one step further, to move outside your own circle of concerns and to help others reach higher heights as well. There is grace that you are here. Be grateful for that and step out with grace into the day.

I have already shared with you that when my kids were at nursery, some colleagues and friends questioned my decision to go to work and leave my kids in daycare. I would respond by saying as long as they are loved, safe, and happy then I am able to do this. If for any reason, I doubt that these three factors are met, I would hand in my notice immediately and leave my job. I hold this same wish for you— that you feel loved, safe, and happy in your relationships, for that is what a thriving people environment creates.

Relationships are so important that they are one of the five elements of Professor Martin Seligman's PERMA (Positive Emotion, Engagement, Relationships, Meaning, and Accomplishment) model.[5]

There are two types of support. In the **Lead** phase, we discussed an aspect of service leadership defined by how you provide support to those with a close relationship to you. These and any other relationships are a two-way process because whilst you are assisting them, and they are also supporting you as a friend, sibling, spouse, or colleague.

One of the first important functions of relationships is to support thriving through adversity, not only by buffering individuals from negative effects of stress, but by enabling them to flourish either because of or in spite of their circumstances. "Relationships serve an important function of not simply helping people return to baseline but helping them to thrive by exceeding prior baseline levels of functioning. We refer to this as a source of strength (SOS) support and emphasize that the promotion of thriving through adversity is the core purpose of this support function."[6]

The other noteworthy function of the people environment is to encourage thriving when adversity doesn't exist by nurturing full participation in life opportunities for exploration, growth, and personal achievement. Positive relationships help people thrive in this situation by helping them to embrace and go for opportunities that boost positive well-being, broaden and build resources, and cultivate a sense of purpose and meaning in life. This type of assistance is referred to as *relational catalyst support*[7] because the people providing the support can be active catalysts for helping others thrive. This help emphasizes that promoting thriving through life opportunities is a core purpose of relationships.

It is worth noting that it is not necessarily merely the provision of support, it is the *type* of support provided— it needs to be meaningful.

RESULTS

Someone who is able to provide support has different behaviors compared to someone who is trying to be supportive but lacks sensitivity in regard to the needs of the other individual. This has several ramifications for shaping our perspective when offering support to others: it directs us to think not only about how we are supporting others, but also to think about the support we are receiving. For you to thrive in your people environment, ideally, you will feel recognized, supported, and loved.

If someone within your circle makes you feel anything contrary to this, then do your best to build a people environment of close friends who will give you what you need. Give yourself permission to contact different people at different frequencies and levels. For example, friends from school may be in touch with you in a different way than friends who live in the same neighborhood as you. You must also give yourself permission to end friendships or let them trail off if they have lived their natural course. You want to have people in your network who are excited about your projects, your aspirations for life, and your vision. I appreciate that it is not always easy to find these kinds of people, which is why we have the RESULTS community, and you are very welcome to join us at any time!

Physical

The **physical** space that you occupy helps to boost or destroy your personal energy. You must be intentional about choosing and maintaining a positive physical space as you create a quality of life that you care about and value. The reality of our current working practices means that you may not have a dedicated desk-space or working area, so how can you create a space that enables you to want to work? More broadly than that, what are your personal preferences for a home space that you love to live in? In all the work I have done with individuals and companies, it is clear that a tidy workspace is important, as is a clean home. You set your own standards, but know that when things feel off in your home or you have a slight resistance to work in the space you have allocated, then it could be as simple as your physical space not being up to your personal standards. Rather than ignore it, please do what is necessary to improve it.

As a former practicing architect, I can tell you that your physical environment has a direct impact on how you feel and experience life. I am sure you already know this, but you may not appreciate its true impact. In 2014, research by Professor Nicholas Bloom from Stanford University revealed that working from home one day a week boost an individual's output by 13 percent.[8] More recently Bloom's research, conducted mid-pandemic, found that more than half of those surveyed who are now working from home are doing so either in shared rooms or their bedrooms.[9] This is why your physical working environment is so key to your ability to thrive. Everyone has a different taste or personal preference regarding the decor or style of their physical environment: modern, traditional, colorful, light, wooden floors, carpets, and I could go on! But research shows that there are some distinct factors affecting the quality of your space that have an impact on your well-being. So, it's worth your time, effort, and energy to be purposeful about your physical space.

Keep your space clutter free; put things where they belong. If it helps, allocate one of your daily 10-minute Pomodoro's to tidying up. When possible, enroll the support of the people you live with in this aim.

Have a dedicated space where you work and make it conducive to working so that you are pleased to sit there with your working tools for two hours at a time. I know your working period may be less, but asking yourself if you can sit there for a two-hour period makes you question the quality of that environment, and you will inevitably remove any resistance in it (i.e. it will be tidier and more conducive to working).

RESULTS

Earmark a couple of different spaces to work in at home—I have written this book at my loft office desk (a former bedroom), the dining table, in the garden, and sitting on the sofa. As long as the environment is favorable for your working, then there is no judgement about the space you are using.

Ensure that there is adequate light in the space. In addition, optimize your electronic devices to avoid eye fatigue by limiting the glare on monitors and turning on any eye-comfort filters.

Consider how your environment smells. Assistant Professor Rachel S. Herz has researched the impact of smell on your creativity and work performance. She says, "In terms of cognition, mood has been shown to influence creativity with the typical finding that people in a positive mood exhibit higher levels of creativity than individuals in a bad mood. Smells can also produce the same effects. When people were exposed to a scent they liked, creative problem-solving was better than it was when they were exposed to an unpleasant odour."[10] Her research also found that people who worked in an environment with a pleasing smell had "higher self-efficacy, set higher goals and were more likely to employ efficient work strategies than those who didn't."[11]

Posture plays an important part in your physical well-being and ability to flourish. Have a good desk and chair, and periodically check in with yourself in terms of how you are sitting. Stretch and move for a moment or two at the end of every Pomodoro. This is even more important now that we are working from home for longer and the water cooler trips have all but disappeared.

Create a physical environment that brings you peace, enables you to be who you are, brings you vitality, gives you a sense of belonging, and motivates you to work and make progress on your projects and tasks. When you consider your physical space from this practical perspective and take action, you are at a competitive advantage because of the emotional and physical benefits from working in a good environment.

You will be happier in the place where you are working, and that will move you from sporadic thriving to a more consistent feeling of thriving.

Psychological

As you know by now, your psychological mindset is critical to getting the results you seek. You have the knowledge (or an understanding of what is necessary), and you have a plan; you also need the psychological attributes to power through the times when you have doubt or uncertainty. Being in a supportive community, having accountability (including to yourself), and looking at your plans every single day will create the psychological foundation you need to move forward and make progress.

So far in the RESULTS Method we have done a lot of work on your mindset and psychology. Building on the work that you did in the **Reach** phase and developing a growth mindset, let us now establish a thriving mindset. When you have a thriving mindset, your mind is calmer, more compassionate, and you have more clarity about where you are and where you want to go. You will find that you have a deeper inner connection to your soul and are able to draw on your inner calm in stressful situations.

I am assuming that you are now regular in your practice of using affirmations, creating permission slips, using a Kanban board, and visualizations to support the daily delivery of your vision and projects. In my experience of working with people who attain the results they seek and who progress according to their true capacity and capability, there is still a lack of self-compassion.

Self-compassion involves acting the same way towards yourself when you are having a difficult time, fail, or recognize something you don't like about yourself as you would with someone else. Rather than continuously fighting the current, pause and acknowledge the difficulties you are facing and honor your humanness. We know that things will not always go the way we want them to. The reality is that you can do all the work I ask you to do and there will still be obstacles and challenges, and you will still do things unsuccessfully, but these instances provide a lesson for the next time; other people call it a mistake, but I call it a learning opportunity!

Self-compassion researcher Kristin Neff says, "You will encounter frustrations, losses will occur, you will make mistakes, bump up against your limitations, fall short of your ideals. This is the human condition, a reality shared by all of us. The more you open your heart to this reality instead of constantly fighting against it, the more you will be able to feel compassion for yourself and all your fellow humans in the experience of life."[12]

There are a number of things you can do to improve your self-compassion (go for a walk, write in your journal, review your affirmations, practice visualization, revisit your values and intention). My go-to reflection when I need to be more self-compassionate is to ask myself, "What would I recommend to a good friend in my situation?" and start from there.

Spend a few moments to reflect on which areas of your three environments you could dial up a notch. Make your three environments as solid as they can be.

Checklists

"The volume and complexity of what we know has exceeded our individual ability to deliver its benefits correctly, safely, or reliably." — Atul Gawande

When it comes to getting it done, our complex environment presents us with two potentially compromising, day-to-day challenges.

One, our memory and attention fail us, especially when we are dealing with run-of-the-mill, mundane tasks that make it easy to be mentally neglectful of the more important things we should be considering. Two, we think we are smart, so we try and skip key steps because "It won't matter," or "I know what I'm doing." Sure, in some tasks it might be okay to forgo certain steps in the process, but it is equally true that missing even the simplest of steps can often cause the biggest problems.

Gawande describes these two gaps as *errors of ignorance* (mistakes we make because we don't know enough) and *errors of ineptitude* (mistakes we make because we don't use what we know). Gawande posits that most of the mistakes we make are because of the latter.[13]

The checklist is a simple system that will help you to respond to the challenges created when you want to keep a higher standard than business-as-usual. By deciding to add projects to your life, even when you have started to optimize how you spend your time, you have taken a huge step. Adding checklists to this venture will enable you to make even more progress. You might not think of checklists as exciting, sexy, or fun, but when you see the impact that they can have on your ability to implement your plan, you may change your mind!

Working harder is no longer the solution.

Working smarter is no longer the solution

Acknowledging your fallibilities and having a plan is the answer.

As someone who is committed to making progress in their lives, you might not like the idea of having a checklist: maybe it makes you feel like your parent is following up behind you or maybe it feels beneath you to use a checklist. But this is not a mindless agreement to an act or tool of protocol, *you* are the creator of *your* checklist. The sole aim is to increase your efficiency and implementation, not to give you a headache. The use of a checklist will help you to avoid simple errors, utilize the knowledge you have, and identify where simple tweaks will help you to be more efficient and use less effort and energy.

Having a checklist can increase your efficiency to the point where you can move a project from breaking point to success.

Atul Gawande's book *The Checklist Manifesto: How to Get Things Right*, presents a very strong case for the importance of checklists. A very important note to make here is that a checklist is *not* a to-do list. To-do lists are lists of things that need to get done, but a checklist takes you through a process step-by-step. Usually to-do lists have no focus, priority, or limit… you can end up with lists of lists of lists! But a checklist is specific and well-defined and process oriented.

To-do list	Checklist
Incidental task (e.g. Buy milk) No order in the steps.	Repeated task (e.g. Weekly house cleaning)
	Any task with multiple steps in succession.
Have your questions ready. Be prepared to ask for clarification or more specifics when they reply.	The process of RESULTS, you go through each phase one-by-one, and create your plans in succession
No structure	Process oriented Prioritized, focused. Has a boundary
Constantly growing	

Comparison of to-do-list and checklists

Gawande explains the impact creating a checklist has had on childbirth in India. This safe surgery checklist was then used in eight hospitals around the world, beginning in spring 2008. The results of this pilot study were released later that year:

- Major surgery complications at all eight hospitals fell 36 percent after the introduction of the checklist.
- Deaths fell by 47 percent—from 435 to 277.
- Infections fell almost by half.[14]

When the results of the study were published in January 2009, many became interested. More than 12 countries publicly committed to implementing versions of the Safe Surgery Checklist in their hospitals. Checklists may seem like a simple concept to use in a complex world, but they obviously work and can have a profound impact on results. Good lists take the obvious routine tasks out of your mind so that you can focus on the difficult things. They may work in all industries—and will work even better in the future, with the increasing complexity of things.

The aim of the checklist is to help you implement what you know, to support you in getting it done, and to deliver at a level acceptable to you.

How can you make an effective checklist that you will use?

Gawande identifies three types of problems:

Simple: individualistic, a set of things to be done (e.g. bake a cake).

Complicated: team based, coordination, involving sequences (e.g. launching a rocket).

Complex: the outcomes might be different even when many people do the same thing (e.g. raise a child).

A checklist can ensure that steps are not missed, skipped, and can be used to communicate tasks with others so that anyone involved is on the same page.

RESULTS

To solve a simple problem like baking a cake you can pick up a book and find a recipe and go with it. Thing is, if you don't check the rating of the recipe perhaps you won't know that the steps have not worked, so it's always a good idea to take a moment to check the feedback from others. The same applies to more complicated and complex tasks. That said, the more challenging a problem becomes, the more essential the checklist is to your overall quality of life. For complex situations checklists are required for more progress to be made.

- A good checklist will be precise, easy to use, doesn't go into unnecessary detail, and includes every step so no one misses it.
- Checklists that are too long, too complicated, hard to understand, or too easy and patronize people will not work because they will just be ignored.
- A good checklist will have five to nine items on it (easy to remember). It will be action oriented and includes a space for you to tick off each item as you do it.
- If you are doing a task from memory, the checklist will require that you pause and confirm that every step needed to be done was done.
- If you are reading a checklist then you will be required to tick off each item.

It is worth noting that the ticking of boxes is not the ultimate goal, but rather it is doing a good job and moving onto the next item. Just having a checklist is not a proven formula for success, and it enables you to be more effective only if you use it. What is truly amazing about a checklist is that it improves your outcomes and results with no required increase in skills. All checklists do are increase your efficiency.

Let me tell you about how I used checklists when my children were five and six years old. This is an age where kids are feisty and yearning for independence—they insist to do things by themselves. Parents want their children to get ready for school as efficiently as they can as just getting the child out of bed can take twenty minutes alone if they are tired (and there, the *they* is for both or either the child or parent!). When my kids were five and six both went to school, and my husband and I had jobs which required us being at work on time for progress or site meetings. Let's say the tasks required by the kids were the following: get up, put on a school uniform, brush their teeth, go to the toilet, put on their shoes, wash their face, eat breakfast, read for 15 minutes, check homework, and comb hair.

I have deliberately written this list a little randomly so it confuses you, as it did me when my children would do it without a checklist.

After weeks and months of trying to get the kids to do things in order, I created a checklist for each of them. It was a simple laminated A4 paper stuck to the fridge. Rather than using words we used pictures to represent each item, and the list was reduced to seven steps:

Wake up.

Go to the toilet.

Brush teeth.

Eat breakfast.

Comb hair.

Put on uniform.

Read for 15 minutes.

You may be wondering why I left out put on shoes and check homework. Kids are less likely to forget to put on their shoes than they are to comb their hair, and the check homework is a task I could do as I put their lunchbox in the bag. This is about focusing on the things that are important, not creating a to-do list or a complex excel spreadsheet—focus on what is critical and important to your project, written in as few words as possible.

Within days of doing this, the kids took responsibility of their own checklist. They would come downstairs and mark off the items that they had done; if they forgot one in the sequence it would remind them to go and do it immediately before proceeding to the next one.

I told them that this was a **do-confirm** checklist. A do-confirm checklist covers tasks you complete from memory. Pilots use a do-confirm checklist to ensure they haven't overlooked anything such as checking the right instruments or locking the plane's brakes. Essentially, this kind of checklist helps the pilot fly a plane safely without relying solely on his or her fallible memory. This was powerful for my children's understanding. You can use do-confirm lists with your children, yourself and your projects.

This is the checklist that you can also use when you are traveling to make sure you have things like your passport, medicines, printed tickets, etc.

Below are a couple of examples of **do-confirm** checklists:

Checking emails
1. Set alarm for 25 minutes.
2. Open laptop.
3. Go to email.
4. Start alarm.
5. Answer emails in priority order.
6. Stop when alarm rings.

Shopping
1. Prepare weekly meal plan.
2. Make list of ingredients that need to be bought.
3. Group items into the shops you will buy from (e.g. supermarket, fruit and veg stall, bakers, meat shop).

4. Schedule when you will go to the different shops or place your order online.
5. Make your order online or go to the store.
6. Set aside time to put items away when purchased.

The other kind of checklist is a **read-do**. If you've ever followed a recipe, you have used a read-do checklist. It sets out the steps required for accomplishing a specific outcome, like cooking lasagna or baking a cake.

This is a **read-do** checklist:

Onboarding new coaching clients
1. Reply to enquiry with email to set up compatibility call.
2. Create virtual meeting for call.
3. Email reminder for compatibility call.
4. Have compatibility call.
5. Either email terms and conditions, confirmation of payment, and link for coaching calls, or email saying thank you and summarizing discussion.
6. Start coaching sessions.
7. Feedback form at the end of the 1st session.

By creating checklists that set out the steps that you want to take, you are taking control of your plans and being more efficient on your follow through and therefore you make more progress. For repeated tasks, checklists will form part of your standard operating procedures and will save you from needless errors when you are in a time of stress or uncertainty. It breaks down the complexities or challenges you are facing into something that you can get done and tick off.

Having a checklist will help you to avoid making common mistakes you have made in the past. Of course, making a mistake often provides you with useful learning, but to do it again without learning is a missed opportunity and will cost you time, effort, and energy in the long run.

Monthly Moves

You may be wondering why I have waited until now to talk about how to create monthly plans (or Monthly Moves as I like to call them), and you are right to ask the question. I believe that people are too hasty in creating a monthly plan, and when that happens, well you know, you don't follow through on it.

Most people have incredibly busy lives and that can be hard to manage, especially when you have taken on new projects. Let's look at how you can design your Monthly Move so that it is effective, and you follow it.

By now you know you must write things down. Use your planner or e-calendar and set out all the time blocks for your various projects and responsibilities. By prioritizing what matters most, you are able to have your projects and goals at front and center when managing your time and effectiveness. Ensure that the time blocks all link with your vision, project goals, and priorities. If you find that you are too busy in one period of the month or at a certain time of the day, move activities around so that there is more balance overall.

Use color to identify different activities in the month. It really helps you to keep track of what is happening at a monthly, weekly, and daily level. You will know, at a glance, what activities are taking up most of your time and where you need to cut down.

Print your monthly plan and stick it to the wall. It is one of the pages that you should spend a few minutes going over every day. If your plan is just in your head, you don't see it, you don't aspire to it becoming a reality, and you certainly do not get it done with the effectiveness and efficiency that is available to you. By spending time looking at it and perhaps even sharing it with someone (a friend, mentor or coach), you increase your chances of follow through. That said, you first need to be accountable to yourself, so spending time breathing it in every day in order to make it a reality.

	Monday	Tuesday	Wednesday	Thursday	Friday	Saturday	Sunday
Week 1							
Week 2							
Week 3							
Week 4							

A sample monthly plan template.

Build in sufficient white space. Some tasks will take longer so white space gives you a contingency in place to help you deal with unexpected circumstances. Other times, things will come up. When you plan for flexibility you increase the chance of success of any plan, and the free time gives you a sense of freedom that you may not otherwise experience.

Have a dedicated place to work on your tasks. As you know, not having a proper workspace will affect your effectiveness and impact your ability to focus on your work. Make sure that your space has natural light and is clean and tidy. When you like your workspace, you tend to get more done. If it is your dining room table or a coffee shop, make yourself psychologically ready to use that space. I also invite you to have a variety of working spaces that you use; a change of environment does wonders to shake up monotony. You can schedule workspace shifts in your monthly plan so you know when you will go to the coffee shop and when you will work from home.

Allow yourself a moment to remember that no one is perfect, and if you do fall off course for a day or so then pause, allow that, but get back to your plan. If you need a break, take it, but get back on track as soon as you can.

Self-Interview

Insight: What is your biggest insight from the **Thrive** phase?

Intention: When you explore your boldest hopes and highest aspirations, what is it that you ultimately want by thriving?

Identity: Why does thriving and overcoming your obstacles really matter to you?

Implementation: What is the smallest or most immediate action you are willing to take to thrive?

Integrity: What can you do to deepen your commitment to follow through?

SUCCEED

HOW DO I SUCCEED AND ~~SUSTAIN?~~
FLOURISH

—REVIEW & RESET

—REST

—REVITALISE

BEFORE   AFTER

REDUCE   INCREASE

SUCCEED

"I don't know what your future is, but if you are willing to take the harder way, the more complicated one, the one with more failures at first than successes, the one that's ultimately proven to have more victory, more glory, then you will not regret it. This is your time."

Chadwick Boseman (1976-2020)

RESULTS

"I lost six months of my life in the past…"

"I'm amazed that you are so calm!" Nicki cut in.

"What do you mean?"

"You've got so much going on, and you look so calm, so in control."

I pause for a moment and smile. I'm meeting Nicki for a virtual coffee, and it's a welcome pitstop in the day. "I suppose I'm trying to bring the swan out in me."

Nicki looks confused.

I respond to her apparent confusion, "A swan moves gracefully in a lake and is often a picture of elegance in motion. What is hidden from the observer's eye is all the work and activity that is going on underneath the surface. We don't see the swan's feet moving fast which are propelling it with the grace. We just see above the water."

RESULTS

Nicki takes a sip from her drink and nods her head. I continue "I've had my fair share of working too hard, not working on the right thing, and listening to other people. I've let my imposter syndrome control me for years. But something happened in March that made me insist Now is my time.'" I turn my head to look out of the window near my desk.

"What happened?" Nicki asks as she leans into her computer screen, her face now taking up the bulk of the Zoom window.

"Well, I had lost six months of my life in the past on three different occasions. One was after a car accident that almost killed me, and I was completely lost and didn't have a plan to aid my recovery. Next was after I decided to leave my role as a director in local government. And third was when I seemed to be living the dream in Egypt, but even though I was highly functioning, I was actually feeling a little depressed." I pause and reflect on the enormity of what I had just realized. "I decided that it was not going to happen again. That there will always be challenges and obstacles, but I decided that I was not prepared to put my life on hold again. And so, I put myself to work."

Nicki said nothing.

"Nicki, are you still there? I can't hear you." I asked, wondering if the connection had been lost.

"I'm still here," Nicki said. "So, you made a decision, that's all?"

"Yes,' I said, "and I decided to reach beyond and asked myself, "What is next?"

#

Let me be the first to tell you that getting to this page is a huge achievement. I am so proud and pleased for you. I know the amount of effort and dedication it takes to get to this stage, and it is not easy. It is not easy to read and reflect on something as life-changing as the RESULTS Method, so I am super pleased that you have done carried through to this final phase—**Succeed**. I am proud of you.

Congratulations are truly in order. You have done most of the heavy lifting to set up your RESULTS systems. And while I know RESULTS is phenomenally potent and practical, it is not the method alone that makes it so effective—it is doing the work and doing it consistently. You may find that as you get to the end of completing your first Quarterly Action Plan and Project3x3, you experience some anxiety about what to do next, or you may feel flat, or you may just think you've done such a good job there is no need for another Quarterly Action Plan. Having gone through the book and applied the learning with the templates that have been provided to you, or even with your notebook, you are in a strong place to make progress, push forward, and get it done.

If you recall the story I told you in the beginning of the book about my son Musa and his Nike trainers, you'll remember that he didn't get his shoes that day, but he also chose not to settle for something unwanted or less than his target. His patience and perseverance paid off because he did eventually get the shoes that he wanted. And yes, they only lasted six months before he outgrew them and the search for a new pair began! Persistence does show unquestionable results, but at the end, you need to restart the process again—you need to renew your commitment to your compelling future vision, or even recreate it because you have now changed.

The personal challenge now is to make the decision and commitment to review, renew, and revitalize. It is an important three step process: missing any one of these steps can cost you years in progress. I know because I have seen the impact of not adhering to this in my own life. In 2016 while living in Egypt, I implemented what I have taught you in RESULTS and impacted the lives of over 100 students and helped a company make $50,000 in sales in six weeks. I followed through and repeated the process, but this time with a team, and we went on to sell $300,000 of training and coach 150 participants. It was a brilliant time in terms of impact, gaining satisfaction as a successful team, and watching people grow and flourish.

The lesson is not in what I did above—it is in what I did next, or rather, what I didn't do. I did not create the next 90-day plan; I did not review, renew, and revitalize. At that point, I actually went back and lost myself in several of the Showstoppers I shared with you in the **Reach** phase. And it took me several years, lots of coaching, and reflection to understand what had happened. Part of the reason I wrote RESULTS is because I want you to avoid *my* mistake. It is essential for you to be an active participant in this **Succeed** phase in order to move from a singular result to plural, multiple, and consistent RESULTS.

Consistent results require a focus on flourishing not sustainability. They demand that you create a new quarterly action plan, necessitating you to take a break so you can revitalize.

How Do I Flourish and Grow?

When I was first thinking about the final phase of the RESULTS Process, I considered using *sustainability* as the theme. As a concept, sustainability felt fine, but it did not seem to align with what I was really looking to put forward—something that would enable the recalibration of the process and support building on what was there, rather than promote sustaining it. Sustainability is being "able to be maintained at a certain rate or level."[1] "Sustainable success" is a term commonly used in personal growth. I, myself, have used it in the past but I always felt some unease about it. As I investigated the word sustainability, I realized exactly where the conflict was. Consider this: if someone is referring to the relationship with their spouse and they say they want to sustain it, does that mean that they want it to be "maintained at a certain level," or do they want it to flourish and grow into the capabilities that the individuals in the relationship have separately and collectively?

I felt uneasy with the concept of sustainability in terms of how the term might be used within the RESULTS Method. The project manager, positive psychologist, and the coach in me knew I wanted to take a *flourishing* approach. I reflected in that, and perhaps realised, true success is knowing that you are using your skills to enhance the flourishing of others and yourself, where you build some level of resilience to stress and burnout. I recognized that when flourishing becomes part of your lived experience, then you *succeed*.

Many of the clients I have worked with, and fellow coaches too, will confirm that in order to be successful you need to focus on your mindset, action, and plan. This is the MAP that will give you true success. The basic elements of this phase remain the same, but the context has a much deeper, flourishing, and positive psychological perspective. I am telling you this so that when you gain a new insight or some new information changes your plan, you don't ignore it, but rather you take the time and consideration to incorporate it, because your results will be better and more consistent.

I believe that succeeding and flourishing, in the context of RESULTS, has three elements: review, rest, and revitalize. These three elements will enable you to pause, take stock, reflect, rest, and then start again, and this process will cause you to have long-term results, not just short-term successes.

But before we look at these three elements, let's understand a little more about success and how it is referred to, the fear of failure and success, celebrations, and intellectual games.

Fear of Failure and Fear of Success

Many of us have experienced these two fears at some point. By now, you may have an idea of what has caused your fear in the past. It could be any of the Showstoppers (as discussed in the **Reach** phase), not having a clear method or process, or not being viscerally linked to your compelling future vision.

What is important to note is that the fear of success and failure is something that will not occur when you are linked to your vision at the very core of your being. Debilitating fear will not be present if you spend the time to look at your plans daily and see your vision becoming real. When you do this, you become more concerned with getting the job done than with the outcome, and that is critical to maintaining your momentum and making progress fear.

Self-sabotage is often rooted in the fear of success or the fear of failure. In fact, these fears can stop projects in their tracks and leave them as mere ideas in your mind, never even making it to paper. Look, let's be straight here: everyone fails. Everyone! Fear of failure can paralyze you—it holds you back from trying something new, from taking a risk, or taking a single step towards your goals. You are vulnerable to this fear when you do not, and sometimes even when you do, have total clarity of your vision.

Guilt is something that will often occur when you fear success. The impact of this is significant and the cycle of feeling fraudulent, guilty, or incapable continues and continues until it psychologically paralyzes you. There are common denominators that bring on feelings of guilt and it is good to recognize these points, not just for you to reflect upon, but to be aware that you may be triggering negative feelings in others. Guilt can be reinforced by:

- Being acknowledged by others for success
- Believing that it is not right or fair to be in a better situation than a friend or loved one
- Being referred to as "the smart one," "the talented one," "the responsible one," "the sensitive one," "the good one," "our favorite," and the like.

Previously when we discussed gaining clarity on your vision, we specified that it does not need to be grandiose, it just needs to be right for you—right now, and neither does it need to match someone else's vision for you. Ironically, fear of failure may be a small hurdle to overcome, but it could be that fear of success is what is really holding you back. The uncertainty of the unknown results success will bring can be terrifying: What will you do? Who will you become? Will the success affect your ego?

Fear of failure or success are feelings to be aware of but not concepts to persuade you to hold yourself back. When you emotionally engage with your vision regularly, you will stop playing intellectual games with yourself because you will have no time for them!

You have the method and process in your hand. If either (or both) of these fears are an issue for you, make sure you go back to the **Reach** and **Evolve** phases for a refresh on who you are.

What Is Success?

Interviewing Arsene Wenger, FIFA's Chief of Global Football Development, for The Guardian, Tim Lewis writes Wenger "often imagines what he will say to God when he dies. In most of these exchanges, God asks Wenger to justify his time on Earth, how he gave meaning to his own life and to others. "I tried to win football matches!" Wenger will explain. God looks at him, sceptical: "That's all?" Wenger goes on: "Winning matches is really hard to do. If you do your job well, you bring joy to millions, a collective euphoria and catharsis."[2]

What will we reflect on at the end of our lives? True success is a life well lived. Earlier in the book I shared with you the top five regrets people have when dying, number one being "I wish I'd had the courage to live a life true to myself, not the life others expected of me." This is the key result we are seeking: one where we are chasing our best self and living our life in integrity with ourselves and our vision.

The job that you have, the relationship you are in, the house you desire, the car you want, the food you eat, the experiences you have are all leading to one thing: satisfaction with life. Your life experience should be one you enjoy every single day. There will be ups and downs, but overall, let's aim for life to be a joyous experience. Abraham Maslow, said that the "good life is a way of approaching life rather than an outcome of life."[3] You are experiencing the good life in the moments that you have joy, and you will feel joy when you are progressing in your projects towards actualizing your vision, and—like Matthew McConaughey— chasing your best self. Don't allow anyone's judgement about you aspiring to more from life affect you. Remember, everyone has their own journey.

Project Management

In project management terms, success is different than project success. Project management success is the completion of a defined project; it is the completion of the change or goal that we were working towards. Project success is different. Project success requires the change or goal to actually work and be effective. For example, one can create an excel spreadsheet for managing your budget, but if you don't use it, for whatever reason, then the project has not really succeeded because it has not met the desired goal which was to manage your budget better.

Project management success is delivering the project to time, with the resources you have and to the expectations or quality target you have set. Even seasoned project managers get caught up with focusing on project management success, and they forget what project success actually means.

Your focus needs to be on both the viability of your project and its goal, as well as its overall success—in other words, its alignment with your vision.

Positive Psychology

Living a life worth living is a key aim of the RESULTS Method. In positive psychology the focus on strengths, optimal performance, and how you feel aligns perfectly with the RESULTS mission. King Jigme Singye Wangchuck, the 4th King of Bhutan, coined the term Gross National Happiness in 1972 when he declared "Gross National Happiness is more important than Gross Domestic Product."[4] This approach has since been explored by countries across the world with a slow, but ongoing, shift taking place towards giving non-economic well-being equal importance to financial well-being. The aspirations of the founding fathers of positive psychology Ed Diener and Martin Seligman support this perspective that more value should be given to an individual's emotional and psychological well-being.

As you progress on your projects and implementation of the process, maintain a focus on your personal strengths, positive emotions, well-being, and other personal factors related to your success and thriving. Having this attention can allow you to connect with an inner sense of hope and an uplifting desire for growth and constructive change. There is an overlap between these concepts and the focus on growth, acquiring new skills, and implementing them.

RESULTS

Researcher Dr Christine Robitschek created the personal growth initiative[5] which provides a useful way to look at personal growth and change. There are four elements to this model which include:

- Identifying areas of growth and the timing of change (you did this in the **Reach**, **Evolve**, and **Select** phases).
- Developing a plan for growth (you created your plan in the **Select** and **Utilize** phases).
- Building awareness and utilizing resources that can be helpful (this work was undertaken in **Lead**, and throughout the other phases).
- Engaging with the intentional behavior of actually following through with the plans for personal growth and engaging in the self-change process[6] (you did this at every step of the RESULTS Method, well done!).

The RESULTS Method is intrinsically a positive psychology based approach, because it is based on your intention, identity, implementation, and integrity; with these in turn being based on your values, innate strengths, preferred communication style, and what you desire for your well-being and impact.

RESULTS Method

Research led by Obhi Hardeep explored the values of lifelong learners and happiness. It found six themes of older adult learners: "need for novelty, generativity [*sic*], spirituality, hedonism, active lifestyle, and family."[7]

Succeeding in the RESULTS Method is flexible and available to all—it is based on your progress. When you have moved forward in your vision, with integrity, and you are able to say that you are putting in the effort, energy, and effectiveness based on your capacity then even the smallest (or most audacious) move forward is worthy of celebration and acknowledgement. You may not always be in the zone; you may sometimes feel that the struggle is too much to bear, but don't give up—instead continue to persevere. Of course, my wish is that you meet all your quarterly goals, monthly priorities, and weekly deliverables. However, if this is your first (or 100th) time using this method then progress is what is important—we are not looking for perfection!

The RESULTS Method has built in flexibility allowing you to move forward at your own pace thus empowering you to live the life you want. Consider just one element, the Capacity and Capability Model, and how it requires you to be true to yourself. Imagine all these ideas layered upon each other. Now you are living a life that is meaningful to you and precludes running a mindless rat race. That is the primary aim of RESULTS— progress at a pace befitting where you are and where you want to go— and also, very importantly, a pace allowing you to experience joy along the way as you get it done.

Celebration

A word about celebration: it's important to find balance here because negative effects arise whether going overboard or underplaying your celebrations. Celebrating too much can cause derailment and underplaying your achievements can cause your soul to feel a little ruffled. Let's begin by considering what meaning you are creating in relation to your progress. You can't just keep running because then you don't get to enjoy the journey. You also can't just be laisse-faire about things, because you will never be satisfied with the pace from that. Ideally, you want to move at an consistent, balanced tempo. And this requires the strategic use of 2-minute tantrums and celebrations.

A 2-minute tantrum comes when you've had enough, need to get it out of your system—it is part of your stride. You know you do it, I certainly do every now and then as it gives me the space to release, reset and carry on. You release frustration and irritation with whatever it was that did not work out in the way you hoped, and then you can move on.

What we miss as human beings is the deep, genuine celebration. We celebrate others, but we tend not to take enough moments to really celebrate ourselves and our own achievements. Acknowledging progress no matter how small is a fundamental part of the RESULTS Process—celebrations and appreciation are proven to increase how happy you feel, how motivated you are, and how positively you view yourself and your work.[8]

I'll be the first to tell you that buying something or eating cake do not do it for me when it comes to celebrating! Reflecting on my love languages, I know that I need something different. Simply relishing and enjoying the fact that you have completed something seems to be missing from the lives of so many. Even those who do celebrate their wins seem to do it just at the end. Why do we forget to celebrate the small achievements along the journey? I don't know but what I do know is when you give acknowledgement to your soul that you are on the right path, you are actively reinforcing what you want on a higher (perhaps spiritual) level. Sometimes we get caught out with our ego when it comes to celebration and either go overboard or do too little. What is necessary is to simply connect with our soul's desire for celebration.

Just as we often suppress our bad feelings, it is also possible to keep your celebratory happiness contained—especially if you are not one to usually celebrate or if you feel it's awkward to celebrate yourself. Give yourself permission to celebrate your successes. The 2-minute celebration (where you give yourself a pat on the back, take a moment to smile in satisfaction for what you've achieved, or a personal acknowledgement of any kind) works for me and for people I've shared it with. It need not be an elaborate affair, but it does fulfill the need for self-recognition. This brief celebration is vitally important to our emotional health, in that we acknowledge our feelings and we don't ignore them or allow them to fester. If you have had a win (small or large) or you've made progress, you owe it to yourself to acknowledge that. Congratulate yourself, and tell yourself, "Good job!" Whatever means you choose to celebrate yourself—do what works for you; in this regard, you are not answering to anyone else.

Remember, I am also here cheering you on. As much as I love big wins, it is the small ones that really make me smile. So keep going, my friend, keep going.

Intellectual Games

So here you are. Almost at the end of the book. And this is the time for me to ask you one of the most challenging questions that I regularly ask myself:

"Are you playing intellectual games with yourself?"

When I sign up for a new course but don't attend to it, end a project because "it's too difficult," buy a book but don't read it, learn something new but don't implement it, read a great idea and go right past it, and every other variation of this un-intentionality, then I have to ask myself if I am playing an intellectual game with myself.

Intellectual games are when you make a very good argument and reason for why you do not do the thing that you, in fact, need to do in order to make progress. Subconsciously, you know that doing the easy thing (i.e. leaving the new book on the shelf, ending a project prematurely, etc) will not give you the progress you desire; doing the easy thing is an active excuse to avoid doing what is important. You also know that because you are busy you will have the satisfaction of feeling that you are making progress, but it is a false satisfaction. And if you look deep enough, you will find that beneath this façade of satisfaction there is disappointment because even though you are busy, in fact, you are not working on what is important.

So, why am I talking now about subconscious avoidance and intellectual games? Because now that we have reached the **Succeed** phase, I am going to stress upon you the importance of reviewing, resting, and revitalizing. But from experience (both personal and with clients), I know that at this point many of you will say, "I don't need to review, rest, or revitalize. I'll just keep going." Please, listen closely. Do you hear that sound? It's me screaming, "Nooooooo!" Why on earth would think that you do not need a break and rejuvenation?

Please stop playing these intellectual games with yourself. I played these games every single day until one day I put a sign on my wall that said, "Intellectual integrity requires putting your ideas into action."

INTELLECTUAL INTEGRITY REQUIRES PUTTING YOUR IDEAS INTO ACTION

Before you move to the end, if you are playing intellectual games then make a conscious decision to stop now. You will thank yourself for it every day for the rest of your life. This was certainly a key part of me sharing my methodology for you in RESULTS—I had to push through, and so can you—in your hands are the tools and strategies I used.

In order to stop playing intellectual games, consider the RESULTS Method from a comprehensive perspective and use the processes I have shared with you. They will either prevent these games or at least, will reduce their impact.

There are three processes to enable you to maximise your success and empower you to flourish in it. They are review, renew, and revitalize. We will now look at each of these in turn.

Review

Taking stock is one of the most important elements of succeeding. It is the acknowledgement of what went well and noting what requires further work or improvement. When you do not find the time to pause and review, you can miss opportunities to improve. This is why, as students, we all had mock exams in school—to assess abilities, to give feedback, and to get a measure of where we were.

There are two main purposes of the review:

1. To check that you have followed your plan and to identify what changes or improvements are needed.
2. To ensure that your plan helped you towards your vision, to evaluate whether your vision is still valid and unchanged, and then to find new projects to work on in line with your vision, values, strengths, and all the new knowledge you have gained about yourself and about what makes life worth living for you.

It is okay if you find that your vision and project aims are different now—life is in a constant state of flux, and so personal visions and projects do undergo change; this happens to most people. Very rarely have I worked with someone whose vision stays intact; mine is constantly being refined and re-articulated with adjustments and amendments.

RESULTS

A regular review process enables you to check in with your projects and yourself, so you stay true to who you are even as you grow and evolve. As your coach and mentor, I do not want you to work on projects that you are not intrinsically connected to. I want everything you do to bring you joy and happiness, as well as progress.

It is worth taking regular time to review your activities against your plans. By now, you know the importance of having the daily 10-minute reviews and 25-minute reviews that are part of your Daily Schedule and Weekly Rhythm respectively. A longer, monthly review supports your Monthly Moves. Every 90 days you will also undertake a 2-day review where you assess where you are, check in with your vision and values, and select your next projects to create your new Project3x3 which will be the next set of plans for your life.

If you review less often than that, you may find that you are not placing enough urgency on your deliverables and developmental activities; you may miss time blocks, and your progress will slip. When this happens a few times, you will either not undertake the review or you will not want to because you will feel that you have not made enough progress. Let me be clear, a day off or so is okay. In fact, any period of time off for self-care is absolutely fine, but what is not fine is giving up on your plans, your desires, and your hopes and aspirations.

About 20 years ago, I had two big projects of which I really only wanted to pick one at the time: get married or do a PhD. Knowing the limits of my own capacity, I recognized that taking on both would have led me to burnout because I was also working full time. Having sought advice from various sources, I decided to focus on getting married. That did not mean studying for my doctorate was on hold, it just meant it became part of my longer-term plan. That is an example of a decision based on long-term success, whilst living a flourishing lifestyle. You will know the areas of your life where you are making decisions like this. Be confident in your decisions, it will enable you to make more progress than you can ever imagine.

In order to undertake a proper review of your Project3x3, I ask you to dedicate two days at the end of the 12-week work period. In that time, you will assess how you have done in relation to your priorities, goals, and project deliverables. You will identify new projects and goals on your march to achieving your vision. The first time you do this, please, take the full 2-day period to carry out a review. I am a big fan of shortcuts when they are proven to work—there are no shortcuts for the 2-day review. By trying to complete it in less time, you do yourself a disservice. If you've ever been inconsistent in your results in the past, you know by now it could be because you didn't plan effectively, or you didn't connect with your values and vision, or because you lost sight of them. This quarterly review is an active measure to keep you planning effectively, keep you aligned with your values and vision, and help you to be consistent in your results.

Performing Your Review

Below is a suggested agenda for the 2-day review (undertaken at the end of a 90-day or 100-day period).

Day One: Review Your Progress

Schedule six hours divided into three 2-hour sessions.

Session 1

Two hours: Review your Weekly Rhythm, Monthly Moves, 90-day goals, Annual Power Plan, and Vision. Conduct a Self-Interview. Write everything that comes to you.

Self-Interview Questions—Session 1:

- What did you achieve?
- How did it feel?
- Did you do something different, but more effective?

RESULTS

- What went well?
- What requires a delta (change or improvement)?

Session 2

Two-hours: Revisit your values, strengths, and communication style. Complete a new Johari Window.

<u>Self-Interview Questions—Session 2:</u>

- What helped you make progress towards your vision and project goals?
- What activities that are slowing you down or will speed up your progress?
- What adjustments do you want to make to your compelling future vision?

Session 3

Two-hours: List all the projects that you are interested in working on.

<u>Self-Interview Questions—Session 3:</u>

- Which three projects do you want to work on? (Take them thorough the Reality Check)
- How much time and resource will they require?
- What external support do you require?

Day Two: Renew Your Processes

Schedule six hours divided into three 2-hour sessions.

On day two, you will review the information from the previous day (day one of your review) and create your new plans all the way from the Quarterly Action Plan through to the Daily Schedule and review your Annual Power Plan (your plan for the year created by collating four Quarterly Action Plans). It is important to set aside time for this because it makes you project forward and create new plans that you are excited about.

If at any point, your vision, project goals, priorities, or deliverables do not excite you then ask yourself, "What do I want to achieve more than anything else? What inspires me to move forward in life and make progress?" Take time out to dig deep and be honest, and then continue.

Session 1

Two-hours: Look at the work from yesterday and identify the top three insights you have.

- What projects do you want to take on next and why?

Session 2

Two-hours: Take those projects and put them into your Project3x3, Weekly Rhythm, and Monthly Moves templates.

Session 3

Two-hours: Review your goals and priorities, and once you are happy with them allocate them to the time blocks in your schedule.

RESULTS

That's it, and it is now time to celebrate in whatever way you wish! You are well on your way to completing your next Project3x3.

But before you do that you must renew and reset.

Rest

Take one week away from any project work. This much needed break will enable you to recalibrate and get a much-needed reset. When you work consistently, you need to rest. I know that you may try and resist this, that would be a very human thing to do, but to move your success from inconsistent to a consistent journey, I suggest that you take the rest, which, after all, you deserve. This can be a few days away, or even a staycation, do whatever feels right. When you are working on an important project, a complicated problem, or feel that you have too much to do, it is easy to convince yourself that you do not have the time to take breaks. This is wrong. In fact, it couldn't be further from the truth.

Whilst we all know the truth that breaks in the day can reduce or prevent stress, research has also found that breaks help to maintain performance throughout your day and reduce the need for a longer recovery period at the end of the day.[9] In addition, taking a break midway in the day (what we have traditionally called the lunch break) enables you to detach from work, increase your level of attention and energy, and reduce overtiredness. Studies show that these lunchbreaks also increase vitality and reduce lethargy levels over a year later![10] These breaks also help you to restore mental energy and reduce the development of fatigue, sleep disorder and heart disease.[11] Research that has been ongoing since 1984, the Framington Heart study, shows that infrequent holidays are an important risk factor in heart disease.

Do I need to say any more to convince you to take breaks?

In my experience, stressed people deplete their psychological energy and their actual capacity. Taking breaks will boosts your creativity and expand your decision-making process, focus, and adaptability to change.[12]

Please ensure that you take a rest period between time blocks of work, once a week, a weekend every month, and a week every quarter. As I said earlier, these can be staycations, reading weeks, or times where you just chill at home. Please, I implore you, take the rest when it is in your schedule.

Revitalize

Revitalize means to "imbue with new life and vitality."[13]

Once you have taken your rest you will most probably be raring to go. You have the process, the plan, you know what you will put into practice, and you are ready to make progress! Get back into your Weekly Rhythm as soon as you are back from your quarterly break. Familiarize yourself again with your Compelling Future Vision, Annual Power Plan, Monthly Priorities, Weekly Deliverables, and Daily Tasks. Hop back into your morning and evening routines if you let them slide during your week of rest, and then go for it!

AM/PM Routine

Throughout RESULTS I have made references to activities you can include in your morning and evening routines; we are now going to bring those ideas together, and, if you haven't already, you will optimize these routines. A solid morning routine is important because it sets you up for the day. How you think and feel first thing has a direct impact on how you approach the day and how much you get done. Some people pray, others bathe themselves in the early rays of the sun to help them get fired-up and ready to go for the day. Others wake up feeling lethargic, overwhelmed, or apathetic. You can change that morning drowsiness and your energy throughout the day simply by having the right morning routine.

Your evening rituals also have a strong impact on your caliber of life and your ability to rejuvenate. Evening rituals contribute to the quality of sleep you get, and the rest that your mind, body, and soul receive is pivotal to your ability to progress towards your goals in the short and long term. Please refer back to the evening routine explained earlier.

The call here is for you to be deliberate about your morning and evening routines, not accidental.

Be meticulous and purposeful about what you do in the first few hours of the morning:

- Have a drink of plain, room-temperature water to hydrate you, then go about your ablutions.
- Pray, meditate, or connect with a higher being.
- Do something physical to get your blood and your body moving: a 5-minute high intensity interval training, stretches, jumping jacks! Whatever it takes to activate your body and tell it is awake!
- Spend 20 minutes reading or learning.
- Journal or write and reflect on your dreams and vision—spend a few minutes breathing in your plans by looking at them, take them in deeply, visualise them as they happen, imagine your day in the best way possible.

There is so much I appreciate about Tony Robbins' work in personal development. One thing stands out in particular is his morning priming process. Priming is the process of amending your thoughts and emotions "so you can live your life in your peak state."[14] I encourage you to take the time to find out more about this and other morning routines so you can what works best for you when it comes to setting you up to bring optimum energy, effectiveness, and effort to your day.

Consistency

The reason consistency is so hard is because of its very nature. The definition of consistent is someone who "always behaves in the same way, has the same attitudes towards people or things, or achieves the same level of success in something."[15] The easier it is to follow through on a behavior without thinking about it, the more likely it is to become a habit: this is "automaticity."[16] It explains why not all rituals develop as easily as others. In RESULTS, we have not spoken about habits because habits require consistency, and contrary to popular belief can take up to 66 (not 21) days to form.[17] In the RESULTS Method we use the word *rituals* to describe what others call habits. Rituals means "a set of fixed actions and sometimes words performed regularly,"[18] whereas habits means "something that you do often and regularly, sometimes without knowing that you are doing it."[19] I want you to be deliberate about the action that you are taking, it is not accidental.

Consistency towards something you don't want to do or enjoy is hard, consistency towards something you want, aspire to and love comes naturally. For there to be consistency in something you are working on you need to have an inherent link to it, and every now and then you need a break. For example, the 90-day plan requires you to be consistent in your implementation for 12-weeks, and then demands that you have a week off at the end. There is consistency in the working rhythm and the rest. Don't leave off or downplay the importance of the element of consistency. It is essential to your success and achieving your desired results.

Lifelong Learning

Before we wrap things up and say good-bye, I want to leave you with a word about committing to be a lifelong learner. This concept of being a lifelong learner was first shared with the world in 1929 by Basil Yeaxlee who said:

> ... adult education must not be regarded as a luxury for a few exceptional persons here and there, nor as a thing which concerns only a short span of early manhood [or womanhood], but that adult education is a permanent national necessity, an inseparable aspect of citizenship, and therefore should be both universal and lifelong.[20]

Personal development, growth, and the RESULTS Method are all forms of lifelong learning. With RESULTS, you are in an ongoing, voluntary, and self-motivated pursuit of knowledge. This enables you to increase your well-being, enhance your impact on those around you, improve your satisfaction with life, and how you experience it. Personal development programs can facilitate well-being, by enhancing self-esteem, confidence, and happiness. Your being here, reading this book, and implementing the RESULTS Method in pursuit of your own self-actualization and achievement is testimony to your drive and willingness to take the necessary steps to enhance your well-being.

Research shows that investing in personal development improves your experience of life.[21] Be deliberate in relation to learning and make it part of your regular practice. As you put time and energy into acquiring a new skill or knowledge you will get better. This book is testimony to my doing just that.

Au revoir.

(French, meaning "goodbye, until we meet again.")

As you reflect on the seven phases of the RESULTS Method—**Reach**, **Evolve**, **Select**, **Utilize**, **Lead**, **Thrive**, and **Succeed**—you may have noticed that they all come back to *you*: who *you* are, what *you* value, where *you* want to go, when *you* want to get there, why it is important to *you*, and how *you* want to live your life. Each step that you take in getting it done requires you to link with your intention, identity, how you implement and maintain integrity. These fundamental anchors show up in the energy, effort, effectiveness and efficiency that you put into play. It is these elements that create your results. The promise of this method is that you are not expected to be superhuman. Taking care of who you are, how you show up, and chasing your best self are all critical to your results.

You have the ability to work it out. You have the tools and templates to create your plan. I know that when you are committed to what you want from life because you *need* it, then you will get out of your own way. As you start to implement what you have learned throughout this book, you will see your RESULTS journey unfold in front of your eyes.

It would be wrong of me to say or lead you to think that gaining results is easy. Throughout this book I have shared that the journey to getting the results you desire will require work and a strong connection to your goals. You know that the aim of creating plans is not to restrict your life or goals, but to enable you to achieve them and to learn and grow at the same time as experiencing joy. It is an incredibly rewarding journey, but it does require you to show-up, fired-up, and to do the work despite the challenges and obstacles that will inevitably come your way.

RESULTS

The path to getting the results you want in life is not predictable, but at least you have a map for the journey ahead. You know the seven phases required for RESULTS, and you now know how to move from one to the other. In each phase you have gained insight, and as you continue your journey—implementing your plans and following and repeating this cyclical method—you will grow in confidence. So, continue the pursuit, and persevere along your journey. You *will* realize the results you seek. You will master *the art and science of getting it done* as you continue to:

- **Reach** beyond the challenges and obstacles of daily life to go deep into the reservoir of your own talent, while overcoming the doubt and uncertainty that you sometimes face when working on change, without letting it derail you.
- **Evolve** on the adventure of fulfilling your latent potential by understanding your values, strengths, communication style, and creating your vision in alignment with who you truly are.
- **Select** three projects to work on each quarter using the Project3x3, so that you are focused on projects with meaning and depth and that have the most impact on your life in the short and long terms.
- **Utilize** your resources properly in a way that builds psychological safety and practical freedom, thus reducing resistance to change and increasing your capacity to implement your plans.
- **Lead** yourself, those around you, and your schedule effectively by taking the right responsibilities, while empowering others to do the same.
- **Thrive** by identifying specific external challenges with the Three Environments so that you can powerfully and positively navigate through the environments in which you live while maintaining your calm despite the volatile, uncertain, complex, ambiguous world we live in.
- **Succeed** so you flourish and guarantee progress longevity by reviewing your goals, aspirations, and agenda, by resting, and by

revitalizing. Experience a values-led, integrity-driven life at work and home.

Reach. **E**volve. **S**elect. **U**tilize. **L**ead. **T**hrive. **S**ucceed.

These are the seven phases you need to embrace in order to get the results that you are seeking so you can flourish in life and work. They will enable you to allocate your energy and effort to be more effective and efficient.

So, what's next?

Look at your quarterly, monthly, weekly, and daily plan every single day—I simply cannot say it enough: breathe it in. In the future, before you plan anything, remind yourself of the seven phases above. Every 90-days check your progress and review your plan. Identify the areas where you need more focus. If you would like additional support, consider joining one of the RESULTS online programs at *results.partners*.

Six months ago, I was stuck. The year 2020 had the potential to cause complete derailment to anyone facing the upheavals that year. Having been thrown off course three times previously in my life, I was not willing to let that happen again. I leaned into what I knew worked well for my clients and me. I learned that at the end of the day you can have big hopes and aspirations for what you want to do in life, but without a plan—and a commitment to that plan—you will keep going round and round in circles. I did that for a couple of months. I didn't like what was happening to me, so I decided to reclaim control of my life and stepped back to look for the best way to go about taking back the wheel. I felt that I had the ability, but something was off. For 10 years I have known that in order to move forward, I had to address imposter syndrome. This global pandemic caused by Covid-19 gave me the chance to do that. It also gave me time to sit down and map out the

RESULTS

RESULTS Process in a structured way so that I could finally present it to you.

I hope that as you come to the end of this book you decide to live with intention, in line with your identity, and that you implement the plans that you have created. I hope that you wake up each day experiencing the joy of living a full life where you flourish and thrive. I hope you are excited and eager to get it done and to see the results that await you. I hope that in a year's time as you look back to the Project3x3's that you have implemented and seen through to completion that you do so with satisfaction and joy, knowing that you understood yourself, created the plans, and did the work that made your goals a reality.

You really can get the results that you seek when you have a plan. We all can. It just comes down to our choices and the decisions we make.

Decide to get the results.

Decide to do the work.

Decide to get it done.

Reach beyond, and ask,

"What's next?"

ABOUT THE AUTHOR

Saiyyidah (pronounced *say-ee-dah*, meaning *female leader*) is a highly experienced coach, project manager, and positive psychologist

Saiyyidah qualified as an Architect at the Mackintosh School of Architecture in Glasgow and went on to have a successful career in local government specializing in regeneration and construction culminating in her role as director of a £300m project. Saiyyidah is a Fellow of the Association for Project Management.

A passionate learner, Saiyyidah graduated in 2011 from The Meyler Campbell Mastered programme where she is now a faculty member, and qualified as a Certified High Performance Coach with the High Performance Institute in 2014. Her clients have included professionals, business leaders, small business entrepreneurs, and individuals in transition who know that they are destined for more.

She holds Masters degrees with distinction in Construction Economics and Management, and Applied Positive Psychology. Saiyyidah is currently reading for a doctorate in positive psychology, coaching, and practical theology.

RESULTS

Having coached and trained clients online for over a decade, Saiyyidah is an advocate of using the right tools to meet the needs of her clients in actual and virtual contexts. She is motivated by knowing that with the right strategies, tools, and coaching, the ability to seize untapped potential exists, and the ability to do extraordinary things is available to anyone.

Saiyyidah has travelled the world with her husband and two children before returning to live in her native North London.

RESULTS

ACKNOWLEDGMENTS

I have written RESULTS standing on the shoulders of giants, supported by giants!

I am truly blessed and grateful to have completed this book so I can share my methodology with you, but I could not have done it alone. I am inspired by knowing that people all over the world are reading and implementing the RESULTS Method.

If you are familiar with my work, you know that I am grateful to my Creator for all that has come my way. Every day I hope to have the ability to utilize the gifts God has given me as a means of being thankful for what I have been blessed with, to be of service to others, and to open the opportunity for new wonders to come into my life.

To my sisters and parents, I would not be the person I am without you. You are the friends I would choose even if blood did not bind us.

RESULTS

Idris, I don't tell you enough, but thank you for being my rock, for always creating a safe space for me to learn, write, and teach, and for being an amazing role model husband who supports his wife. Haleema, when you came into my world you changed my entire perspective on life and made me appreciate so much more! Musa, your silly jokes and curiosity are a reassuring fuel in my life. I look forward to witnessing the results you both will have in your lives.

I have the utmost reverence for my teachers, without whom I would not be the person I am. Thank you to Mr. Trafford who was the first person to believe in me when I said, "I might not know it now, but I will show you I can do it!" and let me study A level Design Technology despite my inexperience. To Professor Andrew Edkins, my master's supervisor at University College London, and Professor Heather Walton of Glasgow University, currently supervising my long-overdue doctorate, your advice and wisdom have helped me flourish—there are no words to demonstrate my appreciation for you. I also thank Muhammad AlShareef who made me realize that there are options beyond a traditional career. Roy Baumeister, Brené Brown, Brendon Burchard, Steven Covey, Ray Dalio, Peter Drucker, Carol Dweck, Edwin Locke, Abraham Maslow, Tony Robbins, Martin Seligman, Jeff Walker, Paul Wong—you are some of the giants upon whose shoulders I stand.

For the last 20 years I have had a tempestuous relationship with personal development, yet since 1 September 2000, I have persevered and immersed myself daily in learning and applying various techniques to further my own personal growth. I thank my coaches Brendon Burchard, Ajit Nawalkha, and Neeta Bhushan for their guidance and support—you are wonderful people to have on my team. Particular thanks to Brendon who in a few words made me realize that I had done something special— 'Did you hear that people? She wrote her book in 2020 lockdown and will launch it eight weeks later!'

I must also acknowledge the support of the Meyler Campbell faculty and community (especially Ann Orton who tutored me through the Business Coach program in 2011 and Catherine Devitt who believed in me from the start), and my fellow High Performance Coaches all over the world—you all inspire me to be a better coach and person! This book is for you and your clients, I hope each of you enjoys it and finds practical benefit in its direction!

In 2020, many of us have spent time being Zoomed out. Yet, it has also provided the opportunity to attend virtual events that would not otherwise be on our radar. I attended an event with Jeff Walker, which led me to Sage, which led me to Jon Bergoff and Xchange. In July 2020, as a participant in an online training session, I was voted by fellow participants as someone they would like to hear more from. Jon duly invited me to speak the next day and share "one word that symbolizes the story of your past and future." I was hesitant at first but selected "imposter syndrome." In that one moment, I made the decision to turn my Achilles heel into my superpower. The comments and support I received afterwards gave me the reassuring fuel to keep going and enabled me to see the impact of what is possible when you believe in yourself, have support, and of course, have a plan! Jon Bergoff, although we are yet to meet face-to-face, I am grateful you and Xchange are in my life.

To my coaching clients worldwide, thank you for the opportunity and for teaching me so much. You make me feel alive.

And it just wouldn't do the year 2020 justice were I to not say a word about Covid-19. Whilst it has been a very challenging time for all including me, it has provided me with the opportunity to sit at my desk and write, and for that I am immensely grateful. They don't know it, but Tim Claire, Neil Gaiman, and David Baldacci were my writing tutors during 2020, and I want to thank you for being my virtual writing coaches!

RESULTS

As I completed writing this book, I received an unexpected lesson—writing is the easiest part! Irada Ronalder, my editor, I had been looking for you forever! Thank you for your excellence and professionalism in editing and making my message come to life; you go beyond the call of duty. Thank you for making me a better writer.

To the many friends, professional coaches, and mentors who helped me shape my thinking around the book and affirmed my analysis, thank you. And a special thanks to those in the High Performance Mastermind—your support and love is boundless.

Finally, to you, the reader, thank you for choosing this book. And thank you for wanting to take your dreams and aspirations and gain clarity on your vision. Thank you for doing the work to make your projects a reality. You deserve to get the results you want in your life. It is my honor to help you.

AUTHORS NOTE

As a new, non-fiction author writing in lockdown I used several books as my 'book role models.' These books included High Performance Habits by Brendon Burchard, The Culture Code by Daniel Coyle, and Principles by Ray Dalio. The research-based and storytelling nature of these books appealed to me as a lay reader and as a researcher. In *this* book I share with you the book I wanted to read and share with my clients. I chose to use the lens of a researcher, coach, project manager, and positive psychologist, looking for individual differences in behavior that help people make tangible progress.

Throughout the book you will find coaching vignettes and personal experiences so that the vital how-to strategies and tactics don't become tedious. Human beings have always used stories to share lessons, deepen learning and provide examples. Musa, my son, gave permission to share the story at the start of the book. In all other vignettes the names and details of the stories have been appropriately changed to mask the identities and protect the privacy of my clients. Any resulting resemblance to personal living or dead is entirely coincidental and unintentional.

RESULTS

Consistent results are not something that anyone can sustain forever but with the RESULTS Method you open yourself up to consistent progress. It is for this reason that I have chosen to favor strategies that we know work, are tried and tested. Throughout my career I have been compensated for getting tangible results for organizations and people. It is the individual that brings the change within the context that they are operating in. This is reflected in the focus of my work and this book. If you are looking for support and advice on how to use the RESULTS Method within a company or for organizational change please contact us at Results Partners and we will support you with a bespoke program.

In this book I have drawn from the wisdom of many sources, theories, concepts, researchers, and books. In every case I have done my very best to find the source material, read it, and understand it before sharing my perspective on it. In a few cases I have come across wonderful ideas that I have found attributed in multiple places but not attributed with a specific source. In those situations, I have tried to give the reader as much information as I could regarding the source of the material.

For more of my personal perspective and stories visit *www.results.partners* where you will find content related to the research and inspirational stories.

329

RESULTS

NOTES

Introduction

1. (Grant, 2012)
2. The phrase 'reduced circumstances' is used euphemistically to refer to the state of being poor after being relatively wealthy. I believe it can apply to a reduction in any circumstance where the lifestyle or experience is less than it once was. (REDUCED CIRCUMSTANCES | meaning in the Cambridge English Dictionary, 2020)
3. (COACH | meaning in the Cambridge English Dictionary, 2020)
4. (Whitmore, 2017)

Orientation

1. (Hadith - The Book of Miscellany - Riyad as-Salihin - Sunnah.com - Sayings and Teachings of Prophet Muhammad (2020) OR Sahih al-Bukhari 1 Book 1, Hadith 1 Vol. 1, Book 1, Hadith 1
2. (Gollwitzer, Sheeran, Michalski and Seifert, 2009)
3. (Critcher and Dunning, 2014)
4. (Steele, 1988)
5. (Cascio et al., 2015)
6. (Dr. Dre, et al. 2017)
7. (Dr. Dre, et al. 2017)
8. (INTEGRITY | meaning in the Cambridge English Dictionary, 2020)

RESULTS

9.   (Ashkenas, 2011)
10. (Williams, n.d.)
11. (Berger, 2016)
12. Appreciative Inquiry, developed by David Cooperrider, is a collaborative, strengths-based approach to change in organizations and other human systems, the aim of which is to bring about positive change in a system.
13. (Lumley and Provenzano, 2003)
14. (Spera, Buhrfeind and Pennebaker, 1994)
15. (Dalio, 2017)
16. (Adams, n.d.)

REACH

1.   (Amazon Prime, 2020)
2.   Measure for Measure, Act 1, Scene 4. (Shakespeare, 1995)
3.   (No Fear Shakespeare: Measure for Measure: Act 1 Scene 4 Page 4 | SparkNotes, 2020)
4.   (Neff, 2011)
5.   (van Gogh, 2020)
6.   The systematic review of imposter syndrome research looked at a total, 62 studies with 14,161 participants. "Prevalence rates of impostor syndrome varied widely from 9 to 82% largely depending on the screening tool and cutoff used to assess symptoms and were particularly high among ethnic minority groups. Impostor syndrome was common among both men and women and across a range of age groups (adolescents to late-stage professionals)." (Bravata et al., 2019)
7.   The term imposter phenomenon was created by Dr Pauline R. Clance and Dr. Suzanne A. Imes in their 1978 article "The Impostor Phenomenon in High Achieving Women: Dynamics and Therapeutic Intervention." (Clance and Imes, 1978)
8.   (Sakulku and Alexander, 2011)
9.   No longer available on the TED website, Valerie Young's talk can be found on TED's Youtube channel: https://www.youtube.com/watch?v=h7v-GG3SEWQ
10. (Young, 2011)
11. (Hoang, 2013)
12. (Ratner, Mendle, Burrow and Thoemmes, 2019)
13. (Markus and Nurius, 1986)

14. (Edmondson, 2019)
15. (King and Hicks, 2007)
16. (Nolen-Hoeksema, 2000)
17. (Ratner, Mendle, Burrow and Thoemmes, 2019)
18. (Goleman, 2009)
19. (Dweck, 2007)
20. (McQuaid, n.d.)
21. (McQuaid, n.d.)
22. (Dweck, 2007)
23. (Kahneman, 2011)
24. (Effort Rubric For Students, 2016)
25. (Prochaska and Norcross, 2001)
26. (Seligman and Csikszentmihalyi, 2000)
27. (Peterson, Park and Sweeney, 2008)
28. (Peterson, 2008)
29. (Seligman, n.d.)
30. (Soots, 2015)
31. (Barnes, n.d.)
32. (APM Body of Knowledge, 2019)
33. (Brown, 2018)
34. (Brown, 2019)

EVOLVE

1. https://www.themyersbriggs.com/
2. (Big 5 Assessments - Psychometric Testing, n.d.)
3. https://www.discprofile.com/what-is-disc
4. https://www.kolbe.com/kolbe-a-index/
5. https://www.hoganassessments.com/assessment/hogan-personality-inventory/
6. (Colan, 2019)
7. (The Values of Humanity, n.d.)
8. Matthew McConaghey's Oscar acceptance speech can be found https://www.youtube.com/watch?v=wD2cVhC-63I&ab_channel=Oscars
9. (Matthew McConaughey's Oscar acceptance speech, 2014)
10. (Peterson and Seligman, 2004)
11. https://www.viacharacter.org/survey/account/register
12. (Rigoni, 2016)

RESULTS

13. (Cooperrrider, 2011)
14. (Rapp, Saleebey and Sullivan, 2005)
15. (McGraw, 2002)
16. (Champman, 2009)
17. (Egbert and Polk, 2006)
18. (Dismukes and Smith, n.d.)
19. (Luft and Ingram, 1955)
20. One notable passage on page seven of the 35-page speech is referred to as "The Man in the Arena," taken from Citizenship in a Republic, the speech given by Theodore Roosevelt, former President of the United States, at the Sorbonne in Paris, France, on April 23, 1910
21. (Alfred Nobel, n.d.)
22. (Covey, 2016)
23. (Ware, n.d.)
24. (Gilbert, 2014)

SELECT

1. The Couch to 5K is a running plan created by Josh Clark in 1996. Clark developed the plan for new runners as motivation with manageable expectations. The plan aims to get the user running for 20 to 30 minutes, three days a week. The daily workouts start with a five-minute warm-up walk and works up to running five kilometres (three miles) without a walking break within nine weeks. (Bower, n.d.)
2. (Oz, 2008)
3. (Fredrickson, 2010)
4. (Fredrickson, 2010)
5. (Worthy, Markman and Maddox, 2009)
6. (Wells, n.d.)
7. (Maslow, 1943)
8. (GOAL | meaning in the Cambridge English Dictionary, n.d.)
9. (Carver and Scheier, 1998)
10. (Higgins, 1987)
11. (Emmons, 1992)
12. (Little, 2000)
13. (Picasso, n.d.)
14. (Aitkenhead, 2016)
15. The Coaches Playbook, Jose Mourinho episode, (Netflix, 2020)
16. (Locke, 1996)
17. (Locke, 1996)

18. (Edith S. Childs, n.d.)
19. (CNN, 2016)
20. (Aaron, n.d.)
21. (Shakespeare, 1595)
22. (Locke and Latham, 1991)
23. (Doran, 1981)
24. (Stajkovic, Latham, Sergent and Peterson, 2018)
25. (Stajkovic, Latham, Sergent and Peterson, 2018)

UTILIZE

1. (Bethune, 2007)
2. (Vierordt's law, 2020)
3. (Ariga and Lleras, 2011)
4. (CHALLENGE | meaning in the Cambridge English Dictionary, 2020)
5. (Alhola and Polo-Kantola, 2007)
6. (Pomodoro Technique, n.d.)
7. **(Vouchercloud, n.d.)**
8. (Seneca, n.d.)
9. (Rubinstein, Meyer and Evans, 2001)
10. (Green and Molenkamp, 2005)
11. (Doerr and Page, 2018)
12. (A History of Kanban | Kanban Tool, n.d.)

LEAD

1. (Bielaszka-DuVernay, 2009)
2. (Hirshkowitz et al., 2015)
3. (Ben Simon, Rossi, Harvey and Walker, 2019)
4. (Walker, 2020)
5. (Perfect Sleep Environment - The Sleep Council, n.d.)
6. (Sissons, 2020)
7. (Wittbrodt and Millard-Stafford, 2018)
8. (Weir, 2011)
9. (Holick and Chen, 2008)
10. (Pareto principle, n.d.)
11. (Parkinson's law, n.d.)
12. (Kahneman and Tversky, 1977)

RESULTS

13. (Koole and van't Spijker, 2000)
14. (Newport, 2016)
15. (Newport, 2016)
16. (Horvath et al., 2020)
17. (The Eisenhower Matrix, 2016)

THRIVE

1. (Achor, 2011)
2. (WHO Constitution, n.d.)
3. (Feeney and Collins, 2014)
4. (Feeney and Collins, 2014)
5. (Seligman, 2012)
6. (Feeney and Collins, 2014)
7. (Feeney and Collins, 2014)
8. (Bloom, Liang, Roberts and Ying, 2014)
9. (Wong, 2020)
10. (Herz, 2002)
11. (Herz, 2002)
12. (Neff, n.d.)
13. (Gawande, 2011)
14. (Gawande, 2011)

SUCCEED

1. (Sustainable | Definition of Sustainable by Oxford Dictionary on Lexico.com also meaning of Sustainable, n.d.)
2. (Lewis, 2020)
3. (Maslow, 1970)
4. (Bhutan's Gross National Happiness Index, n.d.)
5. (Robitschek, 1998)
6. (Conley, 2010)
7. (Obhi, Hardy and Margrett, 2020)
8. (Amabile and Kramer, 2011)
9. (Coffeng et al., 2015)
10. (Fredrickson, 2001)
11. (Geurts, Beckers and Tucker, 2014)
12. (Hennessy & Amabile, 2010)

13. (REVITALIZE | meaning in the Cambridge English Dictionary, 2020)
14. (Robbins, 2020). This video is a great example of how to use the Robbins priming routine in your day https://www.youtube.com/watch?v=faTGTgid8Uc
15. (Consistent definition and meaning | Collins English Dictionary, n.d.)
16. (Lally, van Jaarsveld, Potts and Wardle, 2009)
17. In the study by Lally it took anywhere from 18 days to 254 days for people to form a new habit. (Lally, van Jaarsveld, Potts and Wardle, 2009)
18. (RITUAL | meaning in the Cambridge English Dictionary, 2020)
19. (HABIT | meaning in the Cambridge English Dictionary, 2020)
20. (The 1919 Report, 1919)
21. (Cachioni et al., 2014)

REFERENCES

The following references form a traditional literature review. All these references are cited in the notes and have informed the work. In anticipation of readers wanting to continue learning and exploration on the relationship between positive psychology, project management and personal growth I have included all that we deemed relevant and will continue to provide additional resources at *www.results.partners*

Kanbantool.com. n.d. *A History Of Kanban | Kanban Tool.* [online] Available at: <https://kanbantool.com/kanban-guide/kanban-history> [Accessed 25 July 2020].

Aaron, R., n.d. *The Best Goal-Achievement Strategy | Aaron Website.* [online] Aaron.com. Available at: <http://aaron.com/2013/08/13/the-best-goal-achievement-strategy/> [Accessed 18 July 2020].

Achor, S., 2011. The Happiness Advantage: The Seven Principles Of Positive Psychology That Fuel Success And Performance At Work. Virgin Books.

Adams, K., n.d. *A Short Course In Journal Writing – The Center For Journal Therapy.* [online] Journaltherapy.com. Available at:

<https://journaltherapy.com/lets-journal/a-short-course-in-journal-writing/> [Accessed 12 July 2020].

Aitkenhead, D., 2016. *Usain Bolt: 'I Feel Good Because I Know I'Ve Done It Clean'.* [online] the Guardian. Available at: <https://www.theguardian.com/sport/2016/nov/12/usain-bolt-feel-good-because-know-done-it-clean> [Accessed July 2020].

En.wikipedia.org. n.d. *Alfred Nobel.* [online] Available at: <https://en.wikipedia.org/wiki/Alfred_Nobel#cite_note-Brit1-4> [Accessed 1 July 2020].

Alhola, P. and Polo-Kantola, P., 2007. Sleep deprivation: Impact on cognitive performance. *Neuropsychiatric Disease and Treatment*, 3(5), pp.553-567.

Amabile, T. and Kramer, S., 2011. The Power of Small Wins. Harvard Business Review, [online] Available at: <https://hbr.org/2011/05/the-power-of-small-wins> [Accessed 12 August 2020].

Amazon Prime, 2020. *All Or Nothing: Tottenham Hotspur.* [video] Available at: <https://www.amazon.co.uk/All-or-Nothing-Tottenham-Hotspur/dp/B08G1YYZYN> [Accessed 5 October 2020].

2019. *APM Body Of Knowledge.* 7th ed. Princes Risborough: Association for Project Management.

Ariga, A. and Lleras, A., 2011. Brief and rare mental "breaks" keep you focused: Deactivation and reactivation of task goals preempt vigilance decrements. *Cognition*, 118(3), pp.439-443.

Ashkenas, R., 2011. Why Integrity Is Never Easy. [Blog] *Harvard Business Review*, Available at: <https://hbr.org/2011/02/why-integrity-is-never-easy.html> [Accessed 7 August 2020].

Barnes, M., n.d. *What Is Project Management?.* [online] Apm.org.uk. Available at: <https://www.apm.org.uk/resources/what-is-project-management/> [Accessed 23 June 2020].

Barrettacademy.com. n.d. *The Values Of Humanity.* [online] Available at: <https://www.barrettacademy.com/the-values-of-humanity> [Accessed 15 July 2020].

Barrett Values Centre. n.d. *Barrett Values Centre | Your Organization, Thriving.* [online] Available at: <https://www.valuescentre.com/> [Accessed 15 July 2020].

Ben Simon, E., Rossi, A., Harvey, A. and Walker, M., 2019. Overanxious and underslept. *Nature Human Behaviour*, 4(1), pp.100-110.

Berger, W., 2016. *A More Beautiful Question.* New York [etc.]: Bloomsbury.

Bethune, S., 2007. [online] Apa.org. Available at: <https://www.apa.org/news/press/releases/2007/10/stress#:~:text=%E2%80%9CWe%20know%20that%20stress%20is,to%20obesity%20and%20heart%20disease.%E2%80%9D> [Accessed 12 July2020].

Oxford Poverty and Human Development Institute, n.d. Bhutan's Gross National Happiness Index. Available at: <https://ophi.org.uk/policy/national-policy/gross-national-happiness-index/> [Accessed 23 July 2020].

Bielaszka-DuVernay, C., 2009. Avoid Mistakes That Plague New Leaders: An Interview with Warren Bennis. [Blog] *Harvard Business Review*, Available at: <https://hbr.org/2009/04/avoid-mistakes-that-plague-new.html> [Accessed 18 July 2020].

Big5assessments.com. n.d. *Big 5 Assessments - Psychometric Testing.* [online] Available at: <https://www.big5assessments.com/> [Accessed 19 July 2020].

Bloom, N., Liang, J., Roberts, J. and Ying, Z., 2014. Does Working from Home Work? Evidence from a Chinese Experiment*. *The Quarterly Journal of Economics*, 130(1), pp.165-218.

Bower, M., n.d. *How The Couch To 5K Running Plan Works.* [online] HowStuffWorks. Available at: <https://adventure.howstuffworks.com/outdoor-

RESULTS

activities/running/training/couch-to-5k-running-plan.htm> [Accessed 8 July 2020].

Bravata, D., Watts, S., Keefer, A., Madhusudhan, D., Taylor, K., Clark, D., Nelson, R., Cokley, K. and Hagg, H., 2019. Prevalence, Predictors, and Treatment of Impostor Syndrome: a Systematic Review. *Journal of General Internal Medicine*, 35(4), pp.1252-1275.

British Ministry of Reconstruction, Adult Education Committee (1919). *Final Report* (Chaired by Arthur L. Smith and commonly known as 'The 1919 Report') Cmnd 321. London: HMSO.

Brook, J., 2018. Why strengths-based programs can't ignore weaknesses. [Blog] *Strengthscope*, Available at: <https://www.strengthscope.com/strengths-based-programs-cant-ignore-weaknesses/> [Accessed 4 August 2020].

Brown, Brene. 2018. *Dare to Lead*. London, England: Vermilion.

Brown, B., 2019. *Daring Classrooms | Brené Brown*. [online] Brené Brown. Available at: <https://brenebrown.com/daringclassrooms/> [Accessed 29 July 2020].

Cachioni, M., Nascimento Ordonez, T., da Silva, T., Tavares Batistoni, S., Sanches Yassuda, M., Caldeira Melo, R., Accioly Rodrigues da Costa Domingue, M. and Lopes, A., 2014. Motivational Factors and Predictors for Attending a Continuing Education Program for Older Adults. *Educational Gerontology*, 40(8), pp.584-596.

Carver, C. and Scheier, M., 1998. *On The Self-Regulation Of Behavior*. Cambridge, UK: Cambridge University Press.

Cascio, C., O'Donnell, M., Tinney, F., Lieberman, M., Taylor, S., Strecher, V. and Falk, E., 2015. Self-affirmation activates brain systems associated with self-related processing and reward and is reinforced by future orientation. *Social Cognitive and Affective Neuroscience*, 11(4), pp.621-629.

Dictionary.cambridge.org. 2020. *CHALLENGE | Meaning In The Cambridge English Dictionary*. [online] Available at:

<https://dictionary.cambridge.org/dictionary/english/challenge>
[Accessed 25 October 2020].

Champman, G., 2009. The Five Love Languages: The Secret To Love That Lasts. Moody Press; First Edition.

Clance, P. and Imes, S., 1978. The imposter phenomenon in high achieving women: Dynamics and therapeutic intervention. *Psychotherapy: Theory, Research & Practice*, 15(3), pp.241-247.

CNN, 2016. Obama Tells Story Of Famed Chant: Fired Up, Ready To Go. [video] Available at:
<https://www.youtube.com/watch?v=5AhRqg0ADbk> [Accessed 25 October 2020].

Dictionary.cambridge.org. 2020. *COACH | Meaning In The Cambridge English Dictionary*. [online] Available at:
<https://dictionary.cambridge.org/dictionary/english/coach> [Accessed 23 October 2020].

Coffeng, J., van Sluijs, E., Hendriksen, I., van Mechelen, W. and Boot, C., 2015. Physical Activity and Relaxation During and After Work are Independently Associated With the Need for Recovery. *Journal of Physical Activity and Health*, 12(1), pp.109-115.

Colan, L., 2019. *A Lesson From Roy A. Disney On Making Values-Based Decisions*. [online] Inc.com. Available at: <https://www.inc.com/lee-colan/a-lesson-from-roy-a-disney-on-making-values-based-decisions.html#:~:text=Roy%20E.,%2C%20making%20decisions%20be comes%20easier.%22> [Accessed 20 July 2020].

Collinsdictionary.com. n.d. *Consistent Definition And Meaning | Collins English Dictionary*. [online] Available at:
<https://www.collinsdictionary.com/dictionary/english/consistent#:~:t ext=Someone%20who%20is%20consistent%20always,most%20consiste nt%20of%20players%20anyway.&text=If%20one%20fact%20or%20ide a,do%20not%20contradict%20each%20other.> [Accessed 3 July 2020].

RESULTS

Cooperrider, D., 2011. *Deficit Based Strengths Based.* [ebook] Available at: <http://www.davidcooperrider.com/wp-content/uploads/2011/09/deficit_based-strengths_based.pdf> [Accessed 2 July 2020].

Covey, S., 2016. The 7 Habits Of Highly Effective People. Mango Media.

Critcher, C. and Dunning, D., 2014. Self-Affirmations Provide a Broader Perspective on Self-Threat. *Personality and Social Psychology Bulletin*, 41(1), pp.3-18.

Dr. Dre, Jimmy Iovine, Bono, Allen Hughes, Lasse Järvi, Doug Pray, Sarah Anthony, et al. 2017. *The Defiant Ones.* https://www.netflix.com/gb/title/80214552

Dalio, R., 2017. *Principles.* Simon & Schuster.

Diener, E., & Seligman, M. P. (2004). Beyond money: Toward an economy of well-being. Psychological Science in the Public Interest, 5 (1), 1 – 31.

DISC Personality Testing. 2020. *DISC Personality Testing.* [online] Available at: <https://discpersonalitytesting.com/> [Accessed 24 October 2020].

Dismukes, R. and Smith, G., n.d. Facilitation And Debriefing In Aviation Training And Operations.

Doerr, J. and Page, L., 2018. *Measure What Matters.* Portfolio Penguin.

Doran, G., 1981. There's a S.M.A.R.T. Way to Write Management's Goals and Objectives. *Management Review*, 70(11), pp.35-36.

Dweck, C., 2007. *Mindset: The New Psychology Of Success.* New York: Ballantine Books; Reprint Edition.

En.wikipedia.org. n.d. *Edith S. Childs.* [online] Available at: <https://en.wikipedia.org/wiki/Edith_S._Childs> [Accessed 17 July 2020].

Edmondson, A., 2019. *Creating Psychological Safety In The Workplace.* [podcast] Harvard Business Review. Available at: <https://hbr.org/podcast/2019/01/creating-psychological-safety-in-the-workplace> [Accessed 7 August 2020].

2016. *Effort Rubric For Students.* [ebook] Mindset Works, p.page 1. Available at: <https://www.mindsetworks.com/websitemedia/resources/effort-rubric-for-students.pdf> [Accessed 17 July 2020].

Egbert, N. and Polk, D., 2006. Speaking the Language of Relational Maintenance: A Validity Test of Chapman's (1992) Five Love Languages. *Communication Research Reports*, 23(1), pp.19-26.

Emmons, R., 1992. Abstract versus concrete goals: Personal striving level, physical illness, and psychological well-being. *Journal of Personality and Social Psychology*, 62(2), pp.292-300.

Feeney, B.C., Collins, N.L. (2014). A New Look at Social Support: A Theoretical Perspective on Thriving Through Relationships. *Personality and Social Psychology Review*.

Fredrickson, B., 2001. The role of positive emotions in positive psychology: The broaden-and-build theory of positive emotions. *American Psychologist*, 56(3), pp.218-226.

Fredrickson, B., 2001. The role of positive emotions in positive psychology: The broaden-and-build theory of positive emotions. *American Psychologist*, 56(3), pp.218-226.

Fredrickson, B. L. (2013). Positive emotions broaden and build. In P. Devine & A. Plant (Eds.), Advances in experimental social psychology (Vol. 47, pp. 1 – 54). San Diego, CA : Academic Press.

Gardner, B., 2012. Busting the 21 days habit formation myth. [Blog] *Health Chatter: Research Department of Behavioral Science and Health Blog,* Available at: <https://blogs.ucl.ac.uk/bsh/2012/06/29/busting-the-21-days-habit-formation-myth/#:~:text=The%20bottom%20line%20is%3A%20stay,you%20are%20trying%20to%20do> [Accessed 25 October 2020].

RESULTS

Gawande, A., 2011. *The Checklist Manifesto*. London: Profile Books Ltd.

Geurts, S. A. E., Beckers, D. G. J., & Tucker, P. (2014). *Recovery from demanding work hours*. In M. C. W. Peeters, J. De Jonge, & T. W. Taris (Eds.), *An introduction to contemporary work psychology* (p. 196–219). Wiley Blackwell.

Gilbert, D., 2014. *The Psychology Of Your Future Self*. [video] Available at: <https://www.ted.com/talks/dan_gilbert_the_psychology_of_your_fut ure_self?language=en> [Accessed 24 July 2020].

Dictionary.cambridge.org. n.d. *GOAL | Meaning In The Cambridge English Dictionary*. [online] Available at: <https://dictionary.cambridge.org/dictionary/english/goal> [Accessed 25 October 2020].

Goleman, D., 2009. Emotional Intelligence: Why It Can Matter More Than IQ. Bloomsbury Publishing House.

Gollwitzer, P., Sheeran, P., Michalski, V. and Seifert, A., 2009. When Intentions Go Public. *Psychological Science*, 20(5), pp.612-618.

Grant, A., 2012. An Integrative Goal-Focused Approach to Executive Coaching. *International Coaching Psychology Review*, 7(2), pp.146-165.

Green, Z. and Molenkamp, R., 2005. *The BART System Of Group And Organizational Analysis Boundary, Authority, Role And Task*. [online] Zachary Green and Rene Molenkamp. Available at: <https://www.it.uu.se/edu/course/homepage/projektDV/ht09/BART _Green_Molenkamp.pdf> [Accessed 7 June 2020].

Dictionary.cambridge.org. 2020. *HABIT | Meaning In The Cambridge English Dictionary*. [online] Available at: <https://dictionary.cambridge.org/dictionary/english/habit?q=habits> [Accessed 7 July 2020].

Sunnah.com. 2020. *Hadith - The Book Of Miscellany - Riyad As-Salihin - Sunnah.Com - Sayings And Teachings Of Prophet Muhammad*. [online]

Available at: <https://sunnah.com/riyadussalihin/introduction/1>
[Accessed 23 June 2020].

Herz, R., 2002. *Do Scents Affect People's Moods Or Work Performance?*. [online]
Scientific American. Available at:
<https://www.scientificamerican.com/article/do-scents-affect-peoples/> [Accessed 26 July 2020].

Higgins, E., 1987. Self-discrepancy: A theory relating self and
affect. *Psychological Review*, 94(3), pp.319-340.

Hirshkowitz, M., Whiton, K., Albert, S., Alessi, C., Bruni, O., DonCarlos, L.,
Hazen, N., Herman, J., Katz, E., Kheirandish-Gozal, L., Neubauer, D.,
O'Donnell, A., Ohayon, M., Peever, J., Rawding, R., Sachdeva, R.,
Setters, B., Vitiello, M., Ware, J. and Adams Hillard, P., 2015. National
Sleep Foundation's sleep time duration recommendations: methodology
and results summary. *Sleep Health*, 1(1), pp.40-43.

Hoang, Q., 2013. The Impostor Phenomenon: Overcoming Internalized
Barriers and Recognizing Achievements. *The Vermont Connection*, 34(6),
pp.42-51.

Hogan Assessments. n.d. *Hogan Personality Inventory | Hogan Assessments*.
[online] Available at:
<https://www.hoganassessments.com/assessment/hogan-personality-inventory/> [Accessed 24 October 2020].

Holick, M. and Chen, T., 2008. Vitamin D deficiency: a worldwide problem
with health consequences. *The American Journal of Clinical Nutrition*, 87(4),
pp.1080S-1086S.

Horvath, J., Mundinger, C., Schmitgen, M., Wolf, N., Sambataro, F., Hirjak,
D., Kubera, K., Koenig, J. and Christian Wolf, R., 2020. Structural and
functional correlates of smartphone addiction. *Addictive Behaviors*, 105,
p.106334.

Dictionary.cambridge.org. 2020. *INTEGRITY | Meaning In The Cambridge
English Dictionary*. [online] Available at:

RESULTS

<https://dictionary.cambridge.org/dictionary/english/integrity>
[Accessed 7 November 2020].

Kahneman, Daniel; Tversky, Amos (1977). "Intuitive prediction: Biases and corrective procedures" (PDF). Decision Research Technical Report PTR-1042-77-6. In Kahneman, Daniel; Tversky, Amos (1982). "Intuitive prediction: Biases and corrective procedures". In Kahneman, Daniel; Slovic, Paul; Tversky, Amos (eds.). *Judgment Under Uncertainty: Heuristics and Biases. Science*. **185**. pp. 414–421.

Kahneman, D., 2011. *Thinking, Fast And Slow*. Penguin.

King, L. and Hicks, J., 2007. Whatever happened to "What might have been"? Regrets, happiness, and maturity. *American Psychologist*, 62(7), pp.625-636.

Koole, S. and van't Spijker, M., 2000. Overcoming the planning fallacy through willpower: effects of implementation intentions on actual and predicted task-completion times. *European Journal of Social Psychology*, 30(6), pp.873-888.

Lally, P., van Jaarsveld, C., Potts, H. and Wardle, J., 2009. How are habits formed: Modelling habit formation in the real world. *European Journal of Social Psychology*, 40(6), pp.998-1009.

Lewis, T., 2020. Arsène Wenger: 'I try to read everything that helps me understand human beings. *The Guardian*, [online] Available at: <https://www.theguardian.com/football/2020/oct/11/arsene-wenger-arsenal-manager-football> [Accessed 11 October 2020].

Little, B., 2000. Persons, Contexts, and Personal Projects. *Theoretical Perspectives in Environment-Behavior Research*, pp.79-88.

Locke, E., 1996. Motivation through conscious goal setting. *Applied and Preventive Psychology*, 5(2), pp.117-124.

Locke, E. and Latham, G., 1991. A Theory of Goal Setting and Task Performance. *The Academy of Management Review*, 16(2), p.480.

Luft, J.; Ingham, H. (1955). "The Johari window, a graphic model of interpersonal awareness". *Proceedings of the Western Training Laboratory in Group Development*. Los Angeles: University of California, Los Angeles.

Lumley, M. and Provenzano, K., 2003. Stress management through written emotional disclosure improves academic performance among college students with physical symptoms. *Journal of Educational Psychology*, 95(3), pp.641-649.

Maslow, A., 1943. A theory of human motivation. *Psychological Review*, 50(4), pp.370-396.

Maslow, A. H. (1970). Motivation and personality (2nd ed.). New York: Harper & Row.

Markus, H. and Nurius, P., 1986. Possible selves. *American Psychologist*, 41(9), pp.954-969.

2014. *Matthew Mcconaughey'S Oscar Acceptance Speech, 2014*. [video] Available at: <https://www.youtube.com/watch?v=wD2cVhC-63I&ab_channel=Oscars> [Accessed 4 July 2020].

Dr. Phil McGraw. "Encore Presentation: Interview with Dr. Phil." *Larry King Weekend*, CNN, 26 May 2002.

McQuaid, M., n.d. *Do You Have A False Growth Mindset? | Positive Leadership | Michelle Mcquaid*. [online] Michelle McQuaid. Available at: <https://www.michellemcquaid.com/false-growth-mindset/> [Accessed 23 July 2020].

Neff, K., n.d. *Definition And Three Elements Of Self Compassion | Kristin Neff*. [online] Self-Compassion. Available at: <https://self-compassion.org/the-three-elements-of-self-compassion-2/> [Accessed 25 August 2020].

Neff, K., 2011. Self-Compassion, Self-Esteem, and Well-Being. *Social and Personality Psychology Compass*, 5(1), pp.1-12.

RESULTS

Netflix, 2020. *José Mourinho: A Coach's Rules For Life.* [video] Available at: <https://www.netflix.com/gb/title/81025735> [Accessed 25 October 2020].

Newport, C., 2016. Deep Work: Rules For Focused Success In A Distracted World. Piatkus.

Sparknotes.com. 2020. *No Fear Shakespeare: Measure For Measure: Act 1 Scene 4 Page 4 | Sparknotes.* [online] Available at: <https://www.sparknotes.com/nofear/shakespeare/measure-for-measure/page_38/> [Accessed 7 October 2020].

Nolen-Hoeksema, S., 2000. The role of rumination in depressive disorders and mixed anxiety/depressive symptoms. *Journal of Abnormal Psychology*, 109(3), pp.504-511.

Obhi, H., Hardy, A. and Margrett, J., 2020. Values of lifelong learners and their pursuits of happiness and whole-person wellness. *Aging & Mental Health*, pp.1-7.

Oz, M., 2008. A Brain Scientist's Insight. [Blog] *Oprah*, Available at: <http://www.oprah.com/health/dr-jill-bolte-taylor-explains-her-stroke-of-genius/1> [Accessed 25 July 2020].

En.wikipedia.org. n.d. *Pareto Principle.* [online] Available at: <https://en.wikipedia.org/wiki/Pareto_principle> [Accessed 25 July 2020].

En.wikipedia.org. n.d. *Parkinson's Law.* [online] Available at: <https://en.wikipedia.org/wiki/Parkinson%27s_law> [Accessed 25 July 2020].

The Sleep Council. n.d. *Perfect Sleep Environment - The Sleep Council.* [online] Available at: <https://sleepcouncil.org.uk/advice-support/sleep-advice/perfect-sleep-environment/> [Accessed 25 July 2020].

Themyersbriggs.com. n.d. *Personality Assessment Inventory And Professional Development | The Myers-Briggs Company.* [online] Available at:

<https://www.themyersbriggs.com/en-US> [Accessed 24 October 2020].

Peterson, C., 2008. *What Is Positive Psychology, And What Is It Not?*. [online] Psychology Today. Available at: <https://www.psychologytoday.com/gb/blog/the-good-life/200805/what-is-positive-psychology-and-what-is-it-not> [Accessed 2 July 2020].

Peterson, C. and Seligman, M., 2004. *Character Strengths And Virtues*. Washington, DC: American Psychological Association.

Peterson, C., Park, N. and Sweeney, P., 2008. Group Well-Being: Morale from a Positive Psychology Perspective. *Applied Psychology*, 57(s1), pp.19-36.

Picasso, P., n.d. *Pablo Picasso Quotes*. [online] Pablopicasso.org. Available at: <https://www.pablopicasso.org/quotes.jsp#:~:text=Our%20goals%20can%20only%20be,it's%20always%20in%20your%20face.%E2%80%9D> [Accessed 18 July 2020].

En.wikipedia.org. n.d. *Pomodoro Technique*. [online] Available at: <https://en.wikipedia.org/wiki/Pomodoro_Technique> [Accessed 25 July 2020].

Prochaska, J. and Norcross, J., 2001. Stages of change. *Psychotherapy: Theory, Research, Practice, Training*, 38(4), pp.443-448.

Rapp, C., Saleebey, D. and Sullivan, W., 2005. The Future of Strengths-Based Social Work. *Advances in Social Work*, 6(1), pp.79-90.

Rapp, C., Saleebey, D. and Sullivan PW., (2008) The future of strengths-based social work practice, in Saleebey D (ed) (2006) The strengths perspective in social work practice, (4th Ed) Boston: Pearson Education

Ratner, K., Mendle, J., Burrow, A. and Thoemmes, F., 2019. Depression and Derailment: A Cyclical Model of Mental Illness and Perceived Identity Change. *Clinical Psychological Science*, 7(4), pp.735-753.

RESULTS

Reddie, A., 2017. Subjectivity, Blackness and Difference in Practical Theology in Britain Post Brexit. BIAPT Conference, St Mary's University, Twickenham, London.

Dictionary.cambridge.org. 2020. *REDUCED CIRCUMSTANCES | Meaning In The Cambridge English Dictionary.* [online] Available at: <https://dictionary.cambridge.org/dictionary/english/reduced-circumstances> [Accessed 7 November 2020].

Dictionary.cambridge.org. 2020. *REVITALIZE | Meaning In The Cambridge English Dictionary.* [online] Available at: <https://dictionary.cambridge.org/dictionary/english/revitalize> [Accessed 25 October 2020].

Rigoni, B., 2016. *Strengths-Based Employee Development: The Business Results.* [online] Gallup.com. Available at: <https://www.gallup.com/workplace/236297/strengths-based-employee-development-business-results.aspx> [Accessed 8 October 2020].

Dictionary.cambridge.org. 2020. *RITUAL | Meaning In The Cambridge English Dictionary.* [online] Available at: <https://dictionary.cambridge.org/dictionary/english/ritual?q=rituals> [Accessed 7 November 2020].

Robbins, T., 2020. *What Is Priming? Learn The Impact Of Priming Psychology.* [online] tonyrobbins.com. Available at: <https://www.tonyrobbins.com/ask-tony/priming/> [Accessed 7 November 2020].

Robitschek, Christine. 1998. "Personal Growth Initiative: The Construct and Its Measure." *Measurement & Evaluation in Counseling & Development* 30 (4): 183. doi:10.1080/07481756.1998.12068941.

Rubinstein, J., Meyer, D. and Evans, J., 2001. Executive control of cognitive processes in task switching. *Journal of Experimental Psychology: Human Perception and Performance*, 27(4), pp.763-797.

Sakulku, J. and Alexander, J., 2011. The Imposter Syndrome. *International Journal of Behavioral Science*, 6(1), pp.73-92.

Seligman, M. and Csikszentmihalyi, M., 2000. Positive psychology: An introduction. *American Psychologist*, 55(1), pp.5-14.

Seligman, M., 2012. *Flourish*. Atria Books.

Seligman, M., n.d. *Our Mission | Positive Psychology Center*. [online] Ppc.sas.upenn.edu. Available at: <https://ppc.sas.upenn.edu/our-mission> [Accessed 23 July 2020].

Seneca, L., n.d. *Letters From A Stoic By Seneca: Book Summary, Key Lessons And Best Quotes*. [online] Daily Stoic. Available at: <https://dailystoic.com/letters-from-a-stoic/> [Accessed 25 October 2020].

Shakespeare, W., 1595. *Romeo And Juliet. Act II. Scene II. William Shakespeare. 1914. The Oxford Shakespeare*. [online] Bartleby.com. Available at: <https://www.bartleby.com/70/3822.html> [Accessed 25 October 2020].

Shakespeare, W., 1995. *Measure For Measure (Wordsworth Classics)*. Wordsworth Editions.

Sissons, C., 2020. What is the average percentage of water in the human body?. [Blog] *Medical News Today*, Available at: <https://www.medicalnewstoday.com/articles/what-percentage-of-the-human-body-is-water#where-in-the-body> [Accessed 8 July 2020].

Spera, S., Buhrfeind, E. and Pennebaker, J., 1994. Expressive Writing and Coping with Job Loss. *Academy of Management Journal*, 37(3), pp.722-733.

Soots, L., 2015. *Flourishing - The Positive Psychology People*. [online] The Positive Psychology People. Available at: <https://www.thepositivepsychologypeople.com/flourishing/> [Accessed 4 July 2020].

RESULTS

Stajkovic, A., Latham, G., Sergent, K. and Peterson, S., 2018. Prime and Performance: Can a CEO Motivate Employees Without Their Awareness?. *Journal of Business and Psychology*, 34(6), pp.791-802.

Steele, C., 1988. The Psychology of Self-Affirmation: Sustaining the Integrity of the Self. *Advances in Experimental Social Psychology*, pp.261-302.

Eisenhower. 2016. *The Eisenhower Matrix*. [online] Available at: <https://www.eisenhower.me/> [Accessed 7 July 2020].

Barrettacademy.com. n.d. *The Values Of Humanity*. [online] Available at: <https://www.barrettacademy.com/the-values-of-humanity> [Accessed 24 July 2020].

Lexico Dictionaries | English. n.d. *Sustainable | Definition Of Sustainable By Oxford Dictionary On Lexico.Com Also Meaning Of Sustainable*. [online] Available at: <https://www.lexico.com/definition/sustainable> [Accessed 25 July 2020].

van Gogh, V., 2020. *Vincent Van Gogh To Theo Van Gogh : 28 October 1883*. [online] Webexhibits.org. Available at: <http://www.webexhibits.org/vangogh/letter/13/336.htm> [Accessed 3 July 2020].

En.wikipedia.org. 2020. *Vierordt's Law*. [online] Available at: <https://en.wikipedia.org/wiki/Vierordt%27s_law> [Accessed 3 November 2020].

Vouchercloud, n.d. *How Many Productive Hours In A Work Day? Just 2 Hours, 23 Minutes....* [online] vouchercloud. Available at: <https://www.vouchercloud.com/resources/office-worker-productivity> [Accessed 8 October 2020].

Walker, M., 2020. *BBC Morning Live, Live Broadcast On 26 October 2020*. [video] Available at: <https://www.bbc.co.uk/iplayer/episode/m000nxq8/morning-live-series-1-26102020> [Accessed 26 October 2020].

Ware, B., n.d. Regrets of the Dying. [Blog] Available at: <https://bronnieware.com/blog/regrets-of-the-dying/> [Accessed 27 July 2020].

Weir, K., 2011. The exercise effect. *Monitor on Psychology*, [online] 42(11). Available at: <https://www.apa.org/monitor/2011/12/exercise> [Accessed 25 July 2020].

Wells, T., n.d. Sen's Capability Approach. [Blog] *Internet Encyclopaedia of Philosophy - A Peer-Reviewed Academic Resource*, Available at: <https://iep.utm.edu/sen-cap/#SH3a> [Accessed 19 July 2020].

Whitmore, J., 2017. *Coaching For Performance*. 5th ed. London: Nicholas Brealey.

Who.int. n.d. *WHO Constitution*. [online] Available at: <https://www.who.int/about/who-we-are/constitution> [Accessed 1 July 2020].

Williams, T., n.d. Why Integrity Remains One of the Top Leadership Attributes. [Blog] *The Economist Excede*, Available at: <https://execed.economist.com/blog/industry-trends/why-integrity-remains-one-top-leadership-attributes> [Accessed 72 July 2020].

Wittbrodt, M. and Millard-Stafford, M., 2018. Dehydration Impairs Cognitive Performance. *Medicine & Science in Sports & Exercise*, 50(11), pp.2360-2368.

Wong, M., 2020. *A Snapshot Of A New Working-From-Home Economy | Stanford News*. [online] Stanford News. Available at: <https://news.stanford.edu/2020/06/29/snapshot-new-working-home-economy/> [Accessed 25 July 2020].

Worthy, D., Markman, A. and Maddox, W., 2009. Choking and excelling under pressure in experienced classifiers. *Attention, Perception, & Psychophysics*, 71(4), pp.924-935.

Young, V., 2011. *The Secret Thoughts Of Successful Women*. New York: Crown Business.

RESULTS

GLOSSARY

accepting — The act or condition of willing to allow or approve of something or someone, or to consider something as normal.

Annual Power Plan — An operational plan that indicates specific goals and objectives for a specified program or programs in line with your compelling vision.

avoiding — To consciously or unconsciously stay away from someone or something; to prevent something from happening or to not allow yourself to do something.

confused — Unable to think clearly or to understand something; not clear and therefore difficult to understand.

consistent — Always behaving or happening in a similar, especially a positive, way; in agreement with other facts or with typical or previous behavior; having the same principles as something else.

Daily Schedule — An intentional allocation of time to perform tasks over the course of a day.

deliverables — Within the context of the RESULTS method, deliverables are the weekly targets defined to meet monthly priorities.

evolve — To develop gradually, or to cause something or someone to make incremental, progressive changes.

Evolve phase — The second phase of the RESULTS Method. This phase focuses on identifying your values and strengths and understanding who you really are in order to pave the way for aligning your projects with your identity and intention.

focused — Giving concentrated attention to one particular activity or train of thought.

fulfilled — Feeling satisfied and happy as a result of getting everything wanted from life.

goal — An aim, a purpose, or something that one wants to achieve. Creating specific, targeted goals tied to one's vision, values, strengths, and communication style helps maximize personal output over the quarterly period.

habit — Something done often and regularly, sometimes without one knowing they are doing it.

identity — Who a person is, or the qualities and values of a person or group that differentiate them from others.

impacting — The powerful effect that something, especially something new, has on a situation or person.

implementation — The act of putting a plan into motion or of applying an idea, tool, or process.

increasing — To (make something) become larger in amount or size.

integrity — The quality of being honest and having strong moral principles that you refuse to compromise; the quality of being whole and complete.

intention — The underlying purpose of an action or pursuit; something that you want and plan to do; an aim.

lead — To guide yourself, others, or a process to a defined destination; a busy, normal, quiet, etc. life, to live a particular type of life.

Lead Phase — The fifth phase of the RESULTS Method. This phase focuses on taking responsibility for assuming leadership for self-care, service, and following through on your projects.

Monthly Moves — The clearly identified priorities, activities, and tasks to be undertaken during the month, deliberately organized and scheduled so you are able to make measured progress.

permission slip — Within the context of the RESULTS Method, giving yourself permission to feel or act a certain way; setting an intention for how you want to behave in difficult situations. Writing permission slips is grounded in the belief that you are in charge of your own behavior.

personal growth — The process of improving your skills and increasing the amount of experience that you have while building self-awareness regarding your values and core motivations.

pit stop — Within the scope of the RESULTS Method, a short break or interlude taken between periods of work to refresh, refuel, and recalibrate physically and mentally.

plan — A set of decisions about how to do something in the future; to think about and decide what you are going to do or how you are going to do something.

Pomodoro — A 25-minute time block allocated to focus on a particular task or priority, after which you take a five-minute break before another 25-minute work session.

positive psychology — The scientific study of positive human functioning and flourishing on multiple levels that include the biological, personal, relational, institutional, cultural, and global dimensions of life.

Post-it note — A trademark name for small, colored pieces of paper with a strip of adhesive for temporarily attaching messages or reminders where they will be seen.

practice — The act of doing something regularly or repeatedly to improve your skill at doing it, an action rather than thought or ideas.

priorities — Issues or tasks that are very important and must be dealt with before other things. Within the context of RESULTS, priorities are the monthly goals defined to complete the projects identified in your Project3x3.

process — A series of actions that you take in order to achieve a defined result.

progress — To continue gradually towards an anticipated end; to improve or develop in skills, knowledge, etc.

project — A piece of planned work, activity, or other undertaking that is finished over a period of time and intended to achieve a particular purpose.

project goal — The aim of one of the specific projects you are working on over a three-month period.

project management —The application of processes, methods, skills, knowledge and experience to achieve specific project objectives according to the project criteria within agreed parameters.

Project3x3 — A framework central to the RESULTS Method where you identify three projects you will work on for a period of three months, and within each project you identify three project goals. The Project3x3 is a summary of your plans for the three-month period.

Quarterly Action Plan — A document used to set goals and strategize your three months. The written, personal plan resulting after defining your

Project3x3 and articulating the priorities, deliverables, and tasks to be undertaken over the three-month period.

reach — To arrive at a place, especially after spending a long time or a lot of effort travelling; also means to make a decision, agreement, etc. about something.

Reach phase — The first phase of the RESULTS Method. This phase focuses on reaching beyond perceived boundaries and personal showstoppers to open the way to achieving results.

reducing — To reduce someone or something to a particular state is to cause that person or thing to be in a diminished state.

resisting — To refuse to accept or be changed by something, to stop yourself from doing something that you want to do.

rest — To stop doing a particular activity or stop being active for a period of time in order to relax and get back your strength.

RESULTS GPS —The Goal Positioning System associated with the RESULTS Method; the specific set of questions that can show the position or location of a person in relation to their life, vision, and projects.

RESULTS Method — A structured approach to obtaining meaningful results defined by projects that are strategically selected based on personal values, strength, knowledge of identity, and preserving integrity; developed by Saiyyidah Zaidi.

RESULTS Orientation — Your interests, activities, or aims in relation to intention, identity, integrity, implementation, and how you show up in life.

RESULTS Process — The series of actions that you take in order to achieve a result as developed by Saiyyidah Zaidi.

RESULTS — Acronym for **R**each, **E**volve, **S**elect, **U**tilize, **L**ead, **T**hrive, **S**ucceed referring to the framework developed by Saiyyidah Zaidi to enable individuals and organizations to make progress in their projects whilst flourishing and thriving.

review — The act of considering something again in order to make changes to it, learn from it, improve, and to create a new Project3x3.

revitalize — To give new life, energy, activity, or success to yourself or to something.

rituals — A set of fixed actions and sometimes words performed regularly and driven by purpose and intention.

select — To choose a small number of things or to choose by making careful decisions.

Select phase — The third phase of the RESULTS Method. This phase focuses on selecting the projects that are most suitable for you in this particular stage of life.

showstoppers — Within the context of RESULTS, these are any beliefs, mindsets, or self-defeating tendencies that slow down or altogether halt your progress towards attaining results.

sporadic — Happening sometimes; not regular or continuous.

succeed — Achieving something that you have been aiming for or has been the intended target or desired results.

Succeed phase — The seventh phase of the RESULTS Method. This phase focuses on how you can flourish while building on your initial results to create a cycle of continuously achieving the results you want.

task — A piece of work to be done or undertaken. In context of the RESULTS Method, it refers to the actionable steps done on a daily basis to complete your weekly deliverables.

thrive — To grow, develop, or be successful.

Thrive phase — The sixth phase of the RESULTS Method. This phase focuses on understanding and gaining control of your three environments and learning strategies to overcome obstacles and build resilience.

unfulfilled — If a wish, hope, promise, etc. is unfulfilled, it has not happened or been achieved; state of unhappiness or discontent because you think you should be achieving more in your life.

unorganized — Not planned or carried out in a structured way.

utilize — To use in an effective way.

Utilize phase — The fourth phase of the RESULTS Method. This phase focuses on utilizing the tools and resources available to you in the most effective and efficient way to achieve results.

vision — An experience in which you see things that do not exist physically, when your mind is affected powerfully by something; an idea or mental image of something; the ability to imagine how a country, society, industry, one's personal life, etc. could develop in the future and to plan for this development.

visualization — A mental exercise centered around creating a motivating image in your mind.

Weekly Rhythm — The act of organizing your activities and tasks for the week in a rhythm that suits you.

INDEX

RESULTS

RESULTS

for more resources go to
www.results.partners

Printed in Great Britain
by Amazon